Vital Contradictions

Characterization in the Plays of Ibsen, Strindberg, Chekhov and O'Neill

P.I.E.-Peter Lang

Bruxelles · Bern · Berlin · Frankfurt/M · New York · Oxford · Wien

Dramaturgies

Texts, Cultures and Performances

Series Editor

Marc Maufort, *Université Libre de Bruxelles*

Editorial Board

Christopher Balme, *University of Mainz*
Judith E. Barlow, *State University of New York-Albany*
Johan Callens, *Vrije Universiteit Brussel*
Jean Chothia, *Cambridge University*
Harry J. Elam, *Stanford University*
Albert-Reiner Glaap, *University of Düsseldorf*
André Helbo, *Université Libre de Bruxelles*
Ric Knowles, *University of Guelph*
Alain Piette, *École d'interprètes internationaux-Mons/*
Université Catholique de Louvain
John Stokes, *King's College, University of London*
Joanne Tompkins, *University of Queensland-Brisbane*

Editorial Assistant

Franca Bellarsi, *Université Libre de Bruxelles*

Michael MANHEIM

Vital Contradictions

Characterization in the Plays of Ibsen, Strindberg, Chekhov and O'Neill

Dramaturgies
No.6

© P.I.E.-Peter Lang S.A.
PRESSES INTERUNIVERSITAIRES EUROPÉENNES
Brussels, 2002
www.peterlang.net

ISSN 1376-3202
ISBN 90-5201-991-6
D/2002/5678/17

*CIP available from the British Library, GB
and the Library of Congress, USA.*
ISBN   0-8204-4684-X

Die Deutsche Bibliothek – CIP-Einheitsaufnahme

Manheim, Michael: Vital Contradictions: Characterization in the Plays of Ibsen, Strindberg, Chekhov and O'Neill/ Michael Manheim. – Bruxelles; Bern; Berlin; Frankfurt/M.; New York; Oxford; Wien: PIE Lang, 2002 (Dramaturgies; No.6)
ISBN 90-5201-991-6

To the late Mary Hatch Marshall and to Martha Manheim,
the truest of scholar/teachers

Contents

O'NEILL

Preface

What follows is not uninformed by the historicist criticism of the past decade so much as it sees an older, more personal approach to dramatic characterization as preferable for the kind of drama I am dealing with to an approach which sees the study of character in drama as outmoded and the primary motivators of writers in general the desire to be in sync with political, social, or psychological issues and assumptions of their times. A play like O'Neill's *Strange Interlude*, which I do not deal with, may have been written in part to appeal to its audience's discovery of the fashionably new Freudian psychology, but not a play like *Long Day's Journey into Night*, which was hardly concerned with pleasing an audience or a publisher. And the same may be said of Ibsen's *A Doll House* in contrast to his *Hedda Gabler.* In the former, Ibsen is concerned with the budding controversy over a woman's rights in marriage, in the latter with a person whose inner contradictions destroy her. One might well approach the earlier play primarily from a historicist perspective, but limiting oneself to such a perspective would do harm to the later play. And any approach to the delicately wrought dramatic figures of Anton Chekhov that sees them primarily in terms of the time in which Chekhov lived is bound to distort. A critic's historical sense of a writer's period is important, but more important for me is that critic's sensitivity to what is unique to the human animal regardless of period or place. And I do believe in that uniqueness. I do not believe we are simply by-products of our environments.

I am particularly grateful to my wife, Martha Manheim, for her reading, editing, and advice; and my son, James M. Manheim, who assisted in the preparation and formatting of the manuscript on the computer.

Michael Manheim

Vital Contradictions

My notion of *vital contradictions* in the central characters of early modern drama derives from two connected sources. The first is the idea of character *complexity*, the term complexity often associated with the characters in great literature as opposed to literature that is intended purely to entertain. The term complexity is usually associated with great tragedy, and great tragedy with the great writers of ancient Greece and of the Renaissance. The characters are what we remember best from Greek and Renaissance tragedy. They are characters who have had great impact on readers and audiences but resist easy definition: Sophocles's Oedipus and Antigone, all of Shakespeare's tragic heroes, several residents of Dante's inferno, Milton's Satan, and Goethe's Faust. To these might be added such post-Renaissance figures as Dickens's Sidney Carton, George Eliot's Dorothea Brooke, Stendhal's Eugene Sorel, Dostoevsky's Raskolnikov and the Karamazov brothers, Tolstoy's Anna Karenina, and Faulkner's Quentin Compson. And great comedy fits into this context when one considers Jonson's Volpone, Moliere's Alceste, Fielding's Tom Jones, and Austen's Elizabeth Bennett. The temptation to be definitive about any of these figures can be offset by the recognition of qualities that fight the definitive statement. Oedipus's determination is contradicted by his stubbornness, Antigone's courage by her obsessiveness, Lear's strength by his petulance, Volpone's imagination by his rapacity, Raskolnikov's compassion by his violence. We do not think of any of these figures as *inconsistent* but as made larger as artistic creations by the contradictions that are essential to their natures.

The second source of my notion of vital contradictions in early modern drama derives from the reaction in late nineteenth century Europe and America against *melodrama*, the popular literature of the nineteenth, and twentieth centuries. Melodramatic techniques cover a multitude of factors in drama (and I am now limiting myself to the drama, though much that I say obviously applies to all kinds of narrative literature). Those factors range from plot, to language, to setting and atmosphere, to moral purposes. Character, though not unimportant, is less important in melodrama than are these other factors. The main characters in melodrama are typically the *protagonist,* the embodiment of good, and the *antagonist,* the embodiment of evil. Normally, good triumphs, though there is one kind of melodrama, R. B. Heilman's "drama of disaster," in which evil triumphs.[1] The main interests in melodrama have always been, what is going to happen, and what moral instruction should I get from this? Suspense and clear moral choices are always central. And these are often accompanied by the lurid, often for its own sake. The central figures in melodrama tend to be formulaic. Villains may "reform," fallen women may be "saved," wayward husbands and wives may become faithful spouses; but these normally play-concluding changes in motives and behavior tend to be simplistic.

The four playwrights I shall be dealing with, in their determination to be probing dramatists like their classical ancestors, all attempted to transcend melodrama, even though two of them, Ibsen and O'Neill, used it extensively. Ibsen tried to write non-melodramatic plays early in his career but came increasingly to employ melodramatic techniques because he thought their popularity would attract audiences to his plays and thereby allow him, in the name of a new realism, to more broadly convey his larger vision.[2] And O'Neill, willy-nilly much influenced by the melodramatic American theater of his father, included much melodrama in the plots, language, and characterizations of his earlier drama, but, as I and others have attempted to show, ultimately reached beyond melodrama.[3] As for Strindberg, while melodrama plays some part in his

---

[1]   See *Tragedy and Melodrama: Versions of Experience* (Seattle: U of Washington P, 1968), especially 32–73. I take my lead in this study from Heilman's sense of the inner "dividedness" of the central figures of tragedy as opposed to the absence of inner dividedness that characterizes the central figures in melodrama. That Heilman's view of melodrama in this regard has been extensively and variously revised in recent theater criticism does not displace the truth and clarity of his distinction. For a few of such revisions, see the essays in *Melodrama,* edited by James Redmond (Cambridge UP, 1992), especially those by William R. Morse (17–30) and William Sharp (269–280). See also Thomas Postlewait, "From Melodrama to Realism: The Suspect History of American Drama," in *Melodrama: The Cultural Emergence of a Genre,* edited by Michael Hays and Anastasia Nikopoulou (NY: St. Martin's Press, 1996) 39–60.

[2]   See the chapter on Ibsen in Robert Brustein's *The Theatre of Revolt* (Boston: Little, Brown, and Co., 1964) 35–83. That larger vision for Brustein is shaped by the constant reversals in Ibsen's positions: "For Ibsen ... the ultimate Truth lies only in the perpetual conflict of truths. ..." (48)

[3]   See Jean Chothia's *Forging a Language* and my own *Eugene O'Neill's New Language of Kinship* (Syracuse UP, 1982). In this context, see also Kurt Eisen's *The Inner Strength of Opposites: O'Neill's Novelistic Drama and the Melodramatic Imagination* (Athens: U Georgia P, 1994). Eisen takes his lead from Peter Brooks's *The Melodramatic Imagination* (New Haven: Yale UP, 1976). For the most recent discussion of the "dividedness" of O'Neill's later characters, see Zander Brietzke's

naturalistic plays, it is of minimal importance. And Chekhov all but abandoned melodrama in his close examination of character.[4] All four attempted to de-emphasize melodrama's intricate plots, simplistic characterizations, and, except where it served other purposes, overblown language. And if there is a *moral* to be drawn from any of their plays, at least the ones I look at, it is not an obvious one.

What they turned to, with varying degrees of success, was an emphasis on character comparable to that in the great drama of the past. Rather than emphasizing plot and intrigue, they emphasized the contradictory ways in which their people think and behave, particularly in stressful situations. Their major characters are often inconsistent because that is the way people are. And rather than taking away from these figures, these inconsistencies add to their convincing qualities. One might say these playwrights *reinvent* the human.[5] Three of these playwrights wrote before the influence of Freudian depth psychology on literature, but all of them had an instinctive sense of the multiplicity of often contradictory motives that affect human behavior. And they had a sense that such multiplicity of contradictory motives strengthened their characters as dramatic figures and deepened the plays in which the characters appear.

I have labeled with the phrase *vital contradictions* those contradictions in their natures that essentially identify most of the major figures in the plays I shall look at, and some of the minor figures. Such contradictions are vivid and pronounced, while the figures we encounter is fully wrought, whole, and singular. Such contradictions render the characters convincing while enigmatic, recognizable while indefinable. These characters do not all become Lears (though a couple come close), but their contradictions help them to stand out, especially when the character in question is, or becomes, aware of them. Their contradictions are vital in contributing to the importance of these characters within their individual plays, and vital in contributing to the impact these characters have on us as readers and audiences.

The Aesthetics of Failure: Dynamic Structure in the Plays of Eugene O'Neill (Jefferson, N.C: McFarland, 2001) 164–196.

[4] Harvey Pitcher, in his excellent study *The Chekhov Play* (NY: Harper and Row, 1973), demonstrates how that playwright abandoned a moral outlook, one in which there are heroes and villains, in favor of one which explores the emotional complexities of his characters.

[5] Harold Bloom's *Shakespeare: The Invention of the Human* (NY: Riverhead Books, 1998) is an attempt to re-humanize Shakespeare in an era in which there has been a discrediting of human values as the basis for the study of literature. While I disagree with many of Bloom's interpretations of Shakespeare's plays, I admire what he has tried to do and to some degree emulate him in my approach to modern drama.

To amplify what I have said, let me quickly consider several of these playwrights' better-known figures that I will not later deal with in detail. Ibsen's Dr. Stockmann (*An Enemy of the People*) becomes more human in being both a relentless pursuer of justice and at the same time obsessively self-centered; Strindberg's Captain Adolph (*The Father*) by being both a highly rational figure and at the same time a crazed misogynist; and O'Neill's Con Melody (*A Touch of the Poet*) by being both a genuine aristocrat and at the same time a shanty-Irish brawler. The *at the same time* is important. It is not always easy to assess which side of the contradiction is at work at a particular moment. But in all these figures, an "inner strength" (Kurt Eisen's phrase)[6] is revealed by the contradictions that are always at work between powerful, contradictory forces within them. It is the strength implied by Strindberg's Daughter of Indra in *A Dream Play* when she says of individual human beings that a "conflict of opposites generates power, as fire and water generates steam."

Obviously, I cannot deal with all the significant playwrights and plays of early modern drama whose characters reveal vital contradictions.[7] My selection is based on my impression of a power in the playwrights and plays I have chosen that is largely divorced from what these plays "are saying." Ibsen still strikes many as primarily associated with social protest, Strindberg with the force of the occult in human experience, Chekhov with the changes his society is going through, and O'Neill with fashionable theories of his time.[8] While I do not wish to negate the importance of these factors, I do find these playwrights strongly linked, not by their views on socio-political topics close to their hearts, but by their common perception that vital human beings are most forcefully identified by their contradictions. And the plays I have chosen strike me as ones that most clearly reveal that link.

I begin, with Ibsen, with an unlikely play, but one that is central to my outlook: *Peer Gynt*. I say unlikely because: 1) it is for Ibsen a relatively early effort and, despite its popularity, undeniably long and disjointed; and 2) it is a folk play, not realist drama, as are all but one of the other plays I look at. But if ever there were a central figure who is

---

[6]   See Eisen reference in note 3.

[7]   My selection of playwrights and plays grows out of the historical parameters and prospective length of the study. In addition, my four playwrights—unlike, say, the more cerebral Bernard Shaw—emphasize character as the outgrowth of a multitude of instinctive and psychological forces that cannot ever be fully understood.

[8]   With regard to O'Neill in this context, see Joel Pfister's *Staging Depth: Eugene O'Neill and the Politics of Psychological Discourse* (Chapel Hill: U of North Carolina P, 1995).

full of vital contradictions, it is Peer. I continue with *The Wild Duck,* where I focus on not only on the vital contradictions of Hjalmar Ekdahl, but also on the inner contradictions of the play's intellectual combatants Gregers Werle and Dr. Relling, contradictions that contribute to their being so fierce in their attitudes. And I look at *Hedda Gabler,* that portrait of a woman inhabited by the most vital of inner contradictions of any almost any woman character in literature.

I begin my discussion of Strindberg with a brief look at *The Father,* before discussing *Miss Julie,* in which I consider the ways in which each of the lovers' vital contradictions affect their relationship. Then I move to *Easter,* in which vital contradictions within the central character Elis are seen to parallel contradictory symbols of despair and hope associated with Lent and Easter; and the Expressionist *A Dream Play,* in which contradictions within the figures of the Officer, the Lawyer, and the Poet exemplify oppositions within the human spirit which the Daughter says generate human power. I also look at the inner contradictions the Daughter herself must experience when she assumes her human role as Agnes, the Lawyer's wife.

With Chekhov, I begin with *Ivanov,* the vital contradictions within whose central figure point the way directly, as I see it, to Chekhov's subsequent, better-known plays and characters. I then discuss in succession *The Sea Gull, Uncle Vanya,* and *The Three Sisters,* looking in varying degrees of detail at all those plays' major characters, and some minor ones (if one can say there are minor figures in Chekhov), and conclude with *The Cherry Orchard,* where I concentrate on just four figures. In this section I focus, as I do in discussing *Miss Julie,* on how vital contradictions within the characters affect their relationships with one another. The Chekhov section is the longest in the book because his characters are the wealthiest in vital contradictions.

By O'Neill's own proclamation, Ibsen and Strindberg were his artistic progenitors, and if he discounted Chekhov in the 1920s,[9] I wonder if he would still have discounted him if he had been asked about Chekhov in the late 1930s. It is difficult to imagine the creator of Jamie Tyrone failing to appreciate the creator of the doctor in *The Three Sisters.* After a look at *More Stately Mansions,* I focus on the vital contradictions inherent in almost all the characters in *The Iceman Cometh,* with particular emphasis on Hickey and Larry Slade, before dealing with *Long Day's Journey into Night* and *A Moon for the Misbegotten,*

---

[9] O'Neill denigrated Chekhov in 1924 when in an interview he called the Russian dramatist a writer of "perfect plotless plays." See Oscar Cargill et al., eds., *O'Neill and His Plays* (NYU Press, 1961) 111.

expanding upon and modifying my earlier published discussions of those plays[10] and adding a brief consideration of the one-act *Hughie*. I see the creation of vital contradictions within his characters as the salient aspect of O'Neill's late plays, and I focus most on Jamie (later Jim) Tyrone as the figure whose vital contradictions are the deepest and whose ultimate awareness of those contradictions make him into a genuinely tragic figure.

While melodrama as pure entertainment persists (and always will), and there has been a very self-conscious revival of melodrama in recent years in musicals like *Sweeney Todd* and *Les Misérables*, vital contradictions in their central figures are what most serious dramatists aim for. Witness the work of Tennessee Williams, Arthur Miller, and Edward Albee; and more recent playwrights like Tom Stoppard, David Hare, David Mamet, Sam Shepard and Terence McNally. There is also an increasing number of revivals of plays by the dramatists I deal with.[11] And there has been an increase on screen in the number of plays by these dramatists, along with often popularized versions of the plays of Shakespeare, their chief ancestor. Melodramatic tricks are still employed, as they were by Ibsen to make his serious drama more engaging to popular audiences. This is especially true, for example, of the recent Martin McDonagh two-act *The Beauty Queen of Leenane*, in which emphasis on vital contradictions within the characters in the first act is displaced by an old-fashioned melodrama of blood and horror in the second (seriously marring the play, in my opinion). Theater, like the other arts, seems to have a propensity to run away from the human just as it reaches the point of more deeply probing it. But serious theater today is primarily still in the tradition of the best of the early modern dramatists, and my purpose is to probe that tradition from the perspective on dramatic characterization I bring to some of their major plays.

---

[10] "The Transcendence of Melodrama in Long Day's Journey Into Night," in *Perspectives on O'Neill: New Essays,* edited by S. Bagchee (Victoria, B.C., 1988) 33–42; "The Transcendence of Melodrama in *A Touch of the Poet* and *A Moon for the Misbegotten*," in *Critical Approaches to O'Neill,* edited by J.H. Stroupe (NY: AMS Press, 1988) 147–157; and "The Transcendence of Melodrama in The Iceman Cometh," in *Critical Essays on Eugene O'Neill,* edited by James Martine (Boston: G.K. Hall, 1984) 145–158.

[11] Revivals of *The Wild Duck* and *Hedda Gabler* have in recent years burgeoned in London and New York, as have revivals of all Chekhov's "big four" and of Strindberg's *Miss Julie*. O'Neill's late plays are, of course, constantly being professionally revived—most recently and successfully *The Iceman Cometh* (with Kevin Spacey in London and New York), *A Moon for the Misbegotten* (with Gabriel Byrne in New York), and *Long Day's Journey into Night* (with Jessica Lange in London). In addition are the many revivals of these plays by academic and regional theaters.

IBSEN

Peer Gynt

For many years I did not include *Peer Gynt* in my thinking about modern drama. I had always sensed that everything that follows from *Peer Gynt* in the Ibsen canon in one way or another derives from it—along with its companion piece *Brand*—but because of its folkloristic narrative, its episodic structure, its use of verse, its seemingly unresolvable enigmas, its being so far in setting and mood from Ibsen's naturalistic plays, perhaps even because of the subversive sentimentality of the Grieg music usually associated with the play, I had not felt it worth the time to deal with when there were more apparently "modern" plays to consider. I now realize how mistaken I was.

I want first to stress how important the play is in an approach like mine to some of the large early characters in modern drama, figures who are monumentally contradictory. Ibsen's image of Peer helped lay the groundwork for the approach to the dynamically human figures appearing in his later drama. If we consider Peer a character who says and does irresponsible things that cause others pain and trouble yet alone has the imaginative and psychological energy to make life seem something more than plodding and pedestrian, we might wonder whether we might also be talking about a variety of later Ibsen characters, for example, Hedda Gabler.

The play was quite familiar to the other dramatists I shall focus on, and if they did not often allude to it directly, that is probably because until the second world war, the play was immensely familiar to anyone in Europe and America interested in the drama. So when Strindberg evokes the sexual devil that gets into one on midsummer's eve, he need not make explicit that the second-act mountain scenes of Ibsen's play could well lie behind Miss Julie's impulses. Free spirits as apparently unprincipled yet at the same time guilt-ridden as Chekhov's Ivanov also suggest Peer. And certainly in the irrepressible, not to mention drunken, energies of O'Neill's Jamie Tyrone, who is also crushed by guilt, can be seen a latter-day representation of the Gyntian spirit. Not only are these figures like Peer in being extremely rebellious and at times immoral, they, like him, resist easy assessment and classification. So, in beginning with Peer Gynt, I am not only getting into my discussion of Ibsen, I am getting into the substance of this study.

In my introduction I defined "vital contradictions" in a character as contradictions that are "vivid and pronounced while the character we encounter is fully wrought, whole, and singular." Such contradictions "give depth to the character while rendering him or her both convincing and enigmatic, both recognizable and indefinable." Peer fits this definition better perhaps than any other character I shall look at, but he does so in what I can only call a *raw* way, since the oppositions in his nature seem so bold and abrupt. But he is certainly both convincing and enigmatic, and if he is not always larger than life, he is certainly always different from those around him, as he is to the very end determined to demonstrate.

The best way to get to the heart of Peer Gynt is to look first briefly at his last-act encounter with the button-molder, who threatens to melt Peer down in one of his molds unless Peer can demonstrate, not that he has not led an evil life, but that his evil is anything out of the ordinary. Peer, fearing such a judgment of his moral condition is true, nevertheless believes that he does not *fit the mold,* and spends the remainder of the play trying to prove as much. What Peer is insisting, of course, is that in spite of what the button-molder implies, he, Peer, has never been a nonentity. He has never been good in large terms or evil in large terms, but he has also never been inconsequential.

In suggesting, as I am, that Peer is vitally contradictory, I am suggesting that Ibsen endows Peer's personality with opposing qualities that derive from a source Ibsen would undoubtedly have been familiar with. In *The Sickness Unto Death,* first published before the writing of *Peer Gynt,* Soren Kierkegaard, ignoring traditional morality, discusses the despair associated with "infinitude," which he also calls "possibility," and the despair associated with "finitude" which he also calls "necessity."[1] By infinitude he means behavior that is "fantastical," highly imaginative, unrestrained, and ever seeking the as-yet-undiscovered in life. Finitude by contrast is related to caution, self-interest, and self-discipline. The excess of either, says Kierkegaard, leads to what he calls the *sin* of despair.

I suggest that Peer's contradictions parallel Kierkegaard's dichotomy in that he swings between widely distinct extremes of infinitude and finitude, and that his vitality may be associated with that swinging back

---

[1]   See Soren Kierkegaard, *The Sickness unto Death,* in *Fear and Trembling and The Sickness unto Death,* translated by Walter Lowrie (Garden City, NY: Doubleday Anchor Books, 1954). For a detailed discussion of the play in relation to Kierkegaard's philosophy generally, see Bruce G. Shapiro, *Divine Madness and the Absurd Paradox: Ibsen's 'Peer Gynt' and the Philosophy of Kierkegaard* (Westport, CN: Greenwood Press, 1990). My discussion is limited to *The Sickness Unto Death.*

and forth. The idea may be illustrated by a passage early in Act 4, in which Peer, on his yacht, describes his ambitions, what he calls his "Gyntian self," to a set of unscrupulous guests:

> What's the whole art of daring, of
> Courage in action, what is it
> But to move with uncommitted feet
> Between the pitfalls dug by life—

Thus, Kierkegaard's infinitude. But immediately he swings to an idea suggesting the philosopher's finitude:

> To know for sure that all your days
> Aren't over on the day you fight—
> To know that behind you always lies
> A bridge secured for your retreat. (99)

> [All quotes from the play are from Rolf Fjelde's translation (U of Minnesota Press, 1980).]

After the daring and moving "with uncommitted feet," we get the desire to know that there is always a "bridge secured" for one's "retreat," an aspiration that sounds more like the desire for a pension plan than a dream of the infinite.

The question of self is central to the play. Ibsen seems at pains to insist, especially through Peer's encounter with the button molder, that to look at Peer in traditional moral terms is finally to deny him his self. Yet what is a self, particularly in Ibsen's time, if it cannot be determined in moral terms? The answer must lie outside the terms of traditional morality, and that answer is suggested by Kierkegaard's dichotomy.

In what follows I shall go through the play sequentially, citing lines and events that focus directly on my understanding of it. Everything that Peer is may be figuratively illustrated by his description of his ride on the reindeer buck in the opening scene. Embodied in this famous and startling speech[2] is the essence of Peer's sense of the infinite:

> He and I, on that blade of ground,
> Cut a channel through the wind.
> I've never had me such a run!
> Sometimes in the headlong pace
> The air seemed full of flashing suns.

---

[2] For a description of the speech as an example of Ibsen's ability to write Romantic poetry, see Brian Johnston, *Toward the Third Empire: Ibsen's Early Drama* (Minneapolis: U of Minnesota P, 1980) 177–178. An interesting corollary to my approach to the speech may be found in Charles R. Lyons, *Henrik Ibsen: The Divided Consciousness* (Carbondale: Southern Illinois UP, 1972) 25–27.

In the reeling gulfs of space
Eagles with brown backs would float
Midways between us and the water—
Then fall away like motes. (5)

Then comes the still more startling image of a second, reflected deer:

Downward, endlessly, we go.
But in the depths something shows
Dim white, like reindeers' belly fleece.
Mother, it was *our* reflection
Shooting upward in the lake from
Silent darkness to the glassy calm
On top with the same breakneck
Speed as we were hurtling down. (6)

The vision of the reflected reindeer shooting up to the surface at the "same breakneck speed" that Peer and the buck are "hurtling down" is surely one of the most striking in the play. The whole image is part and parcel of Peer's fired up imagination, something an artist might seek to achieve on canvas or that a "special effects" person might try to create in today's cinema. The shooting up to the surface is a violent countering image to the hurtling down to the surface, and striking countering images are akin to what I am talking about. I would not go so far as to suggest the two images are symbols of the infinite and the finite heading toward some sort of explosive confrontation, but Ibsen clearly intends some extreme confrontation of opposing forces in this vision, and extreme confrontations between emotional counterforces are what define Peer Gynt.

Peer's mother Aase is left gasping by Peer's description, as she is by just about everything about her son. She is herself contradictory in her responses, at one moment telling Peer to behave himself and to get a good wife, at another encouraging the wildness of his imagination. But she is determined to warn others about her son's excesses and insists on following him to the wedding of his former girlfriend to his rival. Equally determined to go and break up the wedding, Peer lifts his shrieking mother onto a millhouse roof, and goes on his libidinous way to the wedding, where not even the appearance as a guest of the innocent Solveig, who is to become the love of his life, restrains him from kidnapping the not altogether unwilling bride for a sexual encounter in the hills.

Contradictions have everything to do with our impressions of Peer throughout his tumultuous, not to say torrid, experiences of Act 2, which culminate with his interview by the Troll King and his eleventh-hour rejection of trolldom. The earlier scenes in the act seem an exploration of the finitude-infinitude opposition in the pursuit and aftermath of sexual fulfillment, the whole subject seen, one might say, at a rudimentary level. In scene 1, we get the aftermath of the crude satisfaction Peer has achieved from the stolen bride and the sour sense of finitude such sexual experience entails; but from there we climb *with* Peer up the alpine slopes to the more lyrical sexuality of his encounter with the three herd girls, and finally to his still more exhilarating but also more perilous affiliation with the Lady in Green (by whom it will be his misfortune to have a child). Again, in still more fantastical terms, infinitude here is represented in the exuberance that accompanies the uninhibited sexuality of youth.[3] Surely nothing in the drama of the period comes closer to dwelling on the erotic for its own sake than these scenes. But the loss of self that rampant eroticism brings in its wake is also implicit, again in rudimentary terms, in these scenes. As the irrepressible drive which sends Peer off in pursuit of these women (and they of him) sets off his most extravagant dreams, so its fulfillment sets off his most profound dejection—the two responses which Kierkegaard equates with the despair associated with both the excess of infinitude and the excess of finitude. To dwell "fantastically" (Kierkegaard's word) on sex is to lose one's self in infinitude, but similarly may one lose one's self in finitude, in this case the regarding of sex solely as an "expense of spirit in a waste of shame." Ibsen seems to understand the idea that with regard to sex, both infinitude and finitude are ever-present and everrenewable—the problem residing in the excess of either.

Next follows Peer's most challenging adventure in the act, his encounter with the trolls, emblems of gross sensuality. That Peer seems an excellent candidate for trolldom has been evident in all his actions from the start. He tells heartily-conceived, magnificently illustrated lies; he drinks heavily and at the slightest provocation; he has no hesitation to engage in fist fights; and, in the episodes we have just been looking at, he enters full-tilt into any kind of sexual encounter that offers itself. At the same time, he has moved beyond the more traditional shapes of trolldom. He fears the disfiguring he might have to endure to become a troll. The king, recognizing in Peer the makings of a troll for the times, assures him, however, that two and three-headed trolls have gone out of fashion. Peer, the king adds, need not even give up his Christian faith,

---

[3]   In the Royal Dramatic Theater of Sweden production of the play directed by Ingmar Bergman and presented in Brooklyn, New York in May 1993, the bride and the herd girls were presented as earthy images, the rape of the bride sordid, the herd girls shrieking and dirty—while the encounter with the Lady in Green was the kind of fantasy associated with adolescent dreaming. For the Lady, Peer produces a mammoth (rubber) erection which bursts out of his fly and remains exposed throughout a good portion of his ensuing encounter with the trolls.

the satiric purpose of which concession is clear. Peer then accedes to the trollian notion that a king's daughter cannot be wooed with a smooth behind. He must wear a tail—another, more Swiftian, satiric thrust.

What, then, does Peer stick at? What is the eleventh-hour issue that saves him, as it might not save other individuals dominated by sensuality? He will not go through the most time-honored trollish rite of all: the splitting of the eyeball, the rite that prevents trolls from accepting the world for what it is in favor of what they wish it to be. This recalls the Lady in Green's earlier observation that among trolls "everything is to be seen two ways." Here we see how that idea works. Peer is asked to witness a dance of what the trolls see as great beauty and elegance but which he recognizes as "A bell cow strumming a catgut lyre,/ And a sow in stockings dancing to her." He refuses to see what the trolls insist is there. And since the Lady in Green has said that trolls see things two ways, it may be assumed that the trolls do know what the figures are, *finitely* speaking. They see things two ways, but won't acknowledge that they do. Peer's problem is that he will not accept their lie. He must recognize illusion for what it is. He may dream of riding a marvelous steed across mountains and fjords, but he never denies, and will not now deny, that dreams are dreams, whatever their attractions and their capacity to alleviate the sufferings of hunger and penury. Peer insists here on the freedom, which a thoroughly debauched life must deny him just as a conventional bourgeois life would have denied him, to see things exactly as they are. In finally refusing to become a troll, he is insisting on the freedom to accept both possibility and necessity, neither one excluding the other. Kierkegaard, of course, might recognize this as evidence of a balanced self.

Then we are introduced to the Boyg, who is, and undoubtedly will remain, the most enigmatic figure of all in the play. Three things stick in one's mind about Peer's encounter with this creature in Act 2, scene 8. First, like all the phantoms and ghosts of tradition, the Boyg has no physical substance. He is impervious to Peer's assaults. Second, he advises Peer to "go roundabout," presumably meaning that Peer should not attempt to confront the central challenges of his life directly. And third, just as it appears the Boyg will overwhelm him, the creature is assaulted and overcome by an ensemble of birds, who are identified by the Boyg with women. (*Boyg*: "He was too strong. There were women behind him." [67]) And here we must associate women with the redeeming Solveig, since it hardly seems likely that the women the Boyg refers to are the herd girls or the Lady in Green.

The Boyg's advice that Peer "go roundabout" is the key to his message. Going roundabout is what Peer does in his youth, and in one way or another continues to do throughout his life. He will not, or more accurately, is unable to, stand and fight against the forces which assail or lay claim to him. He always runs away: from the villagers, from Ingrid, from the troll king, from the Lady in Green and their porcine offspring—and later from an assortment of adversaries. He always "goes roundabout," until the very end. And even at the end his fate remains uncertain because a final judgment is never made about him by the button molder. Peer's being Peer means he avoids traps, and thus the Boyg's advice, which is untenable on moral grounds, actually provides Peer the way to become a hero who lives outside the confines of traditional morality—possibly an embodiment of Kierkegaard's balanced self.

But the Peer we see in Act 4, roughly a quarter of a century later, the Peer who has gone to America to win his fortune in the kinds of crassly materialistic occupations the new world was providing—the import of slaves for the Carolinas and the export of pagan images for China— hardly seems a balanced self. One might say, in fact, that he has actually honored his vows to trolldom in spite of his last minute defection. To be sure, he claims to have compensated for his greed by being "like a father" to his own purchased slaves and sending Christian missionaries to China along with the pagan images, but these are rationalizations the troll king would have been happy to accept. Ibsen simply finds the hypocrisy of European-American imperialism about on a par with that of bourgeois Norway's church-going smugness. But more significantly, and paralleling his sexual experiences as the young sensualist, Peer now seeks the infinite that can come through wealth.

The chief difference between the young Peer of the first three acts and the middle-aged Peer of this act lies in his awareness of self.[4] Part of the young Peer's charm had been his utter indifference to what he was. His loss of that charm, but also the beginning of his movement toward his final destiny, is his search for his identity—his obsession in Act 4 with what he calls the Gyntian self. That self, as he describes it to his fellow-magnates aboard his yacht in the act's opening scene, clearly states his desire to achieve the sense of endless possibility, the sense of infinitude which his preoccupation with hoarding money in America has denied him.

> ... it's an army corps
> Of wishes, appetites, desires.
> The Gyntian self is a mighty sea
> Of whim, demand, proclivity—

---

[4]   See Rolf Fjelde, "*Peer Gynt,* Naturalism and the Dissolving Self," *The Drama Review,* 13 (1968): 28–43.

In short, whatever moves my soul
And makes me live to *my* own will. (99)

But this statement is followed by the treachery of his guests aboard the
yacht and the loss of the gold upon which his aspirations are based. The
sense of infinitude, the Gyntian self Peer pursues through wealth, must
be ever prey to Peer's own basic needs and the greed of others.

The pattern of this first episode in Act 4 is roughly paralleled by the
second and third episodes of that act. Peer enters upon not one but three
attempts to achieve the Gyntian self, each approaching his desire for
infinitude from a different direction, each contradicted by an inevitable
finitude. Following the treachery of his guests (and their own sorry fate),
Peer enters upon his second quest. He again finds gold, paralleling his
American experience, and again he seeks to use that gold to achieve the
Gyntian self, this time in erotic experience reminiscent of his day with
Ingrid and the mountain girls but now burdened by the self-
consciousness of middle age. He this time loses all to the duplicity of
the dancing siren Anitra, who takes him for all he is worth.

Peer's third, and most complex, quest for infinitude in the name of
the Gyntian self is his turn to scholarship in the final scenes of Act 4, the
last of which takes place, significantly, in the madhouse. Faustian in
nature, this quest takes him into the other major sphere of acquisitive-
ness for which humans sell their souls, pursuit of knowledge, and like
Peer's Faustian ancestors, he must pay the price, as he had for its purely
materialistic counterparts. And again, that self will elude him, here even
more painfully than it eluded him in the previous episodes. Again he
finds that he cannot pursue infinitude without a much needed finitude,
which in the process of his pursuit he must lose. What he finds now is
not the loss of his wealth but the loss of his most precious necessity, his
sanity.

Peer's nemesis in this final episode of Act 4 is more threatening and
far more complex than the conniving businessmen and the crass Anitra.
The supreme ironist Begriffenfeldt in fact anticipates the shadowy allegorical figures Peer will encounter in Act 5. He makes fun of Peer's
quest for the Gyntian self, in savage mockery calling Peer the *Emperor*
of self. There is only necessity, he intimates, and anyone who cannot
recognize this must ultimately go mad.

Part of the difficulty in dealing with the scene in Begriffenfeldt's
Cairo insane asylum is that the inmates we hear from are based on specific figures and events of Ibsen's time. Thus, in terms of what these
figures contribute to the larger issues of the play, only their obsessive
concentration on self to the exclusion of any accurate awareness of their

surroundings is immediately relevant to this discussion. And this self-absorption is best symbolized by Begriffenfeldt's image of Munchausen's fox, who in seeking to escape from his captors literally pulls himself out of his skin, casting off its exterior faculties, which here mean primarily the capacity to reason, leaving only an inner body, corresponding to the self in its barest form. This is what madmen do, and Peer is thus a first-class madman in what he is pursuing, the ironist implies. That is, the fox's effort parallels Peer's effort to achieve the Gyntian self, and Peer's mistaking the inmates for a Scholars Club thus specifically links Peer's pursuit of infinitude through scholarship with madness.

Begriffenfeldt is the culmination of all those figures and forces in Peer's life, going back before even the conniving businessmen and enticing dancing girls, who would in one way or another limit his search for the infinite, for possibility, all in the name of necessity (here identified with reason). At the same time, it must be remembered, the troll king would have limited Peer's access to necessity, so that the king parallels Begriffenfeldt from an opposing perspective. That is, as the troll king counseled only infinitude, Begriffenfeldt counsels only finitude. Peer feels hemmed in on both sides, and fears, as we begin Act 5, that his life has been rendered pointless. At least, that is what drives him back to Norway to find out what his origins can tell him about the meaning of his life.

The opening scenes of the final act focus directly on Peer's contradictory nature, for which, from my point of view, the infinitude-finitude division is the ultimate symbol. Now in later middle-age, he is confronted with a life or death situation in a shipwreck within sight of the Norwegian coast. Throughout these scenes his feelings lurch in wildly opposing directions. Before the wreck itself, Peer magnanimously offers to reward the crew for its service during the trip. But upon being told by the Captain of the gratitude the sailors and their families will feel, Peer turning savagely resentful at the fact he has no family, withdraws the offer as spontaneously as he made it. This pattern of magnanimity alternating with resentment is followed in more critical terms when, following the wreck, he struggles with the ship's cook over who will be able to grasp the keel of an overturned lifeboat, the keel apparently providing space for only one, then fruitlessly tries to save the cook, after the latter has been forced to let go. As they have always been, Peer's acts here are utterly impulsive. He has always been quick to shift from good will to injured pride, and back again. Through all this he is observed by a "Strange Passenger," visible to no one but Peer, an allegorical figure anticipating others to follow in the act (the lean one and the button molder), all of them seemingly assessing Peer's moral worth.

Throughout the remainder of the play, Peer's contradictions gradually become subordinated to the larger metaphysical issues of which they are a part. Even though its opening scene and the clearly allegorical nature of the key figures Peer encounters suggest otherwise, the central question of the act is not whether Peer has been a good or a bad person, but whether or not he has been a person, a self, at all—or whether there is such a thing as a self. The central dilemma of *Peer Gynt* thus becomes an anticipation of later absurdist drama, and the central dilemma of O'Neill's *The Iceman Cometh.* Are we not just so much vacuum in the final analysis? That is the question Peer struggles with in trying to defend himself against the button molder, a question which the play never quite answers.

The final scenes move even more chaotically from situation to situation. Peer's return to his native land is not marked by as much realization and fulfillment as he had expected. But a key scene is that in which he hears a pastor's funeral oration for a man who as a youth Peer witnessed cutting off a finger to avoid military service. In spite of the disgrace, the pastor says, the boy had persevered, marrying and building a farmhouse high above a glacier, then having three sons. He used to, says the pastor, lead one son down the glacier, "tied by a line," while carrying the other sons, so that they might go to school—this presumably day after day. The man's story is obviously not Peer's, but it is a corollary to Peer's. It is the two contradictory parts of the man's history that make up his self; and *self,* Ibsen implies, may be made up of quite contradictory impulses. Rather than being a story about the man's reformation—we actually never hear about any reformation—it is about the vitality of the man's contradictions. Thus, through the man's story the possibility of Peer's own redemption is hinted at.

The chief allegorical figure of the last act, the button molder, relates the act significantly to the rest of the play. The button molder is both Peer's nemesis and enigmatic redeemer. Not so much concerned with making a moral judgment on Peer, as have been his predecessors the strange passenger and the satanic "lean one," the button molder seems to offer Peer the best bargain. In death, he suggests, the mold will at least have been better than the inferno. But Peer, growing increasingly panicked that his idea of self be preserved, resists. And unlike Peer's other tormentors, the button molder is ready to temporarily let him off. He will allow Peer to begin a new life (like the man eulogized in the parson's sermon), but he makes clear that the jury is still out.

> We'll meet at the final crossroads, Peer;
> And *then* we'll see—I won't say more. (209)

While the play asserts that Peer cannot be viewed as incontrovertibly good or evil, it does not finally assert that he thereby does not possess a self, which is the core of the button molder's challenge. Through Peer the question of a new kind of identity has been placed squarely before us, a post morality-based kind of identity that in the twentieth century might be associated with, say, a Jamie Tyrone.

But that idea takes us beyond what Ibsen in the 1860s might consciously have been promoting. The struggle over self continues to constitute Peer's angst to the end of the play. Because he would never stay and fight, would never assert a final, incontrovertible, and moral self in the terms of nineteenth-century melodrama—Peer might still be melted down. But the very fact that he is given another chance is what makes Ibsen's perception that humans can be judged by factors outside where they stand in the good versus evil dichotomy so very original. The jury is still out on the Peer of the 1860s. And Solveig's faith and love allow that metaphysical jury time to continue its counsel. It was too early to assert that Peer has demonstrated another kind of self, one which extends Kierkegaard's dichotomy into what might today be called post-modern. But Peer is at least given a chance.

The Wild Duck

My discussion of *Peer Gynt* omitted much discussion of melodrama because since that play is a romantic folk play in verse, melodrama as Ibsen was to use it in other plays was of little concern. Its loose narrative, sudden changes in location, and its covering so long a period of time, make it the very opposite of melodrama in feeling and construction. But Ibsen was both affected by and disaffected with the nineteenth-century melodramatic tradition. This is evidenced by his use of melodrama in his pre-*Peer Gynt* plays (e.g., the bewildering plot intricacies of a play like *Lady Inger of Ostraat*); his abandonment of it once he had swept the dust of Norway from his feet to write his philosophical dramatic poems *Brand* and *Emperor and Galilean* in the Italy of the 1860s; and his ultimate, knowing re-adaptation of it to his major plays, beginning with *The Pillar of Society* and *A Doll House* in the late 1870s. The latter, for example, is a typical French melodrama with a novel, highly explosive ending tacked on; while *Ghosts* and *An Enemy of the People* employ melodramatic devices of plot and characterization to help give the utmost impact to the new and radical ideas underlying those plays. The Ibsen plays that I shall now be looking at are *The Wild Duck* and *Hedda Gabler*. While also employing melodramatic devices, both transcend melodrama, chiefly by an emphasis on contradictions in their major characters, and because they depart radically from the moral blacks and whites that traditional melodrama depends on. I have selected these two because they, among Ibsen's greatest plays, fit so well into the context of this study.

The Wild Duck, written in the early 1880s not long after *An Enemy of the People*, represents for many one of the several reversals in outlook Ibsen went through. Having preached the invasion of the private lives of citizens for their own good or for the good of society in *Ghosts* and *An Enemy of the People*, Ibsen apparently pulled back from the notion that messianic figures could improve the human lot—indeed, he came fairly suddenly to the realization that such figures could do more harm than good. From this perspective, Ibsen was exploding the messianic[1] Gregers Werle and his summons of the ideal in *The Wild Duck*. He was

---

[1] See Robert Brustein's discussion of "messianic drama" in *The Theatre of Revolt* 16–22.

mocking himself in his previous plays by making Gregers the melo-
dramatist with a message, the self-conscious creator of intrigues
intended to show the victims of ruthlessness and corruption the truth
about their pasts and the errors of their present ways. In this interpretation, Dr. Relling is Ibsen's new stand-in, the figure who realizes
that there can be no clear understanding of the rights and wrongs
associated with the past and that the only thing one can do for suffering
humanity is to help it live in the present, even if that means creating
"vital lies"[2] about themselves and their lives as a protection against
despair (Ibsen's equivalent of O'Neill's "pipe dreams" in *The Iceman
Cometh*).

While I in some measure agree with this interpretation of the play, I
do not think it tells the whole story. In Gregers's imagined melodrama,
old Werle's evil manipulation of the Ekdahls will be foiled, and the
victimized Ekdahls will be saved by his, Gregers's, carefully planned
revelations. In this simple construction, there are no grays, only blacks
and whites, and there is no doubt in Gregers's mind who will triumph,
once he sets things in motion. But Relling also sees things in melodramatic terms. In Relling's melodrama, Gregers's manipulation of the
Ekdahls is what needs to be foiled. In Relling's view, as in Gregers's,
there are no grays, only blacks and whites, although in his view it is the
black that will triumph in the end. But evil for Relling goes beyond
Gregers and his summons of the ideal. It is human nature itself.
Relling's insistence upon the need for lying to oneself is the basis of his
melodramatic perspective. Relling's contention that "to rob the average
man of his vital lie is to rob him of his happiness as well"(203) makes
him as melodramatic as Gregers. In Relling's view, human beings have
been defeated from the start, and there is no saving them. There is only
the development of intrigues, not unlike Gregers's intrigues, whereby
human beings might be kept from facing the hopelessness of their lives.
From this perspective, what Gregers does interferes with Relling's fixed
view of existence, just as what Relling does interferes with Gregers's.

At times Gregers and Relling both seem justified, but at other times
both seem unjustified. For example, if the bullet had killed the wild
duck and not Hedvig, or even if the death of Hedvig had not been the
suicide that Relling insists it is but just a terrible accident, Gregers's
view that facing the truth would have seemed justified and Relling's that
illusions are necessary unjustified. Gina has at the point of Hedvig's
death made giant steps in restoring the *status quo* of family life, and the
bequest from old Werle to Hedvig would continue to assure their well-

---

[2]   All quotes from this play and from *Hedda Gabler* are taken from Ibsen: *Four Major
       Plays*, translated by Rolf Fjelde (NY: Signet Classics, 1965).

being, a situation which Gregers might not really deplore, the "summons of the ideal" having been asserted and the "stench of the marsh gas" dissipated. But, of course, Hedvig does die, and Gregers's meddling assumes lethal significance. So Relling's view appears to have won the day. Still, we never really know anything of Hedvig's motives. We never know whether the shot was an intentional act of suicide or not. We can agree with Relling that meddling with a sensitive girl's emotions during puberty is like playing with fire, but in retrospect we can also agree with Gregers that, barring Hedvig's death, the family would be better off with the facts about the past revealed. In short, all that can be said is that any message that might be derived from the play's melodrama, Gregers's or Relling's, is finally left open.

We cannot know what Ibsen intended when he began to write this play, but what he ended with seems a direct challenge to melodrama, whether Gregers's or Relling's. What any approach to the play as melodrama leaves out is what we actually experience.[3] And that has less to do with a moral lesson, Gregers's or Relling's, than simply with people reacting to one another under emotional stress. Reading the play as melodrama also takes little account of the other characters in the play: Hjalmar, Gina, Hedvig, old Ekdahl—and even old Werle, who is presented to us in terms surprisingly broader than the terms in which his son Gregers sees him. Some of these figures play their assigned roles in the competing melodramas of Gregers and Relling as key players, others as bystanders—but in no case do these assigned melodramatic roles come close to fully representing the figures we encounter. Clearly enough, Gina is insufficiently defined by Gregers's reading of her as chief accomplice to the arch-villainy of old Werle, but does Relling's conception of her as the workaday protector and preserver of Hjalmar's "vital lie" necessarily work better?[4] The Gina who is also a person in her own right lies outside the moral structures of Gregers and Relling. And so with old Ekdahl, whose Nordic visions do not quite square with his role as victim in both Gregers's and Relling's schemes of things.

The issue, then, is the characters as they are presented to us in unexpected complexity, not as they are represented by Gregers and Relling. In fact, Ibsen undercuts the efforts of those two to play God by

---

[3] Maurice Valency discusses how the basic melodramatic structure of the play is subverted by what actually takes place. See *The Flower and the Castle* (NY: Macmillan, 1963) 170–174.

[4] Please note that the use of the term "vital" in the play is not the same as my use of it in the phrase vital contradictions. In the former case, Relling is talking about lies that make life bearable, while in the latter I am talking about contradictions that give substance and depth to characters.

revealing the traumas of their own respective pasts. The play makes clear that Gregers may be the way he is not so much because of his idealism as because of his desire to act out his mother's resentments, and Relling may be the way he is not so much because of his cynicism as because of his despair at having earlier been turned down by Mrs. Sorby (who is about to marry old Werle). In other words, Gregers and Relling both have inner contradictions, though their devotion to the melodramatic interpretations of life by which they live subordinates those contradictions.

What follows, then, is a closer examination of the play's other major characters outside the melodramatic contexts of Gregers and Relling, focusing on the vital contradictions in each figure.

Gina Ekdahl

It is important to begin any discussion of characters in this play with Gina, since she is so important to the several actions of the play, while her motives are often misunderstood. One might find in her attempts to bring things back to the *status quo* a third melodrama, one in which Hedvig's well-being, as she defines it, is the good, and any interference with that the evil. But clearly, among the many things that Gina is, she is not rigid about her daughter—provided her daughter is cared for—and she is not rigid about anything else, other than her determination to survive. And survival for her means survival of her family, with no melodramatically moral implications involved.

Gina Ekdahl's essential contradictions make her the most totally herself of any character in the play. She is independent while being dependent, clear while being inarticulate (or, at least, ungrammatical). While always subordinate to Hjalmar in relation to the family photography business, she makes all the arrangements and decisions. As wife and mother, she is submissive to the patriarchal moral values of the times, while in her unashamed attitude to her earlier affair with old Werle she is defiant of those values. She lives practically among the rigidities around her, and that very practicality implicitly defies those rigidities more eloquently than all Nora Helmer's orations.

HJALMAR.

Tell me don't you every day, every hour, regret this spider web of deception you have spun around me? Answer me that! Don't you really go around in a torment of remorse?

GINA.

Hjalmar dear, I've got so much to think about just with the housework and the day's routine.

HJALMAR.
Then you never turn a critical eye on your past!
GINA.
No. Good Lord, I'd almost forgotten that old affair. (183)

Insofar as Hedvig's well-being is concerned, Gina seems an ally of Relling's. She feels that as an adolescent girl, and especially one who is going blind, Hedvig needs to be protected. But she is no more an ally of Relling's than of Gregers's. She is too limited, or perhaps too limitless, to relate to Relling's concept of vital lies. She knows that Hjalmar is not really a scientist, if that means society must recognize him as one. But she also knows in her non-verbal way that a scientist is one who claims to be a scientist, and that if Hjalmar has few results to show for his efforts, how many supposedly legitimate scientists can claim efforts or results greater than his? She also seems intuitively to understand that scientists, like everyone else, escape into figurative attics to care for figurative menageries.

What I am saying is that in Gina Ekdahl Ibsen has created a character who is at peace with herself. It is not that the contradictions in herself and in life do not exist for her; it is that she is not outraged by them, a fact which appalls Hjalmar. She has no sense of irony—she is not cynical—and this may be her greatest saving grace before the deeply cynical understandings of life that underlie the melodramatic manipulations of Relling, and even Gregers.

Hjalmar Ekdahl

While Hjalmar Ekdahl seems quite the opposite of his wife, that he may finally not really be opposite is an important idea in this discussion. He is certainly the opposite of what he fancies himself, or likes to fancy himself: the brave, unrecognized inventor burdened by poverty, a pedestrian wife, and a routine occupation. And it, this fancy, this vital lie, is what Relling encourages as the sole means of preserving the man's supposedly fragile ego. In fact, of course, Hjalmar is lazy, fatuous, and inept. If his ego is indeed as fragile as Relling makes it out to be, it is time for the remaking of that ego that Gregers is so eager to achieve. Hjalmar may simply be one more of the many satirized fools who crowd the pages of comic literature.

But though it contains much satire, *The Wild Duck* is not fundamentally a satirical play. The essential contradiction in Hjalmar's character has little to do with his pretenses and poses, but rather with what he also is in the play, along with the pretenses and poses. He is a fool to *think* the world revolves around him, but in fact several worlds do revolve around him: the world Gregers needs to reform, the world Relling needs to protect from reformers (neither Gregers nor Relling could exist without a Hjalmar Ekdahl to experiment upon), and the world of home and family. The last of these is finally the significant world of the play.

Without idealizing family life, *The Wild Duck*, unlike any other Ibsen play, asserts the family as sole source of stability in a highly unstable, unpredictable, and only faintly knowable existence. And if Gina is the earth of the family, Hjalmar must be its air and fire. Ibsen is seeing the generic family of his time as a group in which fathers are fatuous, mothers are uninformed, and adolescent daughters are troubled. But he nevertheless sees the family as a group which, while dreadfully given to clichés, is beyond plots and melodramas. From this play's perspective, melodramas tend to be forced upon the family from the outside. There is in fact no *story* of family life here; there is essentially only family life itself, invaded by stories constructed out of the memories and predilections of others. What Gina in the final act wants to get Hjalmar back into, and Hjalmar obviously also wants to get back into, is not the control of his vital lie, or the fresh clean air of unvarnished truth, but the rhythm of their life together. Like the rhythm of kinship I have elsewhere identified in the late O'Neill plays,[5] this rhythm is made up of extreme reversals of feeling, and of the shifting rhetoric that accompanies such reversals, though the reversals here are not quite so rapid-fire as we get them in O'Neill.

This rhythm is best illustrated in the play's second act, after Hjalmar's disastrous soiree at old Werle's, but before the invaders, Gregers and Relling, arrive. Hjalmar returns from the party both ebullient and humiliated. He has clearly enjoyed himself, delighted with his borrowed evening dress and still more with the good and ample wine, but embarrassed by his ignorance about wine vintages and still more by the awkward appearance at the party of his father, whose presence he failed to acknowledge at the time. Hjalmar's shame, pretenses, and defenses all at the full, he swaggers and lies upon his return home, not wanting to lose the effect of the evening and determined to deny his humiliation. Inevitably he grows aggressive, attacking his wife for her failure to attract customers and to rent the spare room, and his daughter for her hints about the gift he had promised but neglected to bring her. He tries to make amends to the daughter by reading aloud the menu from the party, then complains about the sour looks he gets in response. But as sobriety begins to get the better of him, and his rashness is

---

[5]   See *Eugene O'Neill's New Language of Kinship*, 22–28.

displaced by guilt, we see him go through a series of rapid emotional changes rhetorically reflected in clichés appropriate to each emotion.

We hear first the clichés of his hurt pride and self-pity (in lines like "What incredible things a family breadwinner is asked to remember" and "I want no pleasures of this world"), and later the rhetoric of the reassurance he alone can provide. That reassurance begins with his concern, presumably genuine, for the animals in the attic, and for his father, toward whom he feels a special guilt; but the most convincing form of this culminating rhetoric of reassurance comes not in the form of words so much as of music. It is not a vital *lie* but a vital *contradiction* that while he bungles almost everything else, he apparently plays the flute well, with, of course, a sentimentality suited to the occasion:

HEDVIG.

... Let me bring you your flute, Daddy.

HJALMAR.

No, no flute. I want no pleasures of this world. (*Pacing about.*) Ah, yes, work. I'll be deep in work tomorrow; there'll be no lack of that ... I'll sweat and strain as long as my strength holds out.

HEDVIG.

Can't I get you a bottle of beer, then?

HJALMAR.

Absolutely not. There's nothing I need. (*Stopping.*) Beer? Did you say beer?

HEDVIG.

... Yes, Daddy, lovely cool beer.

HJALMAR.

Well, if you really insist. I suppose you could bring a bottle.

GINA.

Yes, do that. Then we'll have it cozy.

(*Hedvig runs toward the kitchen door. Hjalmar by the stove stops her, gazes at her, clasps her about the head and hugs her to him.*)

HJALMAR.

Hedvig! Hedvig!

HEDVIG.

(*With tears of joy.*) Oh, my dearest Daddy!

HJALMAR.

No, don't call me that. There I sat, helping myself at a rich man's table, gorging myself with all good things—! I could at least have remembered.

GINA.

Oh, nonsense, Hjalmar.

HJALMAR.

Yes, I could! But you mustn't be too hard on me. You both know I love you anyway.

HEDVIG.

(*Throwing her arms around him.*) And we love you too, so much!

HJALMAR.

And if I should seem unreasonable at times, then good Lord remember that I am a man assailed by a host of cares. Ah, yes! (*Drying his eyes.*) No beer at a time like this. Bring me my flute. (*Hedvig runs to the bookcase and fetches it.*) Thank you. There, so. With flute in hand, and you two close by me, ah! (*Hedvig sits at the table by Gina, Hjalmar walks back and forth, then forcefully begins to play a Bohemian folk dance, but in a slow elegiac tempo with sentimental intonation. After a moment he breaks off the melody and extends his left hand to Gina.*)

HJALMAR.

... So what if we skimp and scrape along under this roof, Gina, it's still our home. And I'll say this; it's good to be here. (*He starts playing again; immediately there comes a knock on the hall door.*) (145–146)

The arrival of no wolf or ogre in folk tale was ever so heralded as is Gregers's by this knock at the door.

The emotional swings indicated by Hjalmar's behavior and lines in this scene lay the groundwork for everything we know of him as he is, unaffected by Gregers's manipulation. He is boastful and humble, accusing and self-pitying, disdainful and affectionate. And it is his affection, however sputteringly recurrent, that carries them all. It is in this sense that Hjalmar rather parallels Gina than opposes her. Despite all the hurt pride and self-protective murk, his and Gina's love for Hedvig and their desire to protect her provide the vitality of this family in its essence, a vitality emanating from contradictory attitudes. It is only when the claims of the ideal penetrate the family, or when the purveyor of the vital lie disrupts its self-assurance, that the vitality dissipates and the play's pathos takes over. This is after all a play about a family, and Hjalmar, warts and all, is the pin that holds that family together.

Still, Hjalmar is and remains every bit as selfish and obtuse as we first take him for. And this is important because his sometimes gross weaknesses are what link him with the other central dramatic figures of this book. His contradictions are what identify him. He never ceases appearing self-centered and greedy even at his moments of genuine feeling, and he never stops being the loving father and husband, even when he is most fatuous. But we must turn now to the other important figures in the play, the older men who blur the past that Gregers is so obsessed with revealing in the precise moral terms of melodrama, and the young girl who arouses so much emotional response, from audience and fellow-characters alike.

Old Werle

When old Werle says that Gregers is suffering from a sick conscience, and that Gregers's words echo his late mother's word for word, he raises the question about the real truth about the past, that there was more to it, far more perhaps, than might fit into Gregers's, and apparently his mother's, construction of it. Certainly there is enough to substantiate the facts that Gregers presents: old Werle's liaison with Gina and old Ekdahl's having taken the rap for a crime in which old Werle had a hand. And there seems no question that old Werle's support of the Ekdahls has been motivated by these events. But what Ibsen is at pains to convey is the more important idea that we are not, and can never be, privy to the emotional substance of these affairs.

No story about the past, Ibsen suggests, ever can have the kind of clear, incontrovertible interpretation that melodrama insists on. We do not know anything at all, really, about Werle's relationship with his wife, as we do not know anything at all about the old relationship between Werle and Ekdahl. And we do not ever really know whether the support Werle has been providing is hush money, guilt money, or simple munificence. Probably it is all three. It is the high-strung, which is what old Werle calls Gregers and his mother, who insist upon melodrama's fixed understandings of the past. We do not see enough of old Werle in the play to say much about the man's emotional state in the present, but without directly denying the facts Gregers presents, the older man feels he is at peace with the past, which might suggest he is heartless (as Gregers sees him), but more convincingly suggests here that he has successfully lived through his struggle with conscience. And to be at peace with the past is to know that remembered episodes are always more complex than they seem, morally as well as factually, always subject to conflicting interpretations. But from his general demeanor (depending, of course, on how he is acted), and especially from his comments about his relationship with Mrs. Sorby, and her remarks about him, we sense the resignation, acceptance, and feelings of anticipated joy that are so absent in Gregers.

The contradictions in old Werle are, then, that he is both heavy and understanding father, cold and sensible businessman, highly ir-responsible and at the same time highly responsible regarding his actions. Ibsen never gives us quite enough about him to make him a full-blown character, but he does give enough to take him out of the role of the melodramatic villain his son has cast him in.

Old Ekdahl

From the perspective of melodrama, Lieutenant Ekdahl is the "broken man," the older figure who once was destroyed by the forces of evil, in this case (from Gregers's melodramatic perspective) by old Werle's greed and treachery. Since the Ekdahl family also sees him as broken, old Ekdahl must be left at the end pretty much as we see him at the beginning, as a self-pitying, aging alcoholic given to periodic withdrawals.

But it is those withdrawals that lead us to the counter-view of this figure. First, the evidence we get is that Ekdahl's alleged crimes at the works up in Hoidal had less to do with forged ledgers than with the pull upon him of the forest and its inhabitants, both mythical and natural. What we get suggests that Lieutenant Ekdahl was never especially attentive to the business, an implication which may throw light on old Werle's willingness to let him take the rap in the first place. Ekdahl's fuzziness about the accounts may have led to a crime, and perhaps Werle should have known about it. But given Ekdahl's general laxness, Werle also perhaps did not feel he should have been held responsible. But we really do not know, and that is the point Ibsen is making. Contrary to Gregers's melodramatic certainties, the only thing certain about the past is that it is clouded in uncertainties, and part of that cloud has to do with old Ekdahl's unusually fecund imagination.

In other words, what we get about the past raises questions about just how broken the old man we see on stage actually is. Old and alcoholic unquestionably, he is also given to pastoral visions centering on his attic menagerie which provide a powerful lure for Hjalmar and Hedvig. And when Hedvig dies, the old man comes up with his mysterious line about the woods taking "their revenge." Ibsen obviously intends old Ekdahl to be something more than a broken-down relic. Similarities with the early acts of *Peer Gynt* are illuminating. In his crusty, truncated, cryptic ways of speaking, the old Lieutenant calls to mind the Troll King: a version, perhaps, of that pastoral trouble-maker now penuriously in city pent. And just as the Troll King draws Peer into his kingdom, toward which he demands Peer's total commitment, old Ekdahl draws Hjalmar and Hedvig away from their worldly responsibilities into his attic (the replacement for the woods the Ekdahls' living conditions have forced upon him), toward which he demands their total commitment.

But even if one accepts this link with *Peer Gynt*, that play's connection with the overall direction of this play remains unclear. What kind of fantasy-escape is Ibsen proposing through the old Lieutenant: one that suggests a neurotic human propensity toward eternal childhood or one that suggests the idea that materialistic man has lost touch with the pastoral well-springs of his better self? Typically, Ibsen is divided. *The Wild Duck* as much as any play in the Ibsen canon is devoted to the here and now, and the here and now is represented by the relationship of Hjalmar Ekdahl and his family. But there is always the call of the woods, which should never be underestimated in an Ibsen play, and that is represented here by what goes on in the mind of old Ekdahl and the fantasy world that emanates from the attic. An escape that world certainly is, but whether for good or for bad remains moot.

Hedvig

Which leads, finally, to the personality and fate of Hedvig Ekdahl. Like her father, Hedvig seems absorbed with the creations of her grandfather's romantic imagination: the attic menagerie, and the wild duck with whose damaged state (because of her oncoming blindness) she identifies. While these inclinations are rooted in an illusion, her own set of vital lies, the stability of the family of which they are a part is finally not illusory. They are one means by which their love for one another is expressed, that love which Gregers, in his obsession with the destruction of illusion, almost destroys.

But apart from her illusions, she also contributes to the family's delicate balance in being the most practical of the lot. I think of such actions as her willingness and clear ability to perform the more tedious tasks involved in Hjalmar's photographic business. And I think of her capacity, at the age of 14, to recognize her father's emotional needs. She embodies in equal measure the contradictory qualities of mother, father, and not insignificantly grandfather and his nordic visions.

When I first encountered this play, I felt that Hedvig was a character conceived solely in sentimental terms whose death was intended to provoke tears of resentment, and little else. I have since come to feel the complexity of her role gives deeper meaning to its ending. Throughout this discussion I have been asserting that *The Wild Duck* transcends the melodramatic constructions of Gregers and Relling. But in fact the play does possess the makings of a melodrama in which a villain brings about the death of a beautiful, helpless child. The only thing that lifts the play above such an interpretation is the characterization of Hedvig. Ibsen creates through her vital contradictions—helplessness versus practical ability, adolescent dreaming versus hard-headedness—a complex human soul with dignity intact. Her death, like that of Shakespeare's Juliet, prompts us to see the play in genuinely tragic terms. And the fact that the play ends with the two melodramatists still trying to argue their opposing views drives the point home. Hedvig's life and death mock their opposing simplicities, and assert the deep complexity of the work.

While written well before his late plays, *The Wild Duck* strikes me as Ibsen's most mature work. There is clarity in its vision that goes beyond even that of the great play I shall discuss next.

Hedda Gabler

If in *The Wild Duck*, Ibsen achieves tragedy by making a genuine tragic hero out of the helpless child-victim of melodrama, he achieves it in *Hedda Gabler* by making a tragic hero out of the traditional villain of melodrama—in this case the central figure herself. And he does so by embodying the play's and her society's contradictions in her character. To this end, Ibsen appears to have appropriated the form, character types, and character relationships of what was (and probably still is) his most popular play, *A Doll House*, with the aim of transforming that play into real tragedy by correcting its numerous oversimplifications, the chief of which were those relating to the personality of its central character.

The melodramatic forms of *Hedda Gabler* and *A Doll House* are remarkably similar. Into the lives of a young married couple come various visitors, if not indeed interlopers, whose arrival ultimately destroys the "peace" of the home. The visitors Thea Elvsted, Judge Brack, and Eilert Lovborg in *Hedda Gabler* directly parallel Christine Linde, Dr. Rank, and the redeemed blackmailer Krogstad in *A Doll House*. Thea and Christine, who are struggling to be independent women, challenge the plays' heroines with the possibility of also being independent; Judge Brack and Dr. Rank are would-be lovers who challenge the plays' heroines with the attractions of adultery; and Lovborg and Krogstad are reformable sinners whose relationships with Thea and Christine challenge the plays' heroines with the redemptive power of dedicated love. That Tesman finally replaces the dead Lovborg in relation to Thea Elvsted complicates but does not destroy the set of parallel character configurations I have proposed.

The plays' melodramatic crises are not so uniquely similar to each other as they are typical of nineteenth-century melodramatic crises in general. The tale of the stolen manuscript in *Hedda Gabler*, like that of the unopened letter in *A Doll House*, is a typical melodramatic situational device. Far less typical, however, are the explosive conclusions of the two plays. In *A Doll House* Ibsen abandons the romantic conclusion of typical melodrama with Nora's declaration of independence and celebrated slamming of the door, while in *Hedda Gabler*, he abandons the romantic conclusion of typical melodrama by having Hedda commit suicide. Both plays, having lured their audiences with typical melodramatic plots, end with unexpected actions, one might even say bombs, proclaiming the author's continuing dissatisfaction with the marital norms of his time. Brack's "People don't do such things!" suits the ending of the earlier play as well as it suits the ending of the later one. Both are in the first, though not the final, analysis thesis plays with essentially the same thesis. People, in this case wives, *can* do such things if denied their basic human rights.

My purpose, then, is in part to implicitly articulate reasons why *Hedda Gabler* is so emphatically a greater drama than *A Doll House*, and I shall do this by linking the later play to my theme of vital contradictions.

Hedda Gabler has intellectual underpinnings which tie it most closely to *Peer Gynt* among Ibsen's earlier plays.[1] In his efforts to de-simplify *A Doll House*, Ibsen seems to have come back to the infinitude-finitude idea discussed in relation to *Peer Gynt*[2]. One need only cite the conflict between Georg Tesman and Eilert Lovborg, and the nature of their scholarly research, to recognize the presence of the idea in *Hedda Gabler*. Tesman's research into "the domestic handicrafts of Brabant in the Middle Ages" seems the epitome of finitude, while Lovborg's inspired but questionably researched set of conclusions about present and future seems the epitome of infinitude, the one being mired in facts and the other being carried away in speculative flight. The idea of Kierkegaard's balance between the two seems also implicit in the play's final, somewhat dream-like tableau of Tesman and Thea working together over Lovborg's notes.

But this approach, which is what Ibsen may have had in mind at the start, tends to make Tesman and Lovborg into stick figures. That they are something more begins to suggest what gives the play its strength. And that something more has to do with contradictions. It is hard to imagine Georg Tesman as a contradictory figure, but that Hedda mocks his research as dry contributes heavily toward its seeming dry. Perhaps there was romantic *possibility* in the handicrafts of Brabant. As for

---

[1]   Its formal roots are, of course, firmly set in the soil of Norse mythology, specifically the story of the Viking warrior-woman Hjordis who cast out her peace-loving husband in favor of her rapacious first lover, which Ibsen dramatized in his early play *The Vikings at Helgeland*. For a discussion of the relationship of the play under discussion to the earlier play, see Evert Sprinchorn, "The Unspoken Text of Hedda Gabler," *Modern Drama* 36 (1993): 353–367. See also Michael Meyer, *Ibsen: A Biography* (Garden City, NY: Doubleday, 1971) 150–151. Another, more recent, discussion of the possible mythic underpinnings of the play is to be found in Elinor Fuchs, *The Death of Character* (Indiana UP, 1996) 61–66.

[2]   See chapter on *Peer Gynt*, pp. 21–31.

Lovborg, it is Hedda who emphasizes the sense of infinitude she finds in him. It is she who has the dreams of "vine leaves in his hair." Lovborg's fatal rage has little to do with vine leaves, i.e., with the infinite. It is at having had a valuable manuscript—the fruits of long, hard, *necessary* labor—stolen. The whole association of Lovborg with the infinite evaporates with Brack's sardonic description of his demise. Having believed that Lovborg has shot himself in the temple, which would be "beautiful" by Hedda's lights, she finally learns that the gun went off accidentally in his struggle with Mademoiselle Diana, fatally wounding him "in the stomach—more or less" (299). From the brain to the bowel: a cataclysmic descent from the infinite to the finite.

If there is a stick figure in the play, at least in the way he functions in the plot, it is Brack more than the two scholars. He comes closer to being the stock villain of melodrama than any other character in Ibsen's plays. Everything traditionally associated with that figure is present in Brack: position, power, manipulative control, consummate hypocrisy. One can imagine him transferred without much modification into the evil banker in an American film western. As such, he should be the epitome of the raw finite: one-dimensional.

But as the first modern playwright who constitutionally found it difficult to create an unadulterated melodramatic figure (outside of the otherworldly Solveig, perhaps), Ibsen did go beyond the ordinary, even with Brack. Taken in the context of the plot, Brack is the absolute villain of melodrama, but in the context of his conversations with Hedda, he becomes something more. What distinguishes Brack from the other male characters in the play is his Machiavellian alertness, his wit. He always appears to respond in morally respectable terms without ever convincing Hedda, or the audience, that he is in any way morally respectable. The subtlest traces of sarcasm are always heard. Brack is the embittered satirist who in seeking to reduce all existence to the material reveals an intelligence which in itself appears to give life a kind of value. In this, of course, he has something in common with Shakespeare's villains—an "alacrity of spirit," which is what attracts him to Hedda despite her profound, and eminently justified, distrust of him.

But all this is only to say that Brack is a more subtly drawn version of the villain in melodrama than the usual; he is not rendered more human by his quickness of mind. If anything, he becomes more convincingly *in*human. The most one can say for him is that he admirably serves Ibsen's most obvious purpose of condemning the bourgeois hypocrisies of his time. But most of what he says and does, at least until he reveals himself as the uncompromising blackmailer late in the play, exists to set up Hedda's responses. Like everyone else in the play his chief function is to get us ever further into Hedda's character. And this play, as has been many times observed, is primarily a one-character play.

Hedda

When one says, as one inevitably does in discussing a figure like Hedda, that she reveals herself in statement or action, the assumption is that what is revealed will somehow clarify something. Much is revealed by what Hedda says, but it rarely clarifies anything. It is important to state at the start that Hedda is and remains an enigma from beginning to end. Her greatness lies in the impact she makes while remaining an enigma. And in pressing ideas about her contradictory nature, I am not saying that these ideas "solve" the enigma. As in discussions of other great characters in literature, my points will I hope be probing and engaging, but the character will, and should, remain inscrutable.

Hedda reveals most, perhaps, in her first private conversation with Brack, the one which begins with her threatening to fire one of her memorable pistols at him—actually firing it, in fact, over his head.

HEDDA.

I really had danced myself out, Judge. My time was up. (*With a slight shudder.*) Ugh! No, I don't want to say that. Or think it, either.

BRACK.

You certainly have no reason to.

HEDDA.

Oh—reasons—(*watching him carefully.*) And George Tesman—he is, after all, a thoroughly acceptable choice.

BRACK.

Acceptable and dependable, beyond a doubt.

HEDDA.

And I don't find anything ridiculous about him. Do you?

BRACK.

Ridiculous? No-o-o, I wouldn't say that.

HEDDA.

Hm. Anyway, he works incredibly hard on his research! There's every chance that, in time, he could still make a name for himself.

BRACK (*looking at her with some uncertainty*).

I thought you believed, like everyone else, that he was going to be quite famous some day.

HEDDA (*wearily*).

Yes, so I did. And then when he kept pressing and pleading to be allowed to take care of me—I didn't see why I ought to resist.

BRACK.

No. From that point of view, of course not—

HEDDA.

It was certainly more than my other admirers were willing to do for me, Judge.

BRACK (*laughing*).

Well, I can't exactly answer for all the others. But as far as I'm concerned, you know that I've always cherished a—a certain respect for the marriage bond. Generally speaking, that is.

HEDDA (*bantering*).

Oh, I never really held out any hopes for you.

BRACK.

All I want is to have a warm circle of intimate friends, where I can be of some use one way or another, with the freedom to come and go—as a trusted friend—

HEDDA.

Of the man of the house, you mean?

BRACK (*with a bow*).

Frankly—I prefer the lady. But the man, too, of course, in his place. That kind of—let's say, triangular arrangement—you can't imagine how satisfying it can be all around.

HEDDA.

Yes, I must say I longed for some third person so many times on that trip. Oh—those endless tête-à-têtes in railway compartments—!

BRACK.

Fortunately the wedding trip's over now.

HEDDA (*shaking her head*).

The trip will go on—and on. I've only come to one stop on the line.

BRACK.

Well, then what you do is jump out—and stretch yourself a little, Mrs. Hedda.

HEDDA.

I'll never jump out.

BRACK.

Never?

HEDDA.

No. Because there's always someone on the platform who—

BRACK (*with a laugh*).

Who looks at your legs, is that it?

HEDDA.

Precisely.

BRACK.

Yes, but after all—

HEDDA (*with a disdainful gesture*).

I'm not interested. I'd rather keep my seat—right here, where I am. Tête-à-tête.

BRACK.

Well, suppose a third person came on board and joined the couple.

HEDDA.

Ah! That's entirely different.

BRACK.

A trusted friend, who understands—

HEDDA.

And who can talk about all kinds of lively things—

BRACK.

Who's not in the least a specialist.

HEDDA (*with an audible sigh*).

Yes, that would be a relief.

BRACK (*hearing the front door open and glancing toward it*).

The triangle is complete.

HEDDA (*lowering her voice*).

And the train goes on. (251–252)

The several ways to approach Ibsen's complex treatment of Hedda are perhaps better suggested by this passage than by any other in the play. The most obvious way is to suggest that Ibsen is protesting society's strictures regarding the whole institution of marriage, from its insistence that the bride not exceed a marriageable age (Hedda at 29 has actually already exceeded it), to the social acceptability of the spouse, to the presumed capacity of the husband to dominate, to the insistence upon early child-bearing (which is heavily emphasized in nearby passages though only hinted at here), to the inevitable hypocrisy generated by all such strictures.

Hedda, at least until her suicide, is determined to adhere to these norms, artificial as she knows they are. She has allowed herself to remain unmarried as long as she did only because she knew her charm and beauty would allow it, but she married at twenty-nine the first accept-able male to come along. The equivocation in her remarks, and Brack's, concerns only Tesman's capacity to dominate. That, I think, and not his being a scholar, underlies their equivocation about Tesman's being "ridiculous." Brack himself, it is implied, who would certainly have dominated, is more interested in illicitly manipulating the system. And Hedda, who carefully measures the reaches of Brack's hypocrisy in this passage, sets limits of her own, limits that apparently, though we are never sure with intimate conversations of the 1890s, will not admit a sexual liaison. Unwilling to "show her legs," she is more than willing to remain "*tête-à-tête*" with Brack, which repeats her earlier described relationship with Lovborg. Hedda reveals a fierce adherence to society's strictures even as she reveals an equally fierce hostility to them.

Ibsen also suggests the possibility/necessity dichotomy in Hedda's responses. Her appetite for the unlimited, here represented as illicit sexuality, is presented as voracious, recalling no figure so much as the youthful Peer Gynt (who unlike Hedda yielded to his appetites). Her reported earlier "bold" inquiries about Lovborg's sexual passions, always "deviously" presented, are to be re-enacted with Brack, "who can talk about all kinds of lively things." But built into every illustration of Hedda's attraction to the infinite is her adherence to necessity, her recognition beyond Peer's that not only are society's strictures unavoid-able but that breaking them can bring one back to the finite with a thud. Her pregnancy is proof of the point. Its cause quite licit—Tesman obviously excited no dreams of the infinite in bed—its effects are just as damaging to her as Peer's impregnating the lady in green was to him. Willing to live a life in which visits from prospective but never actual lovers can make life seem exciting, she is doomed to the necessities of child-bearing and rearing.

But least obvious, yet most important, is the tragic vision implicit in these oppositions. When we treat Hedda simply in terms of the strong divisions within her between defiance of and obedience to societal and biological will, we could still be talking about another version of Nora Helmer. It is the complexity of Hedda's responses that makes this one of the greatest of modern tragedies. In the passage quoted, her enigmatic responses invite us to probe deeper—her "Oh—reasons" while "watch-ing" Brack "carefully" when told she has no "reason" to think herself old; her "Hm" in response to Brock's equivocation about whether Tesman is "ridiculous"; her most significant "And the train goes on" at the end of the passage—all invite an understanding of their conversation from a larger perspective. These responses can all be easily enough explained from single points of view, but they are all subject to conflicting explanations. Is she "watching" Brack when she exclaims about "reasons" because she is curious about whether he thinks she looks older, or because she is contemptuous of the whole question of a woman's age in relation to marriage? Does her "Hm" indicate she believes Tesman is ridiculous or that she is not sure whether she and Brack are perhaps the ridiculous ones—Brack in his equivocation and she in her choice of Tesman? And which is the "train" that "goes on"— the one that signifies her life in general, her married state, or situations in which schemers like Brack can corner a vulnerable woman? That one cannot really decide takes this dialogue beyond the melodramatic nature of the situation itself.

Similarly, as one thinks about the Hedda of this scene and throughout the play, melodramatic certainties tend to dissipate. Moral issues are thrown into a vacuum. Hedda is fascinated by the *possibility* inherent in illicit behavior—she would like to be transported—but she clearly adheres to the *necessity* to protect her reputation, both because of her moral training and the need to protect herself. There are both positive and negative moral forces underlying each of these feelings. She is morally right if she behaves herself, she is morally right if she defies the irrational strictures of society, and she is morally right if she takes responsibility for the fruits of her actions. Hedda is "wrong" to allow society to keep her from being herself, but also would be "wrong" to submit to Brack, and would certainly be "wrong" if she tried to abandon herself without work-a-day skills to the mercies of late nineteenth-century bourgeois society. Ibsen here takes to task the conclusion of *A Doll House*. Conflicting rights and wrongs are implicit throughout the play.

What chiefly makes Hedda's contradictions[3] vital is their intensity. Her treatment of Tesman and his aunt in Act One suggests real contempt for the proprieties of bourgeois life, even to the extent of her insulting Aunt Julie's hat. Yet at the same time she is fiercely determined to live out those proprieties to the letter. Her excuse that she thought the hat was the maid's, while transparent, just manages to keep her behavior within the bounds of the proper. It is the extremes of both her resistance

---

[3]   For a corollary discussion of Hedda's contradictory nature, see Harold Clurman, *Ibsen* (NY: Macmillan, 1977) 150–166. Of course, few discussions of Hedda can avoid pointing out her contradictions. Ibsen's own highly contradictory nature, which is the basis of many of his characters, is discussed clearly and in detail in Einar Haugen, *Ibsen's Drama: Author to Audience* (Minneapolis: U of Minnesota P, 1979) 19-36. The primary Ibsen biographies also inescapably deal with this issue. See Michael Meyer, *Ibsen: A Biography;* and Halvdan Koht, *Life of Ibsen*, translated by Einar Haugen and A. E. Santaniello (NY: Blom, 1971).

and her accommodation that are striking. The insult combined with her near-arrogance regarding Tesman's research and her all-but-hysterical determination not to acknowledge the possibility of her being pregnant reveal feelings that go well beyond ordinary dissatisfaction, but her insistent refusal ever to overtly defy the proprieties is just as intense. Hence she seems in rebellion as much against the unconventionality of an Eilert Lovborg as against the conventionality of her husband and his family. The stasis she has achieved before the complications begin to develop is one of seething contempt (always under a thin veneer of acceptability) juxtaposed with just as seething a hostility toward those who would attempt change—in her or in her society's norms. It is not just the attitude of the person trapped by convention over-adhering to it with a force which is close to scorn. She actually does appear to believe in the necessity of convention. And she is always deeply contemptuous of convention. The two attitudes exist in twain, neither one commenting really on the other.

The complications all follow in the wake of the arrival of Thea Elvsted, the "other woman" of melodrama, whose presence ultimately challenges Hedda to the extent of destroying her. The twists, and contradictions, in our responses to Thea are many. Far from being an enticing creature, she is essentially dull, especially when contrasted with Hedda. But Ibsen makes much of the contradictions implicit in this contrast. Thea has a full head of beautiful hair. Hedda's hair is thin, the difference undoubtedly symbolic of her fecundity versus Hedda's sterility. Hedda as a schoolgirl had tried to burn Thea's hair, as later she will burn the manuscript, the "offspring" of Thea and Lovborg. In the final analysis, in spite of her dullness, Thea is the productive one, Hedda the destructive one. But in the short view, Thea is a mouse, Hedda a lioness. Hedda is the one in whom vigor and imagination, primary requirements of intellectual fecundity, are abundant; Thea possesses neither. It is also perhaps an extension of the irony that Hedda is the pregnant one.

The contrast between Hedda and Thea is richly complex. It is Thea the mouse who has been capable of action, Hedda the lioness for whom action is anathema. It is Thea who has left a heavy Victorian husband and taken the unconventional Lovborg as lover, instilling in him the need to limit his excesses in the interests of his far-reaching goals. Hedda, fully taken up with Lovborg's originality, has earlier refused either to discipline him or accept his advances. And Hedda would never leave a husband, even if he were as ogrish a figure as Sheriff Elvsted. It is dull Thea who will join with dull Tesman in a new "relationship" to attempt a reconstruction of the brilliant Lovborg's work, while the brilliant Hedda withdraws into her parlor with pistol in hand. At every stage, the dull Thea takes action that reaches for the infinite, while the brilliant Hedda, who is in so many ways suggests the infinite, refuses to reach for it.

Thea seems small in the second act, Hedda large as she manipulates Lovborg back into his old ways. If Hedda is evil in what she does, and she is certainly that, it is an evil like that of Shakespeare's villains. It is so fraught with imagination and ingenuity, along with in her case inscrutability, as to pale the surrounding good, here signified by Thea, and indeed Lovborg himself, who also seems like a mouse in this act. It seems here as though evil reaches toward the infinite, good toward the finite. Hedda, like Shakespeare's Richard III, is totally aware of the moral implications of what she is doing, as well as the individual psychology of each figure she is dealing with, including the self-confident Brack and the fussily accommodating Tesman:

HEDDA.

… And besides, I noticed him [Brack] smile and glance at Tesman when you couldn't bring yourself to go to their wretched little party.

LOVBORG.

Couldn't! Are you saying I couldn't?

HEDDA.

I'm not. But that's the way Judge Brack sees it.

LOVBORG.

All right, let him.

HEDDA.

Then you won't go along?

LOVBORG.

I'm staying here with you and Thea.

MRS. ELVSTED.

Yes, Hedda—you may be sure he is!

HEDDA (*smiles and looks approvingly at Lovborg*).

I see. Firm as a rock. True to principle, to the end of time... There, that's what a man ought to be! (*Turning to Mrs. Elvsted and patting her.*) Well, now didn't I tell you that, when you came here so distraught this morning—

LOVBORG (*surprised*). Distraught?

MRS. ELVSTED (*terrified*).

Hedda—! But Hedda—!

HEDDA.

Can't you see for yourself? There's no need at all for your going around so deathly afraid that—(*Changing her tone.*) Now we can all enjoy ourselves!

LOVBORG (*shaken*).
What is all this, Mrs. Tesman?
MRS. ELVSTED.
Oh, God, oh, God, Hedda! What are you saying? What are you doing?
HEDDA.
Not so loud. That disgusting Judge is watching you. (268–269)

And this interchange is followed by Lovborg's drinking a toast and joining the men at Brack's party.

What destroys Lovborg and Thea in this scene is Thea's lack of confidence and the shallowness of Lovborg's up until now subservience. Lovborg's action is not backsliding in the usual sense; the backsliding comes once the alcohol affects him chemically. What Hedda achieves is Lovborg's rejection of Thea, who Lovborg really feels, as does Hedda, is unworthy of him. Yet these responses are placed firmly against the knowledge absolute in everyone concerned that only with Thea can Lovborg project his vision of the future.

Having said this, however, I do not mean to say that what Hedda does in this scene is in any way excused by the fact that she is so perceptive and alert. Too often the very exploration of an evil character's personality or motivation tends to ameliorate the evil, and that is not what Ibsen intends to do with Hedda in this play. He is presenting a woman who does deplorable things to others, and at the same time a woman who is highly intelligent and inventive. We are left stunned by the damage she wreaks, but equally stunned by a magnitude of personality so much larger than that of the others.

Hedda's destructiveness in this scene, of course, directly foreshadows her burning of the manuscript, which all those who see Hedda as the quintessential bitch (which includes most) use as the ultimate illustration. And so it is intended to be. Ibsen carefully forecloses the possibility of viewing Hedda dispassionately with this single act; all attempt to argue this away must fail. Having all but destroyed Thea and Lovborg in the earlier scene, burning their "child" finishes the job. Performed in a moment of near-hysteria, it nevertheless feels premeditated, chiefly by the fact that her destruction of these people is her on-going occupation from the moment Thea enters Hedda's house. This action is its fruition.

All this needs to be stated as emphatically as possible, because what I shall say now may still seem to ameliorate the all-out evil of Hedda's crime. But I think the crime needs to be understood better than it often is, and that understanding forces one to consider the writer's motives. And while I am not using biographical evidence in approaching these plays, it is important to state that the wanton burning of an uncopied manuscript must be the worst thing a writer, especially one who sees his or her whole nature as embodied in their writings, can imagine. Yet it could also very well represent what that writer, in a raging despair, might like to do (and sometimes do). The tremendous amount of emotion generated by this scene gives rise to the idea that its author was in an overwrought state when he wrote it. Its very wildness suggests a wildness in its composition—a state not uncommon for Ibsen. And while in no way justifying her action, Ibsen seems very much to be living it out—to be feeling what Hedda is feeling as she drops the manuscript page by page into the fire. Ibsen, in some rage of the moment, may be thinking about burning manuscripts—perhaps his own, and Hedda's intemperate nature in this scene may suggest Ibsen's intemperate nature. He would shortly write a play about an architect who destroys himself and all he has done in a final, triumphant leap from a tower. Is he perhaps overwhelmingly pained by an awareness that all he has achieved has been thanks to the efforts of a dull, disciplining wife? I am not the first to suggest that Hedda at critical moments reflects her creator, and if so, then the burning of the brilliant work can very well be regarded as Ibsen's vicariously acting against his own achievements.

Ibsen's possible personal investment in this action may account for Hedda's continuing largeness and dignity in the play, despite the fact that what she has done seems on the face of it so petty and cruel. And again we must look at the largeness of such figures as Solness (*The Master Builder*), Borkman (*John Gabriel Borkman*), and Rubek (*When We Dead Awaken*)—all of whom were at one time guilty of in-supportable acts of moral indecency, acts which might have been as bad as burning a manuscript, if not worse. (Solness's attempted seduction of a thirteen-year-old child is the best case in point.) Like Hedda they are all powerful and dominant to the end, dwarfing the personalities around them, including both the morally good and the morally evil. And it is not far-fetched to find the author, with all his pride and all his guilt, at the center of each of these figures.

One more issue needs to be touched on regarding Hedda, and it involves her romantic imagination, comparable to old Ekdahl's. At the opposite extreme from her insistence on respectability lies her dreams of the beautiful deaths of classical heroes with "vine-leaves" in their hair. What she appears to have in mind is a blend of earlier heroes of the Ibsen canon—the Viking woman-warrior Hjordis and the apostate Emperor Julian, who both die gloriously whatever their failures in life— and something akin to old Ekdahl's pastoral visions. As he sees two sides in everything, Ibsen presents Hedda's dream as on the one hand an irresistible vision of an uncorrupted otherworld, and on the other the fantasies of a woman driven mad by her isolation in and entrapment by a narrow, corrupt society. It is difficult to assess what kind of attitude Ibsen intends us to have toward Hedda's horror that Lovborg died from an accidental bullet wound in the bowel and not an intended bullet to the heart or head. In this scene her horrified responses seem extreme. But the beautiful death she envisions does not seem so extreme a way out when she finds herself pushed into the clutches of Brack by the identity of the gun Lovborg used, and the possibility of her having to appear in court. Blatant melodrama seems used here to make viable a quasi-Wagnerian longing for romanticized death.

Nevertheless, the ending of the play is as matter-of-fact as the ending of *The Wild Duck*. Hedda's rather hysterical irony from behind the curtain seems prompted more by jealousy than by dreams of a beautiful death, and the gunshot followed by the "lifeless" body "stretched out on the sofa" bespeak no visions of glory.

As he does elsewhere, Ibsen seems to want to leave us in the balance at the end of the play. Not only does he invite a sharply divided response to Hedda's death, but he leaves us equally uncertain about the other final image of the play, that of Tesman and Thea poring over Lovborg's notes, looking forward to retiring to Aunt Julia's to complete the all-important restoration of Lovborg's manuscript. Can two such pedestrian figures reconstruct a work of genius? Who knows? the play implies. But it also implies that genius is and will always be tied to the pedestrian— as, to achieve the balance needed for a creative life, Kierkegaard's possibility must always be tied to necessity. *Hedda Gabler*, like *Peer Gynt*, may be Ibsen's cry against what his own genius must have but cannot abide. Vital contradictions in theme as in character thus are central to this play.

STRINDBERG

Miss Julie

The Father

Before turning to the play this chapter chiefly deals with, *Miss Julie*, I want to briefly state why I give so little attention to the play that immediately precedes it in the Strindberg canon, the well-known but often despised (by feminists, anyway) *The Father*. It is a play about a brilliantly articulate, headstrong, truculent man, the deep contradictions in whose nature utterly destroy him. Margo Jefferson, unlike many of her fellow feminists, admires the play, feeling it accurately "depicts the reasons that made feminism." She recognizes the leading character's great similarity to the playwright, and precisely describes the character's awesome contradictions in her review of a 1996 production of the play starring Frank Langella. Speaking of the actor, the character, and implicitly the playwright, she says: "You feel his rigor and intelligence, his anguish and cruelty, his bigotry, his dignity, his hysteria, his capacity for suffering and for making others suffer." She finds the play "astonishingly cathartic."[1]

This idea picks up one put forward by Robert Brustein in his excellent discussion of the play: "The two faces that Laura [the wife] shows the Captain lead him to act with tenderness and hostility towards her, an ambivalence reflected in the mood of the play where the energy of battle is occasionally broken by nostalgic interludes, during which the two antagonists pause to reflect, in tones of gentle poetic melancholy, on the mother-child relationship which was their ground for mutual affection."[2] Like Jefferson, Brustein sees Strindberg identifying the battle chiefly in terms of the eternal war between the sexes, and the "pauses" a function of the mother that every woman must become when she takes a husband/lover. But it is not just a generic mother-child situation that underlies the contradictions. Strindberg, as Brustein points out, also suggests that the divisions within the Captain are motivated by his having been the son of highly disturbed parents. In short, both psychological trauma and the universal sexual war underlie the Captain's contradictory behavior and are at the root of his final madness.

---

[1]   *NY Times,* January 28, 1996, section 2, page 5.

[2]   *The Theatre of Revolt,* 108. Discussion of *The Father* is to be found on pp. 103–114.

Brustein sees *The Father* as Strindberg's answer to Ibsen's *A Doll House*, Strindberg's emphasis being on the abused husband rather than the abused wife. Strindberg was always responding to Ibsen, as, in turn, the older playwright began responding to him. The Ibsen play that I sense fired Strindberg up in writing *The Father* was *The Wild Duck*. I say this because of Gina Ekdahl's answer, when asked by her husband whether he was the father of their child: "How would I know?" While Ibsen intends us to accept this as an undebatable reality, one that Hjalmar Ekdahl ultimately comes to accept, Strindberg could, quite violently, not accept it. That refusal may even be what prompted him to write *The Father*. The immediate underlying cause of the Captain's madness is the idea, implanted in him by the scheming Laura, that he cannot ever know, as Strindberg implies no man can ever know, whether he is the father of his own child. The only way the Captain's mind can be relieved of its obsession is for an innocent wife to confess to adultery, something that the rational part of Strindberg realizes is preposterous. And this is, for me, what makes *The Wild Duck* the better play. Ibsen's play makes clear that Hjalmar Ekdahl's kind of obsession is something he needs to overcome. It is not the Ibsen's obsession—as it certainly was Strindberg's.

And this gets me to what I feel is wrong with *The Father*. The play is as powerful as it is because in it Strindberg lives out obsessive personal feelings that are not always successfully rendered into art. The very emotional force with which Strindberg endows the contradictions within and the ultimate madness of the Captain are intended to make him a larger than life character. But what results is too often a bizarre rather than a fully realized dramatic figure. By having the Captain invoke both Shakespeare's Shylock and King Lear near the end of the play, Strindberg lets us know what he wants his character to be. There is no question Shylock and Lear are among Shakespeare's more irrational characters, but there also should be no question that through them and their contradictions Shakespeare attests to what a Harold Bloom might call the magnitude of the human. That, with the Captain, Strindberg fails to achieve this magnitude may result, I think, from Strindberg's inability sufficiently to separate his own insanity from the character's. I agree *The Father* is astonishingly cathartic, but that Strindberg more successfully makes that separation in relation to the leading characters of the three other plays I deal with—plays that are equally cathartic—makes them, for me at least, preferable to *The Father*.

Miss Julie

If Strindberg was intent on answering Ibsen in *The Father*, Ibsen seems in *Hedda Gabler* to be answering Strindberg's *Miss Julie*.[3] Both plays deal with ruthless, disturbed women who have basically already decided at the beginning of their respective plays that their lives are unbearable, and both plays trace what amounts to the last stages of the disintegration of these women. Of all Ibsen's plays, Strindberg must have admired *Hedda Gabler* the most because the play resembles Strindberg's work in the nature of its central characterization, despite the glaring differences between Hedda and Julie in such matters as the social conventions and sexual mores.[4] Yet the plays are finally as different as are their authors, and it seems a useful starting place for a discussion of Strindberg's play to compare them briefly.

Ibsen was certainly not ready to abandon the "well-made play" in *Hedda Gabler*. In fact, perhaps as a counter to *Miss Julie* and certainly as a corrective to his own *A Doll House*, *Hedda* has quite possibly the most efficiently constructed plot, that key element of melodrama, Ibsen ever devised. Strindberg, on the other hand, fought the strictures of "well-made" plot construction with a force equal to his defiance of social convention. While it is inaccurate to say that *Miss Julie* is a plot-less play, just as Strindberg was inaccurate to say (in his "Foreword") that it was a "characterless" play, its plot is so simple as to be practically non-existent. All it tells is of a sexual encounter between a young noblewoman and her father's butler and her subsequent suicide—all taking place within the period of a few hours. It is constructed around the encounter itself, which takes place a little before the middle of the action. What happens before the encounter may be seen as leading up to it, and what happens after it as the effects of it. The suspense in the early part of the play accompanies the sexual passion of the principals (will they or won't they?), and in the later part accompanies the increasing inevitability of Julie's suicide. The third character, the servant Kristin, is important, but not as a complicating factor in the plot—as, say, Christine Linde or Thea Elvsted constitute complicating factors in their plays. She adds some key factual information early in the play, specifically that Julie is having her monthly period, and later prevents the elopement. Yet the play is one of the most complex experiments in

---

3   See Evert Sprinchorn, *Strindberg as Dramatist* (New Haven: Yale UP, 1982) 40.

4   Having said this I should add that on the whole Strindberg despised his Norwegian rival. He felt, for example, that the character of Hjalmar Ekdahl in *The Wild Duck* was created to lampoon him. See Michael Meyer, *Ibsen: A Biography* (Garden City, NY: Doubleday, 1971) pp. 648–649.

dramatic characterization of the past hundred years, more complex in terms of characterization *per se* than Strindberg's later "expressionistic" plays, and more successfully complex than its many latter-day imitations—most notably Tennessee Williams's *A Streetcar Named Desire.*

Strindberg faithfully adheres to what he says about the play in the justly famous Foreword. It is often the case that we are better off not knowing what an artist plans to do in a work. We may find the resultant product either painfully obvious or not at all consistent with what we have been told. Neither is the case with *Miss Julie.* In the Foreword, Strindberg tells us what he plans to do, and he does precisely what he has told us with great control, delicacy, and complexity. More than this, the play has great and immediate impact. It is again "astonishingly cathartic." We are made to empathize with both characters through the full range of their most contradictory feelings.

The main problem in reading Strindberg's Foreword, which is very clear, is that so much of it is written in the context of conventions of the theater of his time he is reacting against, chiefly conventions of plot, characterization, and dialogue he finds in popular French drama of the nineteenth century. The impulse is thus either to dismiss what he says as irrelevant to present-day concerns or to overly historicize both the Foreword and the play. In fact, what he says about French nineteenth-century popular drama is relevant to much popular drama of all ages, and it is the effort to see it only in terms of Strindberg's immediate time period that makes it seem irrelevant. We should, I think, read the Foreword as though it were written today in the context of much popular theater and film.

In his Foreword, Strindberg suggests that his play is more complex than the popular theater of his time. He "congratulates himself on his characters' 'multiplicity of motives.'"[5] "I see Miss Julie's fate," he says, "to be the result of many circumstances: the mother's character, the father's mistaken upbringing of the girl, her own nature, and the influence of her fiancé on a weak, degenerate mind. Also, more directly, the festive mood of Midsummer Eve, her father's absence, her monthly indisposition, her pre-occupation with animals, the excitement of dancing, the magic of dusk, the strongly aphrodisiac influence of flowers, and

---

[5]   *Six Plays of August Strindberg,* translated by Elizabeth Sprigge (Garden City, NY: Doubleday Achor Books: 1955) 64. The Sprigge translation is the primary but not sole translation I have used. I have also used and refer to the Evert Sprinchorn translation (Minneapolis: U of Minnesota P, 1986) and the Michael Robinson translation (Oxford UP, 1998) at times for comparison. But page references, unless otherwise noted, refer to Sprigge.

finally the chance that drives the couple into a room alone—to which must be added the urgency of the excited man" (63).

If language like the "mistaken upbringing of the girl" and the reference to her "weak, degenerate mind" contribute to what makes Strindberg so much under fire these days, the rest of what he says should more than make up for what are the effects of his own, at-times acknowledged, obsessions. Few playwrights have written so precisely and accurately about their own work as Strindberg does in this Foreword. Not only does he include the many motivating factors, but he accurately identifies what he sees as background and what he sees as foreground, placing the sexual excitement of the male in the ultimate foreground, but not so as to lessen the importance of the other factors. It is this multiplicity of motivating factors that I wish to focus on in this discussion.

As I have already pointed out, the play's structure is built around the interlude during which the two have sexual intercourse in Jean's bedroom to the accompaniment of the singing and dancing peasants onstage. The interlude affects the mood and tone of everything they do and say both before and after its occurrence. Before it, all the motivating facts that Strindberg refers to in the Foreword are suspended in the chemistry of their mutual sexual attraction. Contradictions there are aplenty in this portion of the play but here they are motivated as much as by the rituals of flirtation as by the factors Strindberg refers to. In the latter half of the play, their post-coital moods de-emphasize their mutual sexual attraction and intensify Strindberg's other motivating factors, though there, too, the re-arousals of sexual interest intermittently and repeatedly affect what the characters say.

The surest way to illustrate what I have been saying is to concentrate on Jean's story of his pre-adolescent attraction to Julie. Jean tells of seeing her as a pre-adolescent immediately after his adventure in the Count's privy, which he had sneaked into because of his fascination with the pictures on its walls (and also because sneaking into it was forbidden). Hearing someone enter, he had to escape by the only means available—"through excrement," to use Evert Sprinchorn's phrase. He then scrambled through raspberry bushes and a strawberry patch until he found himself on "the rose terrace," where he saw "a pink dress and a pair of white stockings"—Julie—and then hid under a weed pile "among prickly thistles" and on earth which stank from its own rot undoubtedly supplemented by the smell of the boy himself after his recent experience.

> I watched you walking among the roses and said to myself: "If it's true that
> a thief can get into heaven and be with the angels, it's pretty strange that a

labourer's child here on God's earth mayn't come in the park and play with the Count's daughter." (87)

Strindberg's treatment of Jean's story evokes everything from the most general to the most particular: the chivalric romance of forbidden love, the nineteenth century romance of inter-class love, the pre-adolescent boy's love of a pre-adolescent girl seen only as a pink dress and white stockings, and Jean's personal romantic passion of the moment—all of them subject to the savage ironic debasement associated with his escape from the privy. Emphasized on the one hand is the idealization of the love and on the other the excrement. Both are very immediately sensed, neither one undone by the other.

Following the sexual interlude, Jean contemptuously claims his story was in part made up, that he "had the same dirty thoughts as all boy" (94). His response is consistent with his general tone in the second part of the play: arrogant, haughty, and denigrating of the now-vulnerable Julie in every way he can think of. In the second part of the play, the class theme becomes paramount. The upwardly mobile servant denies the aristocrat's idea of the "romantic" except as it might be exploited to further his social aspirations. In the second part, too, Jean uses the word "merde" in response to Julie's calling him a "beast," which, in recalling the excrement in the earlier narrative of his first seeing Julie, further debases the idea of the romantic.

Thus, the basic symmetry of the play seems focused in Jean's opposing responses to his story—responses that embody two sets of fantasies associated with the sensitive servant boy: the first associated with centuries-long romantic folklore, and the second associated with the new romance of inter-class love. On the one hand, there is the fantasy of the boy winning the princess and the later fantasy of the boy trying to move beyond old prejudices, and on the other, the fantasy born of the resentments associated with class repression, what might be called a "getting-back-at-them" fantasy. Both these sets of fantasies, Strindberg would hasten to remind us, accompany "the urgency of the excited man" and the brutality inherent in the release of that urgency.

If Julie seems de-emphasized in this discussion of Jean's story and his contrasting responses to it, she is certainly not de-emphasized in everything that surrounds that story. Having been taken in by Jean's narrative in spite of herself, she later feels the debasement in relation to it that Jean felt earlier. She has her own conception of the little girl in pink dress and white stockings, aware always of her dirty finger nails and unwashed cuffs, but as he relates it she is swept up in the romance of Jean's story (amidst "the aphrodisiac influence of the flowers"). Later she is equally swept up in the sense that she has been as figuratively fouled—in part by her yielding to Jean, but also by her family past, which is never to be overlooked with Julie—as he has literally been by the excrement. The effect of his shouting "*Merde!*" at her elicits shame deeper than simply that associated with her recent sexual encounter. It is not only fear that her relationship with Jean will be discovered that leads to her suicide. It is also shame that she has been betrayed by her class, along with shame that she has betrayed her class.

Going back for the moment to Strindberg's ability to imply historical meaning to a situation presented so potently in terms of the present, Julie's responses suggest the disgust inherent in the entire tradition of courtly love—in which the knight woos the lady amid "the excitement of dancing" and "the magic of dusk," not to mention "the strongly aphrodisiac influence" of poetry—with the sole objective of sexual union. Not only does the lady have nothing to look forward to but debasement by her lover, but she in all likelihood already lives under the debased conditions of either enforced marriage or total subservience to a father rendered insensitive by his class or the despairing emotional conditions of his own life (which is Julie's father's case). The lover's being lower-class modernizes but does not essentially change the situation. Jean would exploit Julie as the knight of old would exploit the lady, now with the up-to-date twist of his wishing to make her a chief attraction in his dreamed-of hotel on Lake Como.

In this play, Strindberg makes us empathetic with the male aggressor even as he makes us empathetic with the victimized female (which is what makes Williams's *Streetcar* so very good an imitation). He makes us love and hate Julie as Jean loves and hates her; he makes us love and hate Jean as Julie loves and hates him. And he makes the motivating forces for their behavior, be those forces autobiographical, historical, societal, psychological, biological, or all of the above, most potently implied.

Yet all this still does not deal with the essence of *Miss Julie*, which is that it is as much a romantic tragedy as Shakespeare's *Romeo and Juliet*, with which it shares several of the same historical and societal dimensions. The fact is, Julie and Jean—quite apart from their class, sexual need, or personal histories—are eminently well-suited to each other. And this is something that possibly Ibsen missed in correcting the play by writing *Hedda Gabler*. (Hedda is not well-suited to anyone.) If it is not customary for the play to be read in this fashion, that is because Strindberg is at such pains both to defy nineteenth-century (and earlier) romantic conventions and to purge some of his irritations with his nobly-born wife. But I find it reasonably clear that in its defiance of romantic convention, Strindberg nevertheless creates characters who have a natural and powerful mutual affinity despite their manifold resentments. And that this affinity is not solely sexual becomes evident at critical moments in the text.

Almost all the numerous productions of the play I have seen over the past fifty-odd years have had in common an image of Julie in physical disarray,[6] if not relative nudity, following the interval in Jean's bedroom. Jean enters "in high spirits," but nothing is said about Julie's appearance. She looks at the "havoc in the kitchen" wrought by the peasants and their dance, "wrings her hands, then takes out her powder puff and powders her face." Strindberg makes no mention of the state of her clothing, and there is little to suggest her emotional condition other than her wringing her hands, and that could be at the state of the kitchen as much as at the possible consequences of her behavior. What we really get at this point is a kind of eye-of-the-storm, a calm which might follow the release of their sexual energies yet precede the resentments that release might engender, and certainly precede the re-arousal of those energies. And in that calm, perhaps we see Julie and Jean in their natural condition, freed briefly from the psychological and biological forces that shackle them to their complex mutual hostility.

Though the first subject discussed following their sexual "interval" is one that will shortly provoke severe recriminations, the discussion appears to begin peacefully:

JEAN.
… Do you still think it's possible for us to stay here?
JULIE.
No, I don't. But what can we do?
JEAN.
Run away. Far away. Take a journey.
JULIE.
Journey? But where to?
JEAN.
Switzerland. The Italian lakes. Ever been there?
JULIE.
No. Is it nice?
JEAN.
Ah! Eternal summer, oranges, evergreens … ah! (90)

---

6   An exception is the film adaptation made in 1999, directed by Mike Figgis, and
     starring Saffron Burrows and Peter Mullan, in which the intercourse takes place in a
     standing position and both characters seem relatively unrumpled after it. The pro-
     duction is in period costumes and scenery but is in other ways very obviously an
     adaptation.

I think the key to approaching this exchange is to recognize the relative absence of tension in it. Julie's responses are in a spirit of pure inquiry—she has never been to Switzerland and the Italian lakes—and Jean's first responses are genuinely lyrical, delighting in his memories of these places while in keeping with his physical calm of the moment. Later in the passage, after Jean imagines their life as proprietors of a tourist hotel, Julie begins to show insecurity but not hostility:

JULIE.
That's all very well. But Jean, you must give me courage. Tell me you love me. Come and take me in your arms.
JEAN., *reluctantly.*
I'd like to, but I daren't. Not again in this house. I love you—that goes without saying. You can't doubt that, Miss Julie, can you? (91)

Then Jean, in explanation of why he cannot call her just "Julie," tells her of his absolute fear of and servility toward the Count—this leading seamlessly into his hurt at his place in life, and this in turn to the shape of his post-coital hostility toward Julie, on whom he will take out his resentment. But the point is that his tone in the quoted passage is loving, confessional, and relatively gentle. I have been told that he is hypocritical here, but I find no evidence of hypocrisy. Certainly, his confession is not hypocritical, and by the same token I find his statement of love unhypocritical. It is also not yet motivated by renewed sexual appetite. Although the flow of such appetite is always a moot issue in this play, at this point one may suppose the feeling he has for her is not governed by it. And if not, and not hypocritical, what can we say of it but that it is genuine. That is, Jean's responses here seem as unaffected by Strindberg's various motivating forces of the Foreword as any of his responses in the play. And the same kind of genuineness seems to underlie her desire for his embrace as well. Certainly their tone here is in sharp contrast to what it will be within minutes—when she calls him a "lackey" and he calls her a "lackey's whore." Both these kinds of response represent their contradictory true feelings, but the responses in the passage immediately following their love-making are the most affected by their direct attention to one another in the present, and the least by their numerous secondary motivators.

Seamlessly yet suddenly (that uncanny characteristic of Strindbergian dialogue) those secondary motivators come to the fore. Having confessed his fear of the Count, Jean lets resentment creep into his description of their forthcoming life as inn-keepers, a resentment he increasingly takes out on Julie, and she becomes at the same time alternately self-pitying, and, in her hurt at his changing tone, class-consciously arrogant—the feelings of both intensified now by post-coital hostility combined with shame and guilt at their particular personal circumstances. (Though he expresses it differently, Jean is just as ashamed at having had sexual relations with a woman of Julie's class as she is at having had them with a man of Jean's class.)

The dialogue that ensues is characterized by what O'Neill identified in Strindberg as the latter's "new language of kinship"[7]: hurt, sharp recrimination, and bullying, subtly varied with defensiveness, concern for the other's feelings, and, admission of their mutual affection—sometimes but not invariably accompanied by renewed sexual engagement. So skillful is Strindberg at mixing these tumultuous responses within the free flow of their conversation that it is sometimes all but impossible to pull them apart, but traces of the shifting reactions are usually evident. For one thing, the impulse to confess to one another—one of the surest signs of their essential compatibility—continues. Picking up, after much shouting of insults and counter-insults, from Jean's confession of his self-abasement before the Count (which itself shared the tone of his earlier tale of his childhood experience in the privy), Julie tells the story of her own childhood, which reveals her to have been shaped far more by her parents' mutual hostilities and betrayals than by her noble breeding. The very fact that Julie confesses to Jean so directly and honestly suggests the nature of a feeling for him not entirely governed by her sexual drives or her far-ranging resentments, but by, for the moment only, trust—and his reactions reflect that mixture of understanding and honesty with his inevitable arrogance that suggests that he genuinely cares about her.

One brief response by Jean in the midst of this stormy dialogue is a clue to the way Strindberg sees the relationship between these characters. Julie asks, in response to Jean's questioning the wisdom of her open confessions to him, "Aren't you my friend"? To which Jean replies: "On the whole. But don't rely on me." (In Swedish: "*Jo ibland! Men lita inte pa mig.*") Sprinchorn's translation, which is better than Sprigge's here, I think, has Jean reply: "I am—sometimes. Just don't count on it." That similar exchanges can be found in Strindberg's other plays— notably in *Easter* and *A Dream Play*—suggests Strindberg's strongly held conviction that close ties, even love, can exist even in the presence of recrimination and even betrayal. The authenticity of human feeling cannot, for him, be measured by its consistency, because human feeling is by its nature inconsistent, often as here made up of vital contradictions. And sometimes the stronger the feeling the greater that vitality.

---

[7]   From O'Neill's program notes for a production of Strindberg's *The Dance of Death* in the early 1920s.

When O'Neill directed his "new language of kinship" to Strindberg's *The Dance of Death*, where a husband and wife are constantly at each other's throats, and the wife is unfaithful, he recognized what I am pointing out for *Miss Julie* in a play a good deal more difficult to see it in. Julie's sense of her basic affinity to Jean is reflected most in her appeals for his help mixed in with the savagery of her attacks. His sense of that affinity, more difficult to identify but just as present, is seen in the fact that he really listens to her, and responds with understanding, which if occasionally bitter, is nonetheless genuine. I think particularly of his caustic but knowing responses to the tale of her mother and father, and his saying, in answer to her appeal that he "speak kindly to her," that "orders always sound unkind." Such responses, in addition to suggesting his knowledge of the world, also indicate an essential under-standing and closeness which are not belied by his adolescent boasts and insults—or his renewed sexual appetites. (What follows is quoted from earlier work):

> At almost every point in their remarkable dialogue, the two main characters ... are moved by multiple, contradictory feelings. These responses include first, though not necessarily foremost, sexual attraction; then the selfless desire to give unconditionally to one another; then disinterested (non-sexual) admiration; then class pride; then fear (of the past, of the present, of the future, of the other sex, of the world); then the rational desire to lead a new life; then the irrational desire to escape; then renewed sexual desire; renewed desire to give unconditionally; and renewed class hostility. These turns of feeling are manifold. ... Jean moves rapidly from his own fear and uncertainty, through contempt for women generally, to genuine concern for her, to a desire for understanding from her, and finally to brutal sexual hostility toward her. ... Since these characters speak what they feel—they rarely deceive, and only early in the play are they hypocritical—what they say reveals the tremendous variations of emotion Strindberg represents in intense human conversation.[8]

I would add, especially in the intense conversation of humans who are very close to one another.

Each frame of mind or mood out of which one of these characters speaks, however short-lived or abrupt, is like a spell or trance which dominates the character while he or she is speaking and then disappears, to be replaced by another spell. The character seems intensely absorbed in the feelings of the moment, then becomes just as intensely absorbed

---

[8]   The preceding extended quotation is from my essay "Eugene O'Neill and the Founders of Modern Drama," in *Eugene O'Neill and the Emergence of American Drama,* edited by Marc Maufort (Amsterdam: Rodopi, 1989) 50. That essay is the basis for this entire study.

in feelings of a very different, in fact often contradictory, nature. And it
is possible to associate these individual spells with one or another of the
character's obsessing concerns: in the case of Julie, family past, high
social position, a frustrated desire to rebel against her surroundings, and
sexual desire or sexual disgust; and in the case of Jean, ambition, resentment at his low birth, general curiosity, a vengeful nature (especially
when it comes to women), subservience to his superior, and of course
sexual excitement.

This trance-like effect is especially important in the final scenes of
the play. The facts of the ending are simple on the surface. Finding that
she can no longer tolerate Jean's brutality after his killing of her pet
canary, that Kristin's vindictiveness will prevent the still-lingering
possibility of escape, and finally that the Count has actually returned,
Julie takes "decent" society's one exit possible for women of breeding
who have "fallen." Julie's sense of entrapment, which began well before
the play's opening in the traumatic memories of her past and has been
building steadily through the emotional ups and downs of her dialogue
with Jean, becomes complete. And that sense finally leads to her act
against herself.[9]

In the last portion of the play, the conflicting emotions become
hysterically contrasting, the highs reminiscent of Peer Gynt's fantasies,
the lows more abject than even Ibsen in his darkest moments ever gets.
Yet the transitions remain fluid. When Julie arrives ready for travel,
carrying her canary (the Sprigge translation has "greenfinch"), the dawn
reveals that Julie, "pale as a corpse," has neglected to wash her face.
Jean's remark that the rising sun "breaks the spell" suggests the way
Strindberg constructs the play's final scene. We get what we have been
getting throughout the play, only now more noticeably—a series of
mutually exclusive, contradictory trances, or "spells." The primary
"spell" throughout earlier portions of the play has been that associated
with Midsummer Eve and all the heady emotions it connotes. Once that
is broken, as it is not only with the fulfillment of their sexual appetites
but also with the realization that they cannot remain where they are,
Julie re-awakens another spell, that of Jean's illusion of escape to Lake
Como. As she dwells on this, however, her ability to become a part of
that illusion quickly wears thin. For example, her reverie of the train

---

9   And Strindberg's biographical novels, supplemented by several recent biographies
    (see those by Michael Meyer and Olaf Langercrantz), show that what Julie goes
    through directly mirrors the playwright's struggles with his own past, both in his
    early life as the offspring of a "serving woman" and an aristocrat and his more recent
    past playing Jean to the Julie-like Siri, and his numerous attempts at escape, and his
    suicidal disposition.

ride south is quickly broken by her recollection of the "memories" that will be "in the baggage car."[10] This realization is immediately followed by the episode involving the canary, which stands for destroyed illusion much as do the shooting of Ibsen's duck and Chekhov's sea gull.

The effect of the canary episode is to throw Julie into another kind of spell, diametrically opposed to her train reverie, but just as unreal. She violently attacks Jean for his brutality, which she now equates with his maleness, imagining herself as his future Mrs. Gate-keeper (fru 'Grindstugan') or Madam Refuse-hole (madam 'Sopbacken') [my translations], the savagely pejorative sexual implications of which are not often noticed. This spell is in turn broken by Jean's abrupt raillery, and is immediately followed by Julie's appeal to Kristin to join them in their escape with its reglamorizing of the proposed venture into the resort business, and the outraged Kristin's stern declaration of her pietistic religious faith, which itself comes across as a sort of spell, one Kristin lives by.

But let what I said at the beginning be re-asserted. The Julie we meet, like the Hedda we meet, is a woman in the last stages of a struggle leading to suicide. There are too many unresolved traumas from her personal past and there is too little to help her in her present for her to avoid it. Perhaps Strindberg intends that her encounter with Jean actually helps precipitate it, as Blanche's encounter with Stanley certainly helps precipitate her suicide in Williams's *A Streetcar Named Desire*; but if so, Strindberg also presents Jean as a means of her possibly avoiding it, were circumstances not what they are. If Julie is in some measure a version of Blanche, Jean is not a version of Stanley— or, at least, of the Stanley we see late in the Williams play. Among the welter of other things Jean is, he is a person capable of being sensitive to the person that is Julie. And the escape they fantasize has a kind of plausibility; the world of the 1890s certainly knew such unions as the kind Jean proposes. The thought of their coming together is not sheer fantasy, although the dreaming about it both indulge in, of course, is.

But Strindberg, at the time he wrote this play, had not yet experienced the real penalties inherent in such an escape. All the play gives us—and gives us with great intensity and great economy—is a highly detailed cross-section of the interaction between two extra-ordinarily complex people in circumstances from which they feel they cannot escape.

---

[10] This reference to memories in the baggage car calls to mind the baggage car that is so important in Jim Tyrone's great confession in O'Neill's *A Moon for the Misbegotten*.

Easter

Easter is made up of a series of shifts in mood and tone. Ranging from the most enervated and depressed of moods to the most energetic and hopeful, it subsumes all the contradictions inherent in human attitudes within the central Christian scheme of sin, repentance, and redemption —and to it ties in the classico-Nietzschean myth of the eternal return. It is Strindberg's most hopeful play without ever denying the centrality of despair in human response. And if despair is treated in the context of the "testing" that must ultimately imply the overcoming of despair, it makes despair so deeply felt and so inevitably recurrent as to leave the final assessment of life's value very much in the balance—like old Lindkvist's blue paper balanced at the edge of the table. It is a play not so much of Easter and redemption as of Easter Eve (the time of its third and concluding act), a point of great hope but still abiding despair—the most vitally contradictory moment. That redemption in this play comes not in the image of a young man nailed to a cross but in the shape of a clownish old man (Lindkvist), who is akin to the ogres of Swedish folk-lore, is one of the several strokes of genius in this play.

The play's reputation among Strindberg's works has suffered from its title and theme.[1] It can be so easily, if superficially, treated as a sort of return to faith on the author's part. And it is easy enough to assume that since plays like *The Ghost Sonata* and *The Pelican*, with their final images of dessication and defeat, appear to assert the triumph of denial over affirmation in Strindberg's work, and come later than *Easter,* those plays are better barometers of Strindbergian attitudes. It is significant that among the various commonly-used anthologies of selected Strindberg plays for classroom use, only the Elizabeth Sprigge anthology includes *Easter.* Few present-day Strindberg scholars I have talked to deny the high quality of the play, but ignoring it in the moral climate of scholarship over the years of Strindberg's burgeoning popularity, has seemed the better part of "wisdom." And certainly it is an inconvenient play for anyone who would rather condemn the playwright's "misogyny" than look carefully at the treatment of women in his work. *Easter*

---

[1]   Harry G. Carlson, for example, finds some of the play "forced," in *Strindberg and the Poetry of Myth* (Berkeley: U of California P, 1982). Nevertheless, he also finds the play's "resolution ... no moment of simplistic mawkishness" (136).

and *A Dream Play* are plays that should affect feminist outlooks on Strindberg as much as the more favored *The Father*.

Easter is important to my approach throughout this study because as much as any play I am looking at, it focuses on the ever-ringing changes and contradictions in the human disposition. But it is also important in that it ranks for me with the playwright's most successful efforts. And a quick comparison of it with the also seemingly optimistic *There are Crimes and Crimes*, which was written around the same time, would support its effectiveness. It is a relatively short play, as are most of Strindberg's naturalistic plays, and perhaps by virtue of that very brevity, it implies a great deal. It is delicately balanced and firmly in control from beginning to end, while it deals with issues as large as those in Milton's *Paradise Lost*.

That the play transcends its basic shape as romantic melodrama is obvious. Yet it is that basic shape that makes the play so deceptive. Using a format not unlike Ibsen's *Ghosts* and *The Wild Duck*, it tells the story of a family enchained by the sins of the father. While the elder Heyst languishes in prison for his unquestioned misdeeds, his wife and son (a high school teacher) go through their individual purgatories of suffering, resentment, and denial—while his daughter, the enigmatic Eleanora, has gone through a transformation from hysterical resentment, which has been perceived by those around her as psychosis, to quasi-saintliness—the resentment only hinted at in the play, the quasi-saintliness what we actually see. Complications come from the son's fiancée, who appears to desert him in the midst of his suffering, and from the son's favored student, who disappoints his teacher by failing a critical examination. In addition, the daughter, who has escaped from the mental institution in which she has been placed, is accused of stealing a flower from a local florist's shop. Everything that goes wrong contributes to the anguish of the son and of his increasingly distracted mother, who continues to deny her husband's guilt. In the end, the son's fiancée returns, the accusation against the daughter is refuted, and the chief victim of the father's dishonesty, his erstwhile business partner Lindkvist, appears, ostensibly to claim all the family's worldly goods in recompense for the evil done him in the past, but actually to release them from their debt.

This plot, taken by itself, has all the elements of the tritest melodrama; but here, as always, to quote Maurice Valency, "Strindberg lapses into sentimentality for a specific purpose."[2] He wants to represent patterns of human guilt and God's forgiveness, in all their mystery and

---

2   *The Flower and the Castle* 313.

complexity, in the most mundane terms he can find. It is not just that Lindkvist is the "brutal creditor" with a "heart of gold" (Valency's phrases), but that he comes, both as creditor and savior, in the most improbable of shapes, anticipating no figure so much as the crazy Doctor O'Neill has Ed Mosher describe *The Iceman Cometh.*[3] He attests to the implausible and the unpredictable in the workings of human behavior and human destiny. To achieve what Strindberg intends for him, he should be played in the broadest manner possible, with the resentful, factual, and unbelieving Elis as straight man and comic butt.[4] If Ingmar Bergman was later to see redemption in the shape of a giant spider (in *Through a Glass Darkly*), Strindberg here sees it in the shape of a consummate joker. That humans are forgiven and saved must come, for Strindberg following Swedenborg, in ways unrelated to the rational. And if Lindkvist is played as he should be, the apparently sentimental structure of the action can be seen as a kind of put-on of all the old sudden-redemption melodramas of the past, which were unconvincing precisely to the degree that their surfaces were stickily endearing. In this play, the irrationality of the manner in which humans are saved is a mirror of the implausibility and irrationality of human behavior itself. To be taken correctly, the play must be seen as August Strindberg's "divine comedy"—the comedy in this case being, through Lindkvist, that associated with the comedy of the music hall.

The name Strindberg gives the play's central character is most important. The name Elis echoes Jesus's final cry of despair on the Cross: *Eli, Eli, naba sabachtani?* (My God, My God, why hast thou

---

[3] The Doctor Ed Mosher describes seems so unlikely a redemptive figure that he has been all but ignored in interpretations of *The Iceman Cometh.* "Old Doc," says Ed, advised for longevity drinking a "pint of whiskey before breakfast. ... It's staying sober and working that cuts men off in their prime." But old Doc himself died "at 80 from overwork." In their last encounter, Ed tells us, Doc had said "You see before you a broken man. ... If I had any nerves I'd have a nervous breakdown. ... [T]his last year there was actually one night I had so many patients I didn't even have time to get drunk. The shock to my system brought on a stroke which ... I recognized was the beginning of the end." The vital contradictions implicit in Ed's description, drawn from a traditional American vaudeville stage routine involving a crazy Doctor, are like Lindqvist's, legion. Lindqvist also comes out of a music hall tradition. [The quotation is from *Eugene O'Neill: Complete Plays 1932-1943* (NY: The Library of America, 1988) 615–616.]

[4] See Martin Lamm, *August Strindberg,* translated by Harry Carlson (NY, 1971) 370, where Strindberg is quoted as saying that Lindkvist should "only pretend to be irascible! Grunting and growling! But good!" My suggestions on the way the character should be played take this idea a step further. His irascibility should be contradicted by his goodness. It should in no way be affected by it.

forsaken me?) At the pinnacle of his suffering Jesus cries out that he is forsaken, and dies. Nothing in the Gospels is more testing of faith than this because it is the last living thought Jesus had. There is no antithesis to Jesus's feeling at that instant. And it is that overwhelming despair Strindberg wants his audience to feel in this play. No simple logic and no single sign can alleviate it. And that the play ends on Easter Eve rather than Easter morning, despite the message of forgiveness that Lindkvist brings, is crucial. At no point in this play does Strindberg give us the absolute assurance of redemption. All he does is give us "intimations" of it—in the Wordsworthian sense. Despair is there and will remain right through the play's final moment.

One other important figure appears to counter the despair that is so much a fixture throughout the play. I refer, of course, to the mystical figure of Eleanora, who made the play such a hit in its own day and is still the figure people talk about most when discussing it. Influenced, by Strindberg's own account, by thoughts of his sister Elisabeth, who was in a mental institution and Strindberg considered his "twin," and by Balzac's Swedenborgian novel *Seraphite*, she, in the words of Martin Lamm, is an "expressive instrument for [Strindberg's] occultism."[5] Her seemingly telepathic ability to communicate with loved ones over long distances can be taken as evidence of the supernatural in her character. But such talents are something she alone claims for herself; and despite the warmth and affection she brings to the play at a time it is most needed, the possibility that she is mad is never denied. And it is that possibility which keeps the play's "feet" on the ground, as it were. She causes great problems, after all, by appearing to have stolen a daffodil from a flower shop. Nothing she says or does indicates that she is anything more than a hyper-sensitive young woman, who while capable of bringing great reassurance to people, once also brought, and is still capable of bringing, great pain through behavior that was as aggressively anti-social as her present behavior is benevolent. In other words, while her kindness and compassion indicate that she acts out Christian good deeds by nature, whenever her supposedly miraculous abilities come up, so does the thought that she really is unbalanced.

Unlike other assessors of the play, I do not see Eleanora as Strindberg's primary indicator of the possibility of human redemption, though certainly she is one indicator. The emphasis that has been placed on her takes our primary attention away from the play's greatest sufferer, Elis. It is possible that thoughts of his beloved sister may have prompted Strindberg to let his characterization of Eleanora get out of

---

5   Lamm 369.

hand. But in a play the focus of which is suffering as a prelude to redemption but not entirely the assurance of it, emphasis should first and last be placed on the characterization of the very Strindberg-like[6] school teacher.

Elis is the true embodiment of what Strindberg wants to communicate in this play just because he still has his doubts at the end. He is literally blackmailed into humility by Lindkvist. He is left "on the edge," like sheets of paper balanced on the edge of the table by Lindkvist. His is finally not so much the spirit of Easter as it is of Easter Eve, as I suggested earlier, the spirit of hope against lingering doubt. And it is in this spirit that we first see him in the play, in the "shaft of sunlight" that falls across the room just before the darkness of Maundy Thursday night. He sheds his heavy coat, which he says has "soaked up all the hardships of winter," anticipating the image of the Doorkeeper's shawl in *A Dream Play*, which soaks up all the hardships of people's lives. He longs to return to his youth on the lake at the edge of Stockholm that he pointedly contrasts with the university town of Lund and its ugly associations with guilt and responsibility. One implicit sign of hope in the play is the anticipated union of Elis the despairing Christ figure with Kristina the soothing Christ figure in a marriage that might join the so far irreconcilable oppositions in human nature. The marriage would be the truest sign of Easter's redemptive power. It would join two human beings as Easter joins winter and spring. But it is a joining that is very much still yet to come at the play's conclusion, despite the implicit hope. The play leaves open the question whether redemption is possible.

The very beginning of the play, then, expresses the hope inherent in the instant that Lent ends and the Easter season begins just as the play's ending expresses that same hope, only more emphatically. Between come the sufferings that Jesus's sufferings on the Cross stand for and Haydn's music at the beginning of the play stands for. Those familiar with Haydn's quartet *The Seven Last Words of Christ* will recall that its piercing intensity is stronger than anything peaceful or redemptive in it, just as the piercing intensity of Elis's suffering is stronger than the sense of redemption in the play, however many signs of redemption Strindberg puts into it. Strindberg loads on the sufferings from the beginning: Elis's shame over his father's guilt, over Eleanora's being sent to the institution, over Benjamin's failing his Latin; his increasing suspicion that Kristina is betraying him; and most of all his guilt over his own failures and denials. All these Strindberg makes grate as few playwrights except O'Neill make suffering grate. Mixed in with the very

---

[6] See Michael Meyer, *Strindberg* (NY: Random House, 1985) 407, where Elis is treated as a Strindbergian self-portrait.

immediately-felt emotions of resentment and self-doubt come varieties of signs and actions, some positive but more negative. The olive branch dropped by the dove seen by Elis on his way home is offset by the arrival in the mail of the box of Lenten birches, and his recollection that he had once similarly received a box of stones; Kristina's steady insistence that Elis is only being tested, that we "are moving toward the light" is offset by her decision to meet with Peter privately for reasons she will not discuss with Elis. All this reason for doubt is accentuated by the sense of a coming not of redemption but of the "rude beast" (Lindvist) outside the door. Little indicators that Lindkvist might not be what he appears are brutally ground under by fear and guilt. Says Elis early in the play:

> Now he's laughing. ... But it's a kind laugh, not a cruel one. Perhaps he's not so cruel after all, even if he does want his money. I wish he'd come in and stop that blessed chatter. ... Now he's waving his stick again—they always have sticks—those creditors that come to dun you—and galoshes that go 'swish, swish'; like a cane through the air. ... like the Lenten birch. But he has a watch chain, with trinkets dangling from it—so he's not quite destitute. They always wear trinkets made of cornelian—like chunks of flesh cut off their neighbor's backs. Listen to the galoshes (*Working himself up into a flagellating frenzy.*) Swish, swish, swish, beast, beasts, hard, harder! (143–144)
>
> [In the original, the still more onomatopoetic: '*vargar, vargar, argar, argare, argast, vitsch, vitsch!*']

And this paroxysm of relentless, reasonless, self-flagellating fear, drawn from the bogey-man images of childhood, possesses Elis through to the last act. He appears calm at times, claiming to be going over the court records of his father's trial for some indication of an innocence he knows does not exist. He claims not to be angry at Benjamin for failing his Latin, or at Eleanora for running away from the institution, or at Kristina for going out with Peter, or at his mother for refusing to believe the truth about her husband—but always his mind is imprisoned by essentially adolescent, intense rage and fear. And this state of mind intensifies as Thursday yields to Long Friday. It is the abyss—a domestic parallel to the suffering of Christ on the Cross.

In the midst of Elis's tantrums and aggressiveness, he retains his dignity. Like the Captains in *The Father* and *The Dance of Death*, he maintains a quality which I can find no better word for than Strindberg-ian: a clarity and spareness of diction and of manner in spite of the repeated irrationality of his outbursts. And in that he does not share with those figures their delight in sarcasm and irony, one might say he is among Strindberg's more attractive male figures—and should be played as such. His irritation with those around him, which is particularly intense toward Benjamin and Eleanora, never makes us question the sincerity of his love for them. He is clearly strong and relentlessly defiant.

One can say, of course, that Elis is simply Strindberg facing his demons, and that the underpinnings of this play, like all Strindberg plays, is autobiographical is a given. Elis is unquestionably the figure the playwright saw in his mirror as he was coming out of his terrible "Inferno" period.[7] The juxtaposition of strength and weakness, attractiveness and unattractiveness, clarity and confusion in his suffering would assure us of that. But I think Strindberg is trying to do something more with Elis. He is closest of all to the Stranger of the *To Damascus* plays, which were written shortly after *Easter*, though he is not quite so self-righteous in his feelings of guilt as that figure. In both these figures, we see at work the Swedenborgian idea that sin and guilt are their own punishment. Obviously, Elis is an over-sensitive man whose guilt over the way life is treating him reaches nearly hysterical proportions. But that very hysteria is itself punishment for that excess. He is punished by feeling hurt by Kristina and Benjamin—and most of all by his resentment at his former student and close friend Peter, whose failure to invite Elis to his graduation party never is resolved in the play. In the fierce diction of the speech about Lindkvist quoted earlier, we see and hear a man, not simply stating his fear and guilt, but in the process of being punished *for* those reactions *by* those reactions.

All this is touched on, of course, by Lindkvist in his moral house-training of Elis in the third act. It is easy to see Lindkvist attacking Elis for the arch-sin of pride, which Elis certainly is guilty of, but Lindkvist is doing more than pointing out to Elis his sinful nature. He is making him live out the sin as punishment for the sin.

LINDKVIST.
Go to the Governor!
ELIS.
Never.
LINDKVIST.
Is that the kind of man you are?
ELIS.
Yes, that's the kind.

---

[7]   See Stephen A. Mitchell, "The Path from Inferno to the Chamber Plays: *Easter* and Strindberg," *Modern Drama* 24 (1986): 157–168.

LINDKVIST (*rising and walking across the room, his galoshes swishing and waving the blue paper*).

Worse and worse! ... I'll begin again from the other end. ... A revengeful person intends to bring a charge against your mother. This you can prevent.

ELIS.

How?

LINDKVIST.

By going to the Governor.

ELIS.

No!

LINDKVIST (*taking hold of Elis by the shoulders*).

Then you are the most contemptible creature I've ever met in my life. Now I shall go to your mother.

ELIS.

No, don't do that.

LINDKVIST.

Then will you go to the Governor?

ELIS (*murmurs*).

Yes.

LINDKVIST.

Say that again, louder.

ELIS.

Yes. (178–179)

The acting of Lindkvist is all-important. If the comic nature of the dialogue can be maintained, its effect comes through best. Lindkvist should be laughing as he shouts these orders, just as he is uproariously playing the children's tale ogre as he swishes about and waves the blue sheet. (A few lines later he says he "can eat children and widows.") He should never appear to be a serious blackmailer. He is punishing Elis with the childishness of Elis's responses by making him live (again) those responses—the sin its own punishment.

Such an approach appears to get us away from the theme of contradiction. But it does not, really. Rather, if sin—or what I have above referred to as the childishness of Elis's responses—is its own punishment, so, clearly, do opposite responses become their own reward. Elis feels better when he responds more positively—a theme that can be found in any cheap pop psychology magazine—but that "feeling better" is associated by Strindberg with Heavenly reward. Thus in the sudden shifts between the antagonistic and the beneficent in Elis do we get hints of the moral structure Strindberg is reaching for in this play. And the key word here is "shifts." People in Strindberg swing eternally between better and worse. Even the "better" that Lindkvist makes Elis feel at the end is qualified by the possibility of shifting back to the worse. There is still doubt abroad, it is still Easter Eve, and all this will happen again— as Elis regularly reiterates.

To explore this idea further, the contradictions in Elis Heyst are the contradictions inherent in everyone projected large. He is patient while impatient, intelligent while obtuse, energetic while phlegmatic, mature while childish, and above all kind while cruel. Contradictions can be seen in the other characters in the play (the Solveig-like Kristina excepted), but their shifts are of smaller proportions. Elis talks about a time when Eleanora was totally different, Benjamin goes from dejection at his failure in Latin to joy at his new acquaintance with Eleanora, and Mrs. Heyst goes through a sudden (perhaps miraculous) shift from total denial of her husband's crime to full acceptance of it. But the shifts that take place in these characters are sudden and individual. A little like the heroes of Greek tragedy, Elis alone embodies in larger proportions than usual the general turbulence the flesh is heir to.

At several points in the play, different characters (Elis, Kristina, Eleanora) allude to the idea that everything happens again, implying that events like those in the play and the emotions associated with them have occurred before and will occur again. This theme, which is obviously most important to the play, can have two possible roots. One is Nietzsche's "myth of the eternal return," which asserts that human life is like the seasons, that there is nothing new under the sun, and that all human experiences—both the good and the bad—are fated to repeat themselves. This idea obviously was a cause for despair in many early twentieth century traditionalists (not to mention the new believers in scientific "progress"), but it was a cause for rejoicing by others. The other possible root is the Swedenborgian idea of "vastation," that scouring of the soul with emotional pain which results in the birth of new life within the soul, in redemption and rebirth.

Evert Sprinchorn discusses this idea at length, while regrettably hardly mentioning *Easter*, in his excellent book *Strindberg as Dramatist.*[8] In *To Damascus* and *The Dance of Death*, Sprinchorn observes the vastation that takes place in the central male characters through the recurrence in their lives of suffering leading to new significance. Since this idea originated with Swedenborg, a Christian philosopher, it must be assumed that it is an idea that supports Christian acceptance.

---

[8] *Strindberg as Dramatist* 109–120.

The idea at first appears to work for *Easter*. Certainly Elis goes through a period of vastation, both in the period in which, as Kristina observes, he is being tested (the Long Friday period), and in the suffering he endures at the hands of Lindkvist. And he appears at the end to be changed. But three factors oppose a strictly Swedenborgian interpretation of the play. One is that we never do actually see Elis having new reactions to relived events (although Mrs. Heyst seems to late in the play). The second relates to the all-important seasonal setting of the play, the Lent-Easter progression suggesting simple recurrence—the good indeed following the bad, but inevitably to be followed by renewed bad and then renewed good. The kind of change revealed through permanently new reactions to relived events that occurs in the Stranger in *To Damascus* is thus missing here.

The third, and most important, factor that supports a more Nietzschean version of eternal return in the play resides in two figures who never appear but are most important to it: the betraying friend Peter (whose name obviously suggests the Christ-denying disciple of the Gospels), and the figure of the imprisoned father, Lindkvist's crooked former business partner. During his long third-act interview with Elis, Lindkvist tells the story of his first meeting with Heyst:

> It was about forty years ago. I came to town to look for a job. Young, alone, unknown. I had next to no money, and it was a dark night. As I knew of no cheap lodging, I asked the passers-by, but no-one would tell me. When I was absolutely desperate, a man came up to me and asked why I was weeping—I was actually in tears. I told him my predicament. Then he turned aside from his own way, took me to a lodging and comforted me with kind words. Just as I was going in, a shop door was flung open and a pane of glass broke against my elbow. The furious shopkeeper grabbed hold of me and said I must pay or he'd call the police. Imagine my despair. A night on the street before me. My unknown benefactor, who had seen what happened, took the trouble of calling the police himself—and saved me. That man was your father. So—everything happens again, the good things too. (182)

So the hope that underlies this play is not the bright hope of permanent conversion, but, following the progression of the Christian year, the psychologically sounder assurance that despair, though inevitably recurrent, will always be temporary. And this idea is tied to the still more important idea that such sequences also reside in the human personality. That old Heyst proved to be a false friend to Lindkvist made him no less a friend. That Peter has been a false friend—to Jesus, to Elis—makes him no less a friend. That Jean was a false friend to Julie made him no less a friend. The reversals, both those involving beneficence and those involving betrayal, are as unexpected and unpredictable as the suffering and resurrection themselves, but that they are inevitable is the ultimate sign in the play.

If the presence of fear and evil constitute a test in this play, it must never seem like one to the tested one while he is experiencing it. Benjamin's failure of his Latin test is quite real, and if redemption comes to him in the form of Eleanora's love, that is an experience not entirely subject to rational analysis. The Latin test is failed and will return to Benjamin periodically as a sign of his failure. That Elis's betrayal by Kristina is never fully explained by her explanation of why she had to meet Peter—she was, she says, helping Peter plan his forthcoming wedding—privately means that it will remain periodically for Elis a sign of his failure, as will the memory of Peter's apparent rejection of him. The test must always be one that is failed, and the suffering must be real suffering. The coming of the redeemer must be, while theoretically assured, always unexpected—like Lindkvist—outlandish and certainly not something that can be counted on. Strindberg's structure of suffering and forgiveness involves a kind of double-think that makes sure of the reality and intensity of evil and despair as it takes us through the final stages of the central Christian myth.

A Dream Play

A Dream Play follows more naturally from *Easter* than from the plays that intervene. And even more than *Easter* is its immediacy and familiarity profound. It digs as deeply into the muck of everyday existence as any play in the western canon, and it does so with a despair that is balanced only by what Martin Lamm has identified as a "warm sympathy that gives [it] its unique position among Strindberg's works." Lamm seems alone in finding in the play a "lightness of touch" that offsets the heaviness of its themes.[1] The work is as broad in the subjects it touches on as are Strindberg's interests, and each subject confirms the bankruptcy of all attempts at rational understanding or the possibility of more than the very temporary abatement of life's essential pain. Yet Strindberg leans against the almost overwhelming push toward the hatred of human life engendered by his episodes with all his artistic weight. In each of the various leading *personae* of the play—the Officer, the Lawyer, the Poet, and the Daughter, each of whom may be seen as different aspects of one person (possibly the author)[2]—there is the sense of disappointed hopes, of directionless aging, of solutions that lead to greater confusion, of agonizing loss—but there is in each something of Lamm's lightness, realizing itself in a variety of ways.

The play opens with the Daughter of Indra finding herself sinking more or less against her will down to earth. Curious to know what life on earth is like, she asks her father whether he might join her in the descent. Indra says he cannot because he "cannot breathe the air," but suggests she continue down and report back to him about whether she finds the persistent "lamentation and complaint" of the earthlings justified. From the start there is the intimation that contradictions govern life on earth, since the complaint, the heaviness of the air, and the darkness are countered by images the Daughter gets of "green woods, blue water, white mountains, yellow fields"—and "shouts of joy." Indra tells her that humans "live on the borderline of folly and insanity," and that she must descend with "courage ... for this is but a test," the test presumably being over whether humans are in any way redeemable.

---

[1]   See Lamm 403, *et passim.*

[2]   See Sprinchorn, *Strindberg as Dramatist* 160; and Elizabeth Sprigge, *Six Plays of Strindberg* 188–189.

(Quotes are taken from 197–199.) She proceeds to go through a series of episodes on earth during which, despite genuinely uplifting moments, she finds herself progressively earthbound and unhappy, finally leading to her return to her father.

Ultimately these episodes must be dealt with, but since Strindberg's summation of the way he sees life is clear, hard, and detailed in the play's later scenes, those later scenes may appropriately be approached first. In those scenes he appears to forsake drama in favor of poetry to make his largest statement, but as in the medieval theological debate, he here, as he had in his earlier *To Damascus* trilogy, uses a two-character format: question and answer, thought and counter-thought (though it often comes out as thought and after-thought). The final scenes constitute the stages of a long poem in dialogue, keeping the audience/reader's mind alive to Strindberg's constantly shifting positions. Strindberg never permits a leaden passivity toward what he says. He is always surprising.

Late in the play, the Poet, the Daughter's final guide on earth, proposes the chief questions growing out of the plot's preceding agonies in a poetic petition read by the Daughter. The Poet is at the same time the least earth-bound of the play's male protagonists and the one most conscious of the degradations life on the planet seems inevitably heir to. While the Officer, her first consort on earth, is most conscious of the degradation inherent in youth—in growing up and courtship, for example—and her second, the Lawyer, is most conscious of the degradations inherent in social inequities and in family life, it is the Poet who has the largest view of the human condition and has the most far-reaching compassion. He is the one the Daughter finally feels most in touch with because he can sense *both* her disgust *and* her other-worldliness. His petition—really a sort of cry—is immensely important to the play because in focusing on the most gaping existential contradictions, it testifies as much to the hard Strindbergian faith at the root of the work as it does to the manifold bases for human despair the play delineates:

> Why wake to life,
> why greet the light
> with a cry of fury and of pain,
> Child of man, when to be glad
> should be the gift of light?
> Why are we born like animals?
> We who stem from God and man,
> whose souls are longing to be clothed

in other than this blood and filth.
Must God's own image cut its teeth? (246)[3]

The Poet's lines about birth and early childhood as an emblem for all human suffering get at the contradictory essence of existence in the most rudimentary terms. Reminiscent of Lear's "When we are born, we cry that we are come/ To this great stage of fools," these lines go a step farther than Shakespeare's. Despite all the blood and pain, human birth, the Poet says, is still a "joy beyond all other joys," and it is *God's* image that "cuts its teeth." It is such constants as overwhelming joy amid the pain that lurk behind most of the play's many dismal enactments of human suffering. Irony abounds, of course, but Strindberg's is an irony that does not share the enervating nihilism of much late twentieth-century irony. Strindberg goes back to Job in never questioning the existence of God as he inveighs against life's outrages.

Later in the final act, the Daughter expands the Poet's thought by explaining the contradictoriness by means of the Hindu idea of the "mingling" of Brahma and Maya, the divine with the earthly. "The mingling of the divine element with the earthly was the Fall from Heaven." Mankind, she suggests, is paying for the presence of the earthly in its nature by the remorse generated by greed and lust. Of primary importance in this, of course, is the idea of deliverance through suffering, but in Strindberg that can only mean suffering without the awareness of deliverance (the idea so entertainingly put forth in *Easter* through the personality of Lindkvist). All that humans can be aware of is the sense of opposites in eternally bitter, restless conflict. But it is that "conflict of opposites" that generates "power, as fire and water create the force of steam." (258) It is the power that is life itself in Strindberg's view, always possessing equal measures of the divine and the earthly. And the former, for Strindberg, is generated first and foremost, in Dantesque fashion, by a woman's beauty, even though it is at the same time for the Miltonic Strindberg, always "woman through whom sin and death entered into life." The contradictory thus pervades every aspect of human existence—beginning with the love that generates the sexual union that generates birth.

---

[3]   Sprinchorn's translation of this last line [in *August Strindberg: Selected Plays II* (Minneapolis: U of Minnesota P, 1986) 714] is "Must the paragon of created beings| cut his eyeteeth and descend into the flesh?" (This translation of the final phrase in the line does not actually appear in the Swedish.) Harry G. Carlson, in *Strindberg: Five Plays* (Berkeley: U of California P, 1981) 251, translates the line as "If we are made in God's own image,|Why must we endure this form"; while Michael Robinson's 1998 translation is the same as Sprigge's. Thus I opt for Sprigge's.

Looking at the rest of the play with these ideas in mind helps one to understand the work as a whole. To begin with is the play's seeming melodramatic center,[4] which I want to be cognizant of but am not concentrating on, that center being the focus on the opening of the clover-leaf door which supposedly will reveal the secrets of the universe, the answers to human suffering. The sense of certainty that opening of the door promises makes this action suspect from the beginning, but its fairy-tale appeal is undeniable. It also creates a framework for the play's bitterly satirical treatment of the conflicting university faculties, each arrogantly confident of its own approach and violently disdainful of the others. And even the "nothing" that is finally revealed behind the door sets off quarrels among them as to its significance. The fascinating interpretation of it by the Daughter, which I shall take up at the conclusion of this discussion, is uniformly dismissed.

It is clearly and only the irrational that concerns Strindberg. There are numerous signs, symbols, and impressions along the way intimating Strindberg's sense of the eternal. Such intimations may simply be in the details of the stage directions: e.g., flowers—the brilliant "giant holly-hocks in bloom: white, pink, crimson, sulphur yellow, and violet" that surround the Growing Castle at the start of the Daughter's earthly excursion and the "giant blue monkshood" growing by the wall of the theater, the giant (again) chrysanthemum bursting from the fire that devours the Growing Castle at the end. Or the intimations may be musical: the *Kyrie* played by the Daughter on the organ at the academic ritual in the Cathedral, the scene melting into that of a sea "grotto" in another scene to be identified with Fingal's Cave, with its "Music of the Waves" and "Music of the Winds" (calling to mind Mendelssohn's unmentioned overture); "Ugly Edith" in Fair Haven playing Bach's *Toccata and Fugue Number 10* (the very specificity signaling the work's confirming force for the author); the music alone of the Daughter's voice as it transfixes the sad, blind shipping magnate (also in Fair Haven), and as it is heard in her "interpretation of the winds" later in the play; and the *Kyrie*, again, sung in perfect four-part harmony by the crew of the sinking ship immediately preceding the appearance of the Savior.

But Strindberg is scrupulously honest in what he puts forward in the face of these signs, which often seem all but lost in the play's flux of suffering. We get repeated counter-signs, like that suggested by the Poet's first appearing carrying a bucket of mud as he stares heavenward.

---

[4]   On the play's formal structure, see Strindberg's own scene designations cited in Sprinchorn, *Strindberg as Dramatist* 156. See also Brustein 126–132; and Sprinchorn's "The Logic of *A Dream Play*," *Modern Drama* 5 (1962): 352–365.

In the same vein, the hollyhocks grow out of a bed of manure; the monkshood withers (though it blooms again); the chrysanthemum (as Sprinchorn suggests) bespeaks implications of lust and orgasm[5]; the solemn academic rites late in the play ignore true worth (the Lawyer) while rewarding pomposity and hypocrisy; the sea grotto is surrounded by treacherous rocks; Bach-playing Edith is "ugly" and cannot attract a man despite her musical proficiency; the shipping magnate is blind and later must have a vision of his son's demise at sea; the *Kyrie*-singing crew (far from being reassured) shrieks in renewed fear at the Savior's appearance. Strindberg is systematic at keeping us uncomforted. All we hear is the Poet's "I have had faith many times, but after a while it drifted away"—although with this playwright it sometimes seems more a blasting than a drifting away.

"It is pitiable to be human," the Daughter's repeated phrase, is demonstrated first in those scenes involving youth, courtship and marriage. There is the persistent progression from hope and promise to disillusionment and despair, from the romantic to the tragic (or perhaps the absurd would be the better word, though Strindberg would hardly have known what to do with that concept as it is now defined). There is always the awareness that to do good in one context involves doing harm in another. The Officer must be led out of the protective confines of a loving parental home to the disillusionments of young manhood. The early scenes are among the lightest in the play, but even then there are repeated intimations of the forbidding in the future. The parents in the home clearly love one another and are ready to forgive everything, but the love and forgiveness do not remedy vaguely alluded to past injustices that poison the atmosphere. Then, in the first backstage scene, as the youthful Officer jauntily woos his Victoria (the opera-singer), the woman Stage-Door Keeper tells the Daughter of her shawl which has absorbed over the years the personal agonies of all the members of the company. The Officer quickly becomes an old man, his wooing flowers withered, the singer still keeping him waiting. But the Officer lives ever in hope, and even if the next adventure will repeatedly undermine that hope, he remains a figure associated with the romantic.

Human suffering intensifies with the second, and longest, episode of the play, that centering on the Lawyer—the figure who lives in a thoroughly Strindbergian "real world." The disillusion here is far more severe than in the previous section because it involves the dashed idealism, not of romantic youth (the Officer), but of doing good in society. A Dickensian figure, the Lawyer is so dedicated to alleviating suffering

---

[5]   *Strindberg as Dramatist* 167.

that he has taken all the suffering and remorse into himself—making him appear old and harsh despite his youth. And because his mien and behavior have rendered him unconventional, he is, at the crucial moment during later rites intended by society to honor the best of its members, humiliatingly denied the honor owed him. This is a man the Daughter feels she can truly honor and perhaps help—but the biggest disillusionment of all lies in store.

Strindberg has always touched the nerve of mutual dissatisfactions in marriage with precision, but here—well after the events and ensuing anguish of his marriage to Siri—the pointed spareness is unexcelled. Nowhere is there such a balance of understatement and despair. Married now, indeed with children, the Daughter and the Lawyer have been discussing the penury that has resulted from his generosity to his clients:

DAUGHTER.

None of it would matter, if only I could have some beauty in our home.

LAWYER.

I know what you're thinking of—a plant, a heliotrope to be exact; but that costs as much as six quarts of milk or half a bushel of potatoes.

DAUGHTER.

I would gladly go without food to have my flower.

LAWYER.

There is one kind of beauty that costs nothing. Not to have it in his home is torture for a man with any sense of beauty.

DAUGHTER.

What is that?

LAWYER.

If I tell you, you will lose your temper.

DAUGHTER.

We agreed never to lose our tempers.

LAWYER.

We agreed. Yes. All will be well, Agnes, if we can avoid those sharp hard tones. You know them—no, not yet.

DAUGHTER.

We shall never hear those.

LAWYER.

Never, if it depends on me.

DAUGHTER.

Now tell me.

LAWYER.

Well, when I come into a house, first I look to see how the curtains are hung. (*Goes to the window and adjusts the curtain.*) If they hang like a bit of string or rag, I soon leave. Then I glance at the chairs. If they are in their places, I stay. (*Puts a chair straight against the wall.*) Next I look at the candle sticks. If the candles are crooked, then the whole house is askew. (*Straightens a candle on the bureau.*) That you see, my dear, is the beauty which costs nothing.

DAUGHTER (*bowing her head*).

Not that sharp tone, Axel!

LAWYER.

It wasn't sharp.

DAUGHTER.

Yes it was.

LAWYER.

The devil take it! ["Oh, for Christ's sake!" in Sprinchorn's translation]

DAUGHTER.

What kind of language is that?

LAWYER.

Forgive me, Agnes [the earthly name the Daughter has assumed]. But I have suffered as much from your untidiness as you do from the dirt. And I haven't dared straighten things myself, because you would be offended and thought I was reproaching you.

DAUGHTER.

It is terribly hard to be married, harder than anything. (219–220)

Harder than anything—as Strindberg well knew. What is so effective about this scene is first that it so accurately pinpoints the nature of the mutual irritations—working through the elliptical quality of such exchanges, emphasizing their oft-repeated subjects with such phrases as "I need air!" "I need a touch of beauty!" "I must have neatness! We must have warmth!" (A Swedish winter, after all.) But more than that at first is the understatement, the implicit effort at self-control, the sincere consideration for the feelings of the other party, the easy flow from one source of mutual torment to the next.

The early portion of the scene bespeaks anything but the melodramatic in the responses of these figures. As one considers the countless expressions of human misery to follow Strindberg's in the century to follow (Pirandello's, for example), one begins to sense not the despair alone that underlies the lines but Lamm's "warm sympathy" very subtly countering it, the "lightness of touch" that makes the compassion for the human that is the play's theme as genuine and penetrating as it is unsentimental. One gets a sense of Strindberg, convinced of the insolubility of the dilemmas at hand, being now beyond the explosions and the tears. "Not that sharp tone, Axel!" says the Daughter, when the Lawyer's tone has seemed anything but sharp. Following this, of course, the Lawyer does explode, but immediately apologizes. Exhausted by his or her own pain, clinging to a determination not to yield, each character seems ever cognizant of the other's pain.

As the scene progresses, however, contradictions of their compassionate tones are immediately heard. They become increasingly recriminatory, and their exchange suddenly takes on one of the tones of traditional melodrama—the Lawyer now assuming the tone of the old-style villain and the Daughter that of his victim. Departing from the understatement and the compassion, the positions of the characters harden and their responses take on the frightening, more conventional characteristics of traditional melodrama. Violence seems threatened. The Daughter confesses she has used what she considers the Lawyer's "unholy" newspaper to light the fire; the Lawyer begins violently and sneeringly to "tidy up." The dialogue (suggesting that Strindberg very much has Ibsen's *A Doll House* in mind) turns inevitably to the subject of the Daughter's obligations as a mother—the most irresolvable of all the issues. In spite of their best efforts, they are dragged into shrill overstatement, with a touch of the surrealism of the dream (this being, one must always recall, a *dream* play):

DAUGHTER.

It is as if you were twisting my heart-strings.

LAWYER.

I twist, I twist!

DAUGHTER.

Don't!

LAWYER.

I twist ...

The sense of disillusionment in this scene, then, is not solely in the fact that the married people, for all their ideals, cannot get along, but that inevitably they must lose their dignity, moving from compassion to rigidity to monstrosity, a kind of movement Strindberg was later to use still more emphatically in *The Ghost Sonata* and that Ingmar Bergman followed him in so effectively. Strindberg presents these characters as thoroughly admirable so long as they remain mutually understanding, but destroys that admiration at the point their hurt deprives them of their willingness to give, makes them revert to the basically childhood figures of monster and maiden—the basic figures of one kind of melodrama.

The Officer re-appears at this point, playing the role of the hero in melodrama appearing just in time to rescue the heroine from the fiend. His appearance leads into the next portion of the play. The Daughter runs off with him, feeling that with him, rather than with the Lawyer, she will find happiness. They seek out Fairhaven, a kind of earthly paradise, but on the way they must withstand a test, the test being a requisite in much early melodrama. They must first visit Foulstrand, which lies just across the bay from their earthly paradise.

Foulstrand is a purgatory where all human diseases, including moral ones, are "cured" by being scoured and bleached. It is overseen by the savagely ironic Quarantine Master, in whom the author may be representing his youthful self, seeking to correct the abuses he saw around him with verbal assault and blistering satire. But the attempt to better the human condition in this fashion only renders it more unpalatable—an idea Strindberg represents by making Foulstrand the waiting area of a hospital, dominated by the odor of disinfectants, its very cleanliness having driven out all living warmth.[6] Humanity's self-generated efforts to improve seem to do more harm than good.

But the ultimate explosion of the romantic dream is Fairhaven, the affluent suburb populated by well bred, educated, seemingly happy people, the foreshadower of the American Dream. Here the contradictions, if more subtle, are just as devastating in that they are more familiar to the typical Strindberg audience/reader. Here Ugly Edith plays her Bach *Toccata* but cannot get a dancing partner, and the blind shipping tycoon lives in comfort but must endure the loss of his son at sea. It is also the place where the Officer must relive the humiliations of grade-school life. It is in the schoolroom sub-episode (which Bergman recreates in *Wild Strawberries*), with its dream-like distortion, that Strindberg details the precisely-remembered and still-open wounds of childhood and school:

SCHOOLMASTER (*to the Officer*).

Now, my boy, can you tell me what twice two is?

(*The Officer remains seated, painfully searching his memory without finding an answer.*) You must stand up when you are asked a question.

OFFICER (*rising anxiously*).

Twice two ... let me see ... That makes two twos.

S. MASTER.

Aha! So you have not prepared your lesson.

---

[6] This is a theme Strindberg will treat late in *The Ghost Sonata* in the image of the cook who drains all nourishment from the food she prepares.

OFFICER (*embarrassed*).

Yes, I have, but ... I know what it is, but I can't say it.

S. MASTER.

You're quibbling. You know the answer, do you? But you can't say it. Perhaps I can assist you. (*Pulls the Officer's hair.*)

OFFICER.

Oh, this is dreadful, really dreadful!

S. MASTER.

Yes, it is dreadful that such a big boy should have no ambition.

OFFICER (*agonised*).

A *big* boy. Yes, I certainly am big, much bigger than these others. I am grown up. I have left school ... (*As if waking.*) I have even graduated. Why am I sitting here then? Haven't I got my degree?

S. MASTER.

Certainly. But you have got to stay here and mature. Do you see? You must mature. (232–233)

The theme of the clinging immaturity, the psychological suffering associated with childhood, so often the sad song of the affluent, is as telling here as are the themes of marital misunderstanding preceding it and the poverty of the coal-heavers following it. And the seeming villain of the exchange is only a villain from the perspective of the child. The School Master may be a profound ironist, but his understanding and restraint are as great as that of the Lawyer early in the marriage scene. The anti-melodramatic thrust of these scenes is in part that the apparent villain is in fact the one with the greater awareness, villainous only from the perspective of the one who feels victimized.

Nevertheless, the point has been made. Fairhaven is only fair on the outside. Essentially all walks of life are characterized by the vividly-detailed suffering of these scenes, and if that suffering may always be perceived in contradictory terms, it is no less suffering for that. Which is perhaps why the Poet now becomes the Daughter's consort. The Officer is the central figure of a romantic melodrama; but he cannot grow up, and the happy ending he expects (as he previously did with his opera singer) is unattainable. The Lawyer is the central figure of a social(ist) melodrama, but the happy ending he seeks in alleviating the suffering of others is unachievable, and he cannot live successfully as a husband. Their melodramas are exploded. The Poet, on the other hand, by his very nature goes beyond melodrama. He is in tune with the contra-dictory in life, always focused at the same time on both the Keatsian beauty that is truth and the sordidness that is human existence. He seeks no happy endings, while his perspective acknowledges the "strange world of contradictions" of things as they are.

The Daughter does not immediately take up with the Poet, but as it becomes clear that the Officer will never give up his pursuit of romantic chimeras—late in the play he is still courting his Victoria—and the Lawyer keeps insisting she fulfill her wifely-maternal obligations, the Poet seems, for the moment, her only answer. Convinced that life on earth can only be the endless successions of tedious repetitions the Lawyer predicts, she decides she must return to her ethereal home, and the Poet is the most appropriate one to accompany her through the earthly portion of that final journey.

The opening of the door, as suggested earlier, is the play's melodramatic (and false) denouement. Even though it has not been mentioned through the many intervening scenes, it seems ever the anticipated explanation of and resolution to all the agony. Yet anyone familiar with Strindberg then and now knows it will resolve nothing, and on the surface it appears not to. Its primary purpose—to emphasize the arrogant, violent bickering of the competing university faculties—this time focuses on the dilemma posed by the "nothing" they find once the door is opened. The four representatives cease their quarreling only when there is something they can agree on, and that comes in the person of the Daughter, whom they turn on violently, first because she mocks their endless bickering, and finally in response to her assertion of their incapacity to comprehend what they have seen:

CHANCELLOR.

Will the Daughter kindly inform us what her idea was in having the door opened.

DAUGHTER.

No, my friends. If I told you, you would not believe it.

MEDICINE.

But there's nothing there.

DAUGHTER.

What you say is correct. But you have not understood it. (254)

The contempt of the four in response to this releases the Daughter (and Strindberg) from the responsibility of further explanation, but the Daughter's enigma is tantalizingly important to the scene and to the play. What is it about the "nothing" that exists behind the door that the academicians do not understand? The theologian's view that what is represented is the "nothing" out of which "in the beginning God created heaven and earth" has been implicitly rejected in that his is one of the four positions of the wrangling scholars. Yet something of the sort seems implied, inasmuch as Strindberg in writing the work was plainly affected by a Hindu perception of the universe, which has within it a similar concept to the theologian's. Oversimply put, understanding the meaning of life is dependent on that which transcends *things*. Still, Strindberg does not allow for that kind of speculation—beyond the implication that the Daughter is speaking of issues which by their very nature will not yield to rational human understanding.

The scene's other thrust, and perhaps in view of the inaccessibility to humans of what the Daughter knows, its primary one, is its attack on the "righteous," who are in the background for the door-opening. The pharisaical righteous, the Poet suggests, while represented by the conflicting intellectual positions of the scholars, are one in being hypocritical, smug and insensitive. And the conclusion of the righteous, spoken through the scholars, is that the Daughter must be stoned however she answers the riddle of the door because she raises doubts in the young. Thus is she linked not only to the previous offspring of God who assumed human form in order to take on the sufferings of humankind, but to the Greek philosopher Socrates at his trial.

The Daughter's statement to the Poet that she will solve the riddle for him, privately in the wilderness, foreshadows the final scenes of the play, with which this discussion led off. And that "solution" almost accomplishes what it cannot accomplish. The Poet, like the winds and waves, can only bewail the varieties of human suffering in the face of the wonder of the human form and intellect. But in the end, the daughter's one piece of comprehensible evidence is that the conflict of opposites, which is at the heart of the Poet's lament, is what preserves life. It is the "power" that generates the "steam" by which humanity endures; and at the earthly level, she implies, "that is all ye know and all ye need to know."

That the play's final, much-discussed symbol—that of the burning castle the top of which bursts into a giant chrysanthemum—is the ultimate emblem of that assurance is an idea not inconsistent with the phallic/orgasmic implications suggested by others. It is another version of the fire and water bursting into steam image, the result of the mingling of the divine element with the earthly. Any other kind of assurance is the assurance of melodrama—the black vs. white kind of assurance that the playwrights I am discussing devote themselves to offsetting. All humankind can see—other than in epiphanic flashes such as that wrought by old Lindkvist—is its own suffering, and all it can "realize" is that the suffering is always somehow contradicted. Humans, despite their incipient good will toward, and even love for, one another, find their frustrations making them into monsters. Still, the Poet's faith, ever faint, flickers on and off—and very occasionally there is the kind of bursting into flame of the play's ending. Not quite acceptable as a ground for faith in Strindberg's time or our own, it is nevertheless the inevitability of contradiction and the unexpected in human affairs that finally sets this play apart as much from the nihilistic melodrama, the "drama of disaster" that was to grow out of it, as it did from the romantic melodrama that preceded it.

CHEKHOV

Ivanov

A good deal has been written in English about Chekhovian drama, some of it clear and some of it less than clear. The clearer criticism tends to focus on individual aspects of the plays: their reflections of the culture of their time, their focus on social change, their connections with Chekhov biography, their theatrical innovativeness. The less clear criticism (or much of it) grows out of unstinting admiration of the playwright and tends to be stated in more sweeping generalities. The earlier twentieth-century English critics J. Middleton Murry and William Gerhardie typify such criticism.[1]

Surprisingly, perhaps, the criticism that is less clear seems often better at getting at the essence of the playwright than that which is clear. This is because the nature of Chekhov's art is always greater than the sum of its parts, and the clearer critics want to focus on the parts. To those who love Chekhov, the generalities of the less clear sound wonderful on first reading, but quickly pale with the realization that those generalities are insufficiently rooted in specifics. And they tend not to emanate from a focused context (i.e., biography, culture, theater etc.) other than that implicit in their admiration for the playwright. But two of the most ardent of Chekhov's admirers of the past thirty years, J. L. Styan and Richard Gilman, look at the plays in extensive detail; and the result is a pair of critical studies that probe farther than most the inscrutabilities of the playwright's vision.[2]

Deferring to none as an admirer of the playwright's, I hope to emulate Styan and Gilman by treating the plays in detail comparable to theirs, my ideas emanating from the perspective established by this book: that the four major playwrights who founded modern drama saw the large magnitude of the human that is expressed by and ultimately transcends their major characters' contradictions. I hope to suggest, moreover, that nowhere in the works of those playwrights are the con-

---

[1]　See Murry, "Thoughts on Tchekhov," in *Aspects of Literature* (London, 1920); and Gerhardie, *Anton Chekhov: A Critical Study* (NY: St. Martin's Press, 1974).

[2]　See J. L. Styan, *Chekhov in Performance: A Commentary on the Major Plays* (Cambridge UP:1971), and Richard Gilman, *Chekhov's Plays: An Opening into Eternity* (New Haven: Yale UP, 1995).

tradictions and the transcendent magnitude presented with greater force
and clarity than in the plays of Anton Chekhov.

By beginning with *Ivanov*, I am suggesting that in its essence it is no
less a work than the later plays. The play is usually given short shrift.
Styan all but omits it entirely, and most other critics seem satisfied to
avoid the play by citing the playwright's letter to A. S. Suvorin in
January 1889 in which he describes it as merely a work of satire against
a type of individual (the "despondent man") and castigating its "execu-
tion" as "worthless."[3] My own reading of the play prompts feelings
quite different from those in Chekhov's letter (which should not in any
case be considered the final word, since an author's letters need not
indicate final judgments on issues regarding their work). Far from being
the satire of a particular type, the play's central figure is the first of
Chekhov's major representations in drama of a figure who is greater
than the sum of his contradictions and inadequacies. Clearly there are
satirical portraits in *Ivanov*, as there are in all Chekhov's plays, but
Ivanov himself can hardly be dismissed as one of them. I once cited as
the three characters who most typify the view of the human central to
these playwrights Ibsen's Peer Gynt, Chekhov's Ivanov, and O'Neill's
Jamie Tyrone. It is my primary objective in what follows to support that
idea in relation to Ivanov.

Ivanov

While Styan, along with most others, dismisses *Ivanov* as merely
satirical, what he says of the central characters of *The Sea Gull* applies
precisely to the character of Ivanov as well. "We are neither to like nor
to loathe [them] …, but to hold them in what might be called his
'balance of sympathy' by which we are forced to come to some sort of
judgment. Our contradictory responses to the play hold the secret of the
play's theme."[4] In a comparable vein, and here directly assessing
Ivanov, Gilman discusses the play's "balances and shifting perspectives."[5] The big difference between *Ivanov* and the plays to follow
is that while Styan's statement applies to many of the central figures of
the later plays, it is more true for the single central figure in *Ivanov* than
for the others, as Gilman's discussion makes clear. We neither like
Ivanov nor loathe him but are forced toward some sort of judgment by

---

[3]   In *Letters of Chekhov*, selected and edited by Avrahm Yarmolinsky (New York: The
      Viking Press, 1973) 107. Maurice Valency discusses various letters relating to the
      play in *The Breaking String* (Oxford UP, 1966) 82–100.

[4]   *Chekhov in Performance*: 17.

[5]   *Chekhov's Plays:* 56.

an intricate balance of sympathy and shifting of moral perspectives toward him. And that judgment is as difficult to make as it is toward any figure in Chekhov's plays. As throughout the play Ivanov reveals more and more about himself, we feel less and less ready to make a final assessment of him.

The play's other characters should not be summarily dismissed, however. Some tend to be mere satirical portraits, like characters from Chekhov's earlier short plays and stories—for example, the outrageous steward Borkin, who bores Ivanov with his bluster and scheming; or the uproariously stupid money-lender Zinaida Savishna, who unrelentingly duns Ivanov to pay his debts; or the gold-digging young widow Babakhina; or the excise officer Kosych, who is totally obsessed with his bridge hands; or the viciously gossiping card-players. But others are complex in ways that, like the lead, look forward to the characters of the later plays. Ivanov's one true friend Lebedev is noble in his willingness to give Ivanov some of the money he needs (out of his secret savings) but craven in the face of his miserly wife (the money-lender). More Chekhovian still, in the sense the later plays give that word, is Count Shabelsky, Ivanov's dependent uncle, whose viciously anti-semitic railings at Anna Petrovna, Ivanov's consumptive Jewish wife, are quite undercut by an instinctive good will toward that wife. The positive force of the balance of sympathy Chekhov creates toward him is perhaps best seen in the sense of harmony created by his routine playing of musical duets with her.

Other cases in point are the young doctor, Lvov, seemingly so sure of himself in his abhorrence of what he considers Ivanov's cruelty and hypocrisy toward his wife yet essentially quite unsure of himself, as revealed in part by his own statements when alone, and in larger part by the sound of his public attacks on Ivanov, which have the effect in their overstatement of the do-gooder in a melodrama seeking to root out the corruption around him. His counterpart is Ivanov's young admirer and lover Sasha, whose voluble defense of Ivanov before others sounds as much like youthful defiance of a stupid, hypocritical society as it is evidence of the supposed genuineness of her love for him (a pose which breaks down just before they are to be married). And then there is the wife Anna Petrovna herself, whose sincerity in the allowances she makes for her husband (presumably out of a genuine love for him) are offset by her determination to embarrass him.

But with the possible exception of Count Shabelsky, all these characters serve more as catalysts for and agents of Ivanov's downfall than of full-blown Chekhovian characters in their own right. In the context of this study especially, this play begins and ends with its central figure—a

statement which cannot be made of any of the later plays—and if that
makes it a lesser play than the others, it is still a superbly crafted lesser
play.

Aside from his conversational responses to those around him, which
tend for the most part to be evasive or pacifying, all that Ivanov says is
of a piece. His longer speeches are confessional, self-accusing, and
guilt-ridden. They are rarely self-justifying, and they always reveal,
sometimes with seeming calm, sometimes almost hysterically, the
depths and suffering inherent in his self-awareness. He is everything the
young doctor accuses him of being—cruel and selfish—yet at the same
time he is totally free of the hypocrisy the doctor accuses him of. Responding to the doctor's first appeals to him, he speaks with an honesty
that becomes increasingly enmeshed in its own depths:

> I suppose I am terribly guilty, but my thoughts are muddled, my soul is
> under the grip of a kind of apathy, and I am no longer able to understand
> myself. [...] Here you tell me she is going to die soon, and I feel neither love
> nor pity, but only a sort of emptiness and lassitude. To anyone looking at me
> this must seem appalling; I don't understand what is happening within my
> soul. ... (32)[6]

Ivanov here anticipates Jim Tyrone telling of his response to his
mother's death in *A Moon for the Misbegotten*[7]—another seeming
emptiness of response born of an overwhelming guilt. And Ivanov picks
up the theme later with the rapt Sasha:

> I tell you in all honesty, I can bear anything: depression, mental illness, ruin,
> the loss of my wife, my own premature old age and solitude, but I cannot
> bear, cannot endure, the contempt I feel for myself. I could die of shame that
> I, a healthy, strong man, have turned into some sort of Hamlet, or Manfred,
> or superfluous man. [...] There are those persons who are flattered at being
> called Hamlets or superfluous men, but for me it is—ignominious! My pride
> is outraged, I am weighed down with shame, and I suffer. ... (59)

Ivanov's is a passion of the "emptiness and lassitude" of which he
speaks, of self-contempt and guilt growing out of sources more obscure
than his apparent betrayal of his wife. It is perhaps key that he compares
himself to Hamlet—obviously the Hamlet who "has of late lost all [his]
mirth." Commentators in our century have ascribed the reasons for the
prince's mood to one or another cause—his disillusion with his mother
(the leading one), the existential angst of the times, a possibly psychotic
nature given to great mood swings—but with possible truths in all such

---

[6]   All quotations from Chekhov's plays are from *Chekhov: The Major Plays*, translated
      by Ann Dunnigan (NY: Signet Classics, 1964).

[7]   See my discussion of this play: pp. 191–201.

causes, none adds up to the prince who speaks to us, who so forcefully invades us with his person.

And so with Ivanov, of whose mother we know nothing (though we might well speculate), whose angst at his debts and social down-sliding perhaps constitute an emblem of the deterioration of the landed class in late nineteenth-century Russia, and whose mood swings are less pronounced but ultimately more psychotic than the prince's. The point is that with the same muddle of motivations, the same willingness to confess all that he knows about himself yet incapacity to reconcile the rudely conflicting nature of what he knows, the same facility in expressing his thoroughly overwrought feelings, he also penetrates us deeply.

And in the face of the charges, including Chekhov's own in his letter to Suvorin—that he is no more than a satirical portrait of a type sometimes called the "despondent man" (as in Chekhov's letter), sometimes the superfluous man (Ivanov's own word and that used by others describing the type in question)—Ivanov says that his shame includes the idea that he may be a "Hamlet," in the sense that Chekhov uses it here, the embodiment of despondency and superfluousness. That shame and the very awareness Chekhov gives Ivanov of what he appears to be is proof alone that he is something more. Perhaps Chekhov indeed tried to create a Hamlet for his time, then threw up his hands (as have so many at Hamlet), and decided such people are superfluous. But the character created is one of those few in modern literature who does approach the melancholy prince in his comparable angst and especially the depths he probes in the listener while conveying it.

And at the root of Ivanov's self-awareness, as it is at the root of the melancholy prince's in the past and of Jim Tyrone's to follow, is the awareness that his "emptiness and lassitude" exist side by side his intense and unbearable compassion. It might seem sufficient in all three cases to say, simply, side by side with hysterical guilt, but in all three, it is the guilt and then some. In the case of Ivanov, it is the guilt, but also the fear of social displacement, plus the pressures on him of every kind from those around him, plus his awareness of the wild mood swings seemingly inherent in his nature. The extent of his incredible self-awareness is nowhere better revealed than in his most telling chastisement of the self-assured young doctor:

> No, Doctor; in every one of us there are far too many wheels, screws, and valves for us to be able to judge one another by first impressions, or by two or three external signs. (77)

And he goes on to add, most significantly for anyone trying to get into Chekhov's plays: "I don't understand you, you don't understand me, and we don't understand ourselves." But, he might add, it seems inherent in our natures to keep on endlessly trying to understand one another and ourselves.

It would almost seem that there is a stasis created by the roiling contradictions and Ivanov's painful awareness of them, and there is such a stasis, but only up to a point. That point is the crucial, and in this case, baldly melodramatic exchange between Ivanov and his wife closing the third act. When Ivanov says, shortly before the passage quoted above, that he feels like "putting a bullet into my head," few would think he means it. Most would see this as simply an outburst not unlike Lebedev's saying he feels like "sticking a knife in himself" an act later. But Ivanov does put that bullet in his head at the end of the play, and his last conversation with Anna Petrovna tells us why. As Edmund Tyrone's goading by his mother excites him into calling her a dope-fiend in the penultimate act of *Long Day's Journey into Night*, so Ivanov's goading by his wife prompts his calling her "Jewess" and telling her she is going to die, an exchange which concludes the penultimate act of this play. And the effects in both are a new, genuinely suicidal guilt. In the case of Ivanov, that guilt grows out of one of the few breaks in his pattern of total honesty alongside total self-contradiction. Anna Petrovna accuses him of lying—and he knows he never lies. She accuses him of enticing Sasha so that he may escape his large financial debt to her mother. He knows that nothing could be farther from the truth. And she accuses him of having never loved her, when he is certain that he did love her once but that the love died. All these accusations enrage him because he is sure they are not true. But they also enrage him because he knows they may at the same time *be* true. In short, the one thing he is really certain about is the existence of equally true opposites in his nature—and this, of course, without a shred of the hypocrisy the doctor accuses him of in that nature. And that certainty breaks his self-control as has nothing before. He explodes into the worst kind of cruelty—into killing his wife with words, as Edmund feels he kills his mother with words. And then follows the words that generate the inescapable guilt.

IVANOV.

You may as well know, then, that you ... you are going to die soon. ... The doctor told me that you would die soon ...

ANNA PETROVNA (*sits down, her voice failing her*). When did he say that? (*Pause*)

IVANOV (*clutching his head*).

How guilty I am! God, how guilty I am! (*Sobs*) [End of Act 3] (85)

The Ivanov of the final act sounds very much like the Ivanov of the preceding acts. The big change that has come over him in the year since his direct cruelty to Anna Petrovna does not sound like that much of a change—Ivanov is still Ivanov—but the change is great. His self-accusations have deepened; his awareness of the "other side" of his self-loathing has dwindled. How he has come to be on the brink of marriage to Sasha is unclear, but one may safely conclude, from what she says to Ivanov and others during the final act, that it has been Sasha's doing—in spite of her own eleventh hour loss of nerve. Growing out of his earlier vision of himself, that image has darkened considerably. What Sasha calls his "whining" (she is really pretty exasperated with him by this time) "has become," she says, "a mockery." Ivanov responds:

> No, I am not whining now. But mockery? Yes, I am mocking. And if I could mock myself a thousand times more violently and make the whole world laugh at me, I would! I saw myself in the mirror, and it was as if a bomb had exploded in my conscience! I began to laugh at myself and nearly went out of my mind with shame (94–95).

This represents a big change from the earlier Ivanov, but even this is not yet suicidal. That final shift comes, not in response to Sasha (who has become something of a combination of saint and nag in this act), but to the doctor, who talks of challenging Ivanov to a duel and accuses him in public of being a scoundrel. That accusation pushes Ivanov into desperation, as his wife's accusations an act earlier had. Again he feels he is anything but a scoundrel, but at the same time, he feels that he is a greater scoundrel than even the doctor imagines. And he is not mad. Now, he says, he sees things "in their true light."

Ivanov's shooting himself is comparable to his telling his wife she is going to die. He is goaded to both as much by the contradictions in his own nature as by the accusations themselves. Like that of Strindberg's Captain in *The Father*, Ivanov's terrible self-awareness is one he cannot get beyond.

The Sea Gull

Before beginning my discussion of *The Sea Gull*, I want to make a general statement about the structure of the four Chekhov plays that succeed *Ivanov*—in short, about the heart of Chekhov's dramatic canon. All are focused on life on country estates that are falling on bad times. Before the plays begin, the residents of these estates have been having trouble with money, with boredom, and especially with one another; but they have been managing to plug along—aging, having difficulty with their servants, wondering what they are doing with their lives, wondering if they will ever find suitable spouses, falling in love with the wrong people—but also sporadically satisfied with existence. The plays themselves deal with the effects of prolonged visits to these estates by outsiders, usually relatives and usually from the city, who have a profound effect upon the estate residents before they, the visitors, depart, leaving things something like they were before the visits, except that certain of the residents' lives have been shattered. In each, either an old *status quo* returns, or a new, similar one takes its place. (Just how this structure works for *The Three Sisters* will be explained later.) In the case of *The Sea Gull*, of course, the visit is followed by a second visit two years after the first one, which has an effect even more shattering than its predecessor; but the visitors will presumably again depart following the play's action, leaving things pretty much as they were—except that one of the residents will have killed himself.[1]

The purpose of this structure, as I see it, is to see how the everyday reactions of both the residents and the visitors are intensified by the visits. Things that were previously just bearable for both groups suddenly seem unbearable. Memories of the past cannot be suppressed, causing the characters to reveal themselves to one another (and to themselves) as never before. These visits make the characters in both groups into the dramatized figures we see in the plays. Normally able to escape themselves when in Moscow or Petersburg or Paris, or when performing the routine tasks of the farm, they cannot escape themselves when confronting one another. In addition, of course, the pull of their "normal"

---

[1]   My analysis of the structure of these plays is a variant of that recognized by Harvey Pitcher in *The Chekhov Play* (NY: Harper and Row, 1973), especially pp. 14–16, where he discusses the "framework of disruption" (16) in the plays.

lives is also always present. The visitors need to get back to their lives as actresses, writers, professors, or simply lovers; the residents need to get back to taking care of the complex affairs of the estate in the country.

In *The Sea Gull*, the feelings of all the characters are intensified (deepened and speeded up, as it were) by the visit of the successful actress Arkadina and her successful writer and lover Trigorin to the country estate owned by Arkadina and her brother Sorin. The estate is inhabited by Sorin and Arkadina's would-be writer son Treplev (known familiarly as Konstantin, or Kostya) and their usual visitors, their friends and associates, who include Nina (Kostya's beloved, who is later seduced by Trigorin), Dorn (the local physician), Masha (who hopelessly loves Konstantin but is engaged and later married to Medvedenko, a schoolmaster), Shamreyev (the dictatorial estate manager), and his wife Polina (who has hopelessly loved the physician Dorn for many years). My discussion will touch on all these figures, but will concentrate on Medvedenko, Sorin, Dorn, Trigorin, Arkadina, Nina, and Konstantin.

But before I can discuss the characters and their contradictions, that seemingly all-important, yet finally unimportant, matter of plot, or melodrama, must be disposed of. Styan aptly quotes Robert Corrigan to suggest that while all the "plot devices" of melodrama—revenge, suicide, illicit love—are amply present in Chekhov, they "are not ends in themselves ... but ... indirect means of focusing our attention on the inner lives of the characters ... ."[2] I would go farther to suggest that the moral conclusions inherent in melodrama have been all but submerged in the examination of the ways the figures respond. The clear case in point in *The Sea Gull* is its chief melodramatic action: Trigorin's seduction and abandonment of Nina. The play does not revolve in moral terms around this evil deed or really its consequences. It focuses on Trigorin, as it does on everyone else, as a complex creature with sharply contradictory impulses. We may be invited to detest him, but the play does not revolve about his story or that detestation so much as it revolves about the inner lives of all the major characters.

And inner lives in Chekhov means essentially what it meant in Ibsen and Strindberg, and will again in O'Neill: the sometimes wildly contradictory characteristics that make their people tick. The internal conflicts of the characters are not the conflicts they are thoroughly conscious of and consciously struggle with: e.g., shall I or shall I not try to seduce this attractive young woman? Or, shall I or shall I not abandon my

---

2   Quoted in Styan: 14.

family commitments in the interests of my career? The inner lives I am talking about involve contradictions the characters are usually either unaware or only vaguely aware of. Occasionally characters—for example, Ivanov, and later Dr. Chebutykin—are keenly aware of them, however, and such figures may be seen as the most memorable in the Chekhov canon.

In my discussions of Ibsen and Strindberg, I have been able to focus directly on the three or four most important characters of a play, glossing over or omitting the play's lesser figures. But it sometimes seems that there are no lesser figures in Chekhov. At least, in dealing with the opposites at the core of his characters, it is difficult to leave anyone out. The problem in writing about Chekhov's characters is that he catches so much about them that trying to assemble all we understand is daunting. Hence, for the sake of clarity, I am resorting to an approach I have always more or less deplored: the use of what might be seen as "thumbnail sketches." But while the usual thumbnail sketch attempts to get at a single distinguishing quality of a character, and where that character stands within the moral structure of the play—i.e. the identification of heroes and villains—my sketches focus on the strength or vitality given the characters by their contradictory natures.

Medvedenko

It might seem strange to begin with a figure who has been shown so little attention in criticism of this play and who seems at first glance one of its least effective characters. But dealing with him first rather vividly illustrates my approach.

Everyone else in the play tends to ignore Medvedenko, and the woman he loves and eventually marries treats him scornfully throughout. Unquestionably he is clumsy and speaks haltingly. His being a convenience for Masha, a transparent means by which she can wallow for the rest of her life in her unrequited passion for Kostantin, are givens. As a schoolmaster and husband, he may be compared to a later husband, the schoolmaster Kuligin in *The Three Sisters,* though that figure is also finally more complex than first appears.

But Medvedenko, despite his clumsiness, is not at all obtuse. In ignoring him, the other characters in the play miss something important. He is astute, and his judgments are usually accurate and original. He is one of the two characters who attempts to understand Konstantin's aborted play-within-the-play of the first act on its own terms, observing that the unity of "spirit" and "matter" implicit in its lines is an engaging idea. It may be, he says, that spirit is itself an "aggregation of material atoms." (117) This is a startlingly advanced idea for its time, one that physicists only today are seriously pondering. Yet of course no one listens to him. He again feelingly refers to that play in Act Four when he says he thinks he hears someone crying on the long-abandoned out-door stage. This rather poetic insight from the play's chief non-entity constitutes a vital contradiction. His intelligence and understanding stand in opposition to his ineffectiveness.

Similarly, clumsy Medvedenko astutely suggests to the doctor that Sorin's health problems may have to do with his excessive smoking (which no one else has thought of). And he realizes without histrionics that the children he and Masha have had by Act Four need parental attention, willingly walking the ten versts home in bad weather (Shamreyev having denied him a horse) to see to their care. Yet for all this, Medvedenko is, and must always be, a minor figure. That is his condition, effectively contradicting his astuteness and sensitivity. As much as we may come to appreciate those latter qualities in him, his very minor-ness in the face of those qualities constitutes the essential contradiction of his nature.

Sorin

Sorin, Arkadina's brother and the resident owner of the estate, tries us with his persistent complaints about his physical condition, and with the hackneyed terms he uses in dealing with everything and everyone around him. Yet that he himself recognizes better than anyone the hackneyed quality of what he says is seen in his incessant tag-lines: the "and so forth"s and "and all that"s which punctuate or conclude almost every one of his speeches. But without being self-aware exactly, he seems instinctively aware of the clichéd nature of what he says. He is appalled by his pathetic overuse of the kind of language he speaks ninety percent of the time. At one point late in the play he actually mimics his own tag-lines: "I speak abominably: (*mimicking himself*) 'and all that sort of thing, and so forth and so on ... .'" (155) Yet he ends that very speech with the same tag-lines. At this point the instinctive self-awareness of the way he speaks becomes intellectualized—but it quickly reverts to its usual form. And in that instinctive self-awareness set against the clichéd vapidity of his tag lines lies the essential contradictoriness of this fundamentally decent man.

Dorn

The ancestor of Chekhov's doctor figures to follow (though, typically, different from each of the later ones in critical ways), Dorn is anxious to give the impression of seeing everything with great objectivity while maintaining an amused irony about what he sees. He is compassionate and understanding while at the same time as self-absorbed as anyone in the group. His sympathy with Konstantin's aborted play stands out as one of Chekhov's truest instances of one character's appreciation of another. His calling the aborted play "fresh" and "ingenuous" is authentic and certainly welcomed by the young playwright. But immediately following that statement Dorn begins to forget about the boy, speaking vaguely about how "a work of art should ... express a great idea." (122) To which Konstantin, as a sort of prompting of Dorn to give a more specific response, asks: "So you're telling me to keep at it?" Instead of emphasizing the "Yes" that follows, however, Dorn continues to make overblown generalities about the "important and eternal," and worse yet starts talking about his own failure to "soar" like the artist. His essential contradiction lies his total self-absorption in the face of his understanding and empathy.

Trigorin

The writer Trigorin derives from the traditional villain of melodrama— the seducer of young women (and perhaps some older ones). A weak-willed philanderer to the bone, he revels in this role. Yet set against Trigorin's lechery is his sensitivity—as a writer and observer. The two are not necessarily opposed, of course. Sensitive artistry and philandering are often natural partners (in literature as in life). But Chekhov has made them feel like opposites in this play by placing unusual emphasis on Trigorin's self-awareness as a writer, giving him one of the most self-referential passages in the canon. In one famous passage Trigorin describes the writer's art precisely as Chekhov might describe his own as a writer of short stories:

> I see that cloud, it looks like a grand piano. ... Must remember to put into a story somewhere that a cloud floats like a grand piano. There's a smell of heliotrope. I make a mental note: cloying smell, widow's color, use when describing a summer evening. I catch up every word and phrase we utter, and lock in my literary storeroom—they may be useful. (134)

Chekhov intends us to identify with Trigorin in this long description: his obsession with his craft, his intense responses to the natural world, his fear of those around him. One cannot help but hear the author making this speech—and in hearing the author inescapably empathizing with the speaker and his amused irony.

Yet the passage also foreshadows what is to follow in Trigorin's relationship with Nina.

> I have no rest from myself, and I am consuming my own life, that for the sake of the honey I give to someone in a void, I despoil my finest flowers of their pollen, tear them up, trample on their roots. (134)

Trigorin, as he obviously has before, will despoil a "finest flower ... and trample on [her] roots" in the interval between Acts Three and Four, and for a time-honored reason that has nothing to do with his writing.

Most revealing is Trigorin's imagined story of the sea gull which is shot by a man with "nothing better to do"—that sea gull standing for Nina and his treatment of her. At times he speaks lines that reveal a genuinely compassionate nature, but his responsiveness is trumped by his need to use it, his awareness by his self-focus as a writer. A "presentiment of sorrow ... wrings" his heart (146), yet he despoils Nina because he has nothing better to do. He yields willingly to his lust. Each of the opposing sides of Trigorin's nature is as basic to it as the other. This contradictoriness is as true for Trigorin as it is for Medvedenko or Sorin, except that in his case we must detest him for that negative side, as we do not detest Medvedenko and Sorin. (All characters are not equal in Chekhov just because they all have opposing sides.)

Arkadina

The opposing sides we see of Arkadina are the opposing sides of a dedicated professional woman: She must put her career before everything; she must love her son, who implicitly denies her that single-minded pursuit. When we first see her in Act One, her responses are her essential ones and almost predictable. She implicitly resents the fact that Konstantin's being 25 focuses on her being middle-aged, and she overtly resents the challenge to the kind of popular drama she acts in inherent in the avant-garde nature of his play. (She may also resent the attractive young Nina playing the leading role.) But having disrupted the performance, which prompts Konstantin to abort it and run out, she is overcome with guilt, both at having hurt his feelings and having been so childish in her responses.

The basic contradictions in her character in Act One, as it were, go with the territory: the *artiste* unable to control either side of her emotions. But in a crucial scene in Act Three, Chekhov expands on this opposition, significantly deepening both the selfishness and the love.[3] Following Konstantin's attempted suicide, Arkadina's responses are deeper and more genuinely frenzied. She begins by changing Konstantin's head-wound bandages, and ends with an attack on him as a "decadent" and "nonentity"—even illogically a "petty bourgeois" like his shadowy father—prompting Konstantin to tear off the bandage she has so tenderly applied. In the midst of their exchange, there are moments of tearful reconciliation, followed by renewed attack, these ever-more explosive outbursts set off by Konstantin's jealous attacks on Trigorin and her defense of him. Chekhov comes closest in this scene to what I have called the "language of kinship" in O'Neill:[4] in which the very intensity of the attacks countered by the equal intensity of the short-lived reconciliations become the essential evidence of how close these people are.

This scene with her son is followed by a sort of parody of it in a disingenuous exchange with Trigorin, who pleads with her to release him so that he may be carried off into a "world of dreams" by pursuing his "youthful, alluring, poetic" love of Nina. (147) Her shifts in emotion here are studied. She knows exactly why Trigorin wants Nina and puts on a hysteria that successfully puts him down. Then, having mastered Trigorin with emotional display, as she always has, she suddenly becomes cool and reasonable. For his part, he plays the romantic adolescent sadly capitulating to a domineering lover. Their histrionics here feel as artificial as the emotional responses between mother and son a scene earlier felt genuine.

One part of Arkadina's conversation with Konstanin may tell us more about her than anything we actually see in the play. During one of their reconciled moments, Konstantin recalls an incident "a long time ago," when:

> there was a fight in our courtyard, and one of the tenants, a washerwoman, was badly beaten. Do you remember? She was picked up unconscious. ... You looked after her, took medicines to her, washed her children in the trough. Don't you remember? (143)

---

[3] See my article on this scene entitled "Mother-Son Dialogue in Chekhov's *The Sea Gull* and O'Neill's *Long Day's Journey into Night*," *Eugene O'Neill Newsletter* 6 (1982): 24–29. See also Robert Louis Jackson, "Chekhov's *Seagull*," in *Chekhov: A Collection of Critical Essays* (NY: Prentice-Hall, 1967) 99–111. Jackson observes that what he calls the "duel" between Konstantin and his mother throughout the play is "marked ... by alternating acts of hostility, magnanimity, and submission." (102)

[4] See p. 18, n. 10. See also Pitcher's discussion of the emotional "network" in the plays generally, a network characterized by periods of great disharmony and alternating with periods great harmony among the characters.

To Arkadina's blunt answer "No," Konstantin also recalls there were two ballet dancers living in the same house, who used to come and have coffee. This Arkadina does remember.

Here in essence is the woman we encounter in this play—genuinely compassionate in actions she can quickly put out of her mind—equally sincere in pursuing her pleasures to the extent of hurting those close to her. Chekhov leaves our responses to her much as he left our responses to Trigorin. While we sense the deep contradictions that govern her responses and actions, we finally may hate her for denying even basic necessities to her son, as we hate Trigorin for taking advantage of Nina. But again, what we see in Arkadina is not hypocrisy so much as instinctive following up of contradictory sets of motivations.

Nina

Nina seems at first almost non-Chekhovian in her relative simplicity, her seeming freedom from the complexity that dominates the others. But this view of her tends to look too superficially at the Nina we see in Act Four, where she has provoked not a little controversy about her character. Some feel she has been "destroyed" by Trigorin, especially in light of her lost baby and subsequent abandonment—events that take place between Acts Three and Four. Some see her disoriented responses in the return encounter with Konstantin in these terms—the confusion and depression that seem to have overwhelmed her in Act Four in their opinion evidence of incurable psychological damage.[5] Yet Richard Gilman and others argue the opposite[6]—as I shall try to do in the terms of the overall argument of this book.

To see Nina as the "ruined" woman is to see her essentially in melodramatic terms, as the innocent ingenue victimized by the villain. Her early appearances invite such an outlook—her innocence in relation to others, her naive ambition to be an actress, her girlish early love for Konstantin, her being so easily drawn to Trigorin—even the nature of her rebellion against her domineering family. During the first three acts we naturally feel she is not very complex. She is simply the graceful but abused sea gull.

Act Four presents her in a very different light. Everything that happened to her in Moscow, and in her sputtering nascent career as a

---

[5]   Styan says that Nina's repeated phrase, "But that's not it" "is almost like a symptom of mental derangement." (85)

[6]   Gilman finds Nina to be saved by her dedication to her art (91–94); Jackson talks about Nina's "tragic perception" in the last act (109); and Pitcher suggests that Nina seems to have gotten hold of herself psychologically (63–65).

third-rate actress, has constituted a massive shock to her system. The greatest evidence of that shock is her repeated reference to herself as a sea gull, followed by the phrase, "But that's not it." Then, of course, there is her emotional reaction to the realization that Trigorin is in the next room. It is easy enough to believe that she has been permanently maimed by what she has experienced.

Yet, what are the facts? Deeply troubled, but still working at her career, she has returned to her home—not the family home, where she knows she will be rejected—but to the home represented by Konstantin. It is too easy an assessment of her character to say she does not love Konstantin. She has not been seduced by him as she was by Trigorin, but who else has she really come back to see in the act? Whose breast does she lay her head upon? Obviously, such an action might be that of a sister to a brother, and obviously Trigorin still deeply affects her. (Why wouldn't he?) But the central opposition within Nina in this act is between the power Trigorin continues to have over her set against her abiding, and not unhappy, feeling for Kostya. That is the central contradiction in her character. And who is to say which is the "immature" love—when the immaturity of her capitulation to Trigorin is all too evident?

Above all, there is, rightly or wrongly, Nina's continuing belief in herself as an actress. Her seeming rejection of Kostya at this point is entirely focused on her determination to succeed, even in the seedy provincial theaters, with the pawings of the merchants, she must act in. Our sense of her "failure," it should be remembered, is primarily from that which is described by Konstantin, who tells Dorn of her history over the period between Acts Three and Four—Konstantin, whose assessments are incisive yet affected by his own experience. And her invitation to Kostya to come see her when she has achieved some success, which she seems really to believe she will achieve, can be seen as perfectly sincere—even if it gives him little satisfaction. Seeing Nina as the helpless victim, totally ruined by what the villain has made of her life, is to see the play in the melodramatic terms Chekhov, like the other playwrights looked at in this volume, is trying to get beyond. She is almost crushed between deeply opposing concepts of herself—one, that which her sense of victimization by Trigorin fosters, the other her determination to be an actress—but her feelings for Konstantin provide a constant that seem to help her bridge the gap.

Treplev

Konstantin Treplev is another matter, however. He commits suicide. Any discussion of the play must look squarely at that fact—especially as it follows so closely upon Nina's departure.

The first thing to dispose of in relation to Konstantin is his aborted play in the first act. This play-within-the-play has been long assumed to be something the author is mocking—the overly abstract, sophomoric effort of a self-absorbed neurotic suffering from what would later be called an Oedipus complex. Of course, we do not know how the play might have continued after Kostya, prompted by his mother, closes down the production. Perhaps we do not need, or want, to know. But I do not find that the action surrounding Kostya's play support Arkadina's negative view of it, and the reactions of first Dorn, who says he has been deeply moved, and later Medvedenko, who admires the original thinking in the play, suggest a response that is hardly one of condemnation. Rather, it seems, from what we see and hear of it, to represent an experimental beginning effort of an original young playwright. Far from making me feel more distant from him, it makes me feel initial and increasing empathy with him.

From the productions of *The Sea Gull* I have seen—one a good number of years back with Montgomery Clift in the role of Konstantin and another more recently with Frank Langella in that role—I have gotten the impression of an attractive, if rather moody, young man who engages my sympathies from the start. Certainly his early relationship with Nina makes me feel this way, as do his attitudes toward others: Sorin, Medvedenko, and even at times Trigorin, his great nemesis. When not confronting his personal crises, he seems to possess a general magnanimity similar to that of his great model Hamlet. So, far from contempt, it strikes me that deep feelings of sympathy are what Chekhov seeks to arouse. In short, I do not feel that in any way Chekhov is "attacking" Treplev or what he might represent in this play.

But having said this, I want to stress that Konstantin is an immensely complex figure who it would be difficult to say we ever fully understand. He is a serious artist of no small talent, yet he lacks the determination to try getting out of the country rut fate has placed him in. (Not that such an escape would be easy—but there seems never a thought that he might, say, "go to Moscow.") Certainly, like the Hamlet he is fond of alluding to, he is immature about his mother. At the very point of Nina's departure in the last act he seems more worried that his mother might be disturbed than by that departure itself. But I also get the impression, perhaps a mistaken one, that if Arkadina would follow her brother's suggestion that she buy Kostya some decent clothes, the son's feelings might lighten towards her.

The contradictions in Konstantin's character run deep, but are difficult to pinpoint. He may finally be the play's great enigma. Certainly a basic contradiction resides in the juxtaposition his genuine care for others set against his wretched insecurity, especially regarding his mother. But there is something else about him we are not quite sure of. And what we are not sure of leads directly to our response to his suicide.

Are we prepared the suicide of this character? I find it believable but not entirely plausible. Unlike Gilman, I find it as shocking as Ivanov's. It does not square with what we know about him. He seems when we see him following the return of the other characters after two years to be much more in control of himself than he was earlier. And he seems to understand and be ready to help Nina. Yet her departure and his awareness of the others playing a parlor game in the next room plunge him into an irreversible despair. This goes beyond what I have been calling a vital contradiction in character. It is terribly disruptive without being entirely accounted for. Yet are suicides ever? I suspect Chekhov, without trying to fully account for Konstantin's action, may be trying to characterize someone with a suicidal nature, and psychologists today still cannot determine who has that and who does not. Plenty of people more troubled than Konstantin do not take their own lives. Perhaps we need to recall his own statement to his mother in Act Three—explaining that he wounded himself in "a moment of insane despair." (143) That seems an evasive statement at the time, intended to reassure Arkadina, but perhaps it is finally the author's only statement on the subject.

The Other Characters

As for the other characters in the play, I find less to say about them in the context on this study than their first impressions might seem to invite. The chief case in point is Masha, who opens the play with her famous observation that she is dressed in black because she is "in mourning for [her] life," which too many in the West refuse to recognize as comic: possibly Chekhov's put-on of heavy Russian pessimism. But there is little to say about her other than: 1) that she is Chekhov's take on the young would-be intellectual trying to be a city decadent—using drugs (snuff and vodka) and decrying life, and 2) that she feels an overpowering love for Konstantin, which is just that—overpowering—without much real awareness of the other party. Her love is entirely focused on herself, very much unlike Kostya's for Nina. She is in no way so complex as she would have us believe, since she seems always to be singing the same tune, and her marriage to Medvedenko seems a gross abuse of that good man's fundamental decency, the abuse and the decency both illustrated by her refusal to be concerned about his ten verst walk home in winter to look after the children. She is the true daughter of her passionate but shallow mother, Polina, whose hysterical love for the doctor clearly has set the pattern for her daughter's for Kostya. By the last act, the mother seems to have learned something about life, however, which it is doubtful the daughter ever will.

Both mother and daughter, of course, are victims of the most one-dimensional character in the play, Shamreyev himself, the heavy-handed estate manager. That a streak of hysteria seems to run through the family is suggested by the tone of his refusal to let anyone have any horses— even Arkadina, who is strictly speaking his boss. And his daughter's pseudo-intellectual affectations seem patterned on her father's insistence on recalling, at inopportune moments, all the famous actors and singers he has known. In someone else such recall might be considered a sign of a complex nature; in him it simply confirms his shallowness.

My focus has been on oppositions and contradictions within the key personae of *The Sea Gull*. As he did with the character of Ivanov, Chekhov achieves the sense of an inner strength of opposites in figures as different from one another as Sorin, Trigorin, Arkadina, and Konstantin: strength that makes the play a monumental advance over the emphasis on the well-made plot, stock figures, and moral certainties of melodrama, placing Chekhov in direct line from Ibsen and Strindberg, and directly anticipating O'Neill.

Uncle Vanya

The framing structure that I briefly discussed in relation to *The Sea Gull* is evident as well in *Uncle Vanya*. The action of the play deals with a visit which seriously disrupts the everyday lives of the hard-working residents of a country estate whose chief residents are Voinitsky (the Vanya of the play's title), his mother ("Maman"), his niece Sonya—and a still-youthful country doctor, who is not a resident but visits on a regular basis. The complications which are the meat of the play are brought on by the visit from the city of a professor, brother-in-law of Vanya and Sonya's father, and his young wife. The young wife's sexual allure is one cause of the complications in that both Vanya and the country doctor are very much affected by it.

As in all Chekhov's plays, it is characterization rather than plot (or melodrama) that is important, and the characters all reveal deep oppositions in their natures as a result of the visit. Although Vanya is the main character, as the title suggests, there are really five central characters, with three strongly supporting ones in the background. The five, in the order in which I shall look at them, are Vanya, Serebryakov (the professor), Elena (the wife), Astrov (the doctor), and Sonya. The background figures are Vanya's "Maman," Telyegin (a friend who seems always to be present at the Voinitskys), and Marina (an old nurse).

Vanya

Uncle Vanya's character is contradictory in the extreme. He is adolescent and mature, obtuse and brilliant, irritating and reassuring— these opposing elements frequently being present in him simultaneously. He also has a recognizable and most familiar personality. In a sense, he is everyone's *uncle*.

From the beginning of the play, Vanya's exasperation with the professor is the primary motivation of Vanya's responses and ultimately actions—and it is an exasperation based partly on truth and partly on jealous envy. To an extent the professor is what Vanya says he is—a pompous charlatan who has wasted his life in empty scholarship and in pursuit of uncritical adulation. There also seems little doubt that he married Vanya's late sister in the first place to get a controlling interest in the family estate, and that he married soon after her death to get possession of a young beauty who idolized him. Yet Vanya's overblown responses to the professor are equally the result of his own frustration—including that over his failure to find a suitable profession and a beautiful wife—and the professor's blatant defects. And overblown they are, leading him to an action which is at the same time roaringly comic and potentially disastrous. The scene in which Vanya fires his pistol point blank at the professor—and misses!—is one of the most farcical in the Chekhov canon. All the contradictions roiling inside this figure are caught up in that single instant—a sort of still point (though hardly still) of his character.

> ...Where is he? Ah, there he is. (*Shoots at him.*) Bang! (*Pause*) Missed him! Missed again! Oh, damn, damn! (*Throws the revolver on the floor and sits down exhausted.*) (218)

Of course, it is important to remember what Vanya has just been through preceding his blow-up at the professor. Not only does the professor's suggestion that the estate be sold assault the very basis of Vanya's existence, but immediately before the professor's calling the family into counsel, Vanya has witnessed the kiss between Astrov and Elena.[1] That alone has put him on the edge of losing control. The professor's self-interested proposal merely pushes him over the edge.

But it must be understood that Vanya could never kill the professor—or anyone else. His missing him at point-blank range—twice—is surely evidence of that. Yet he is not play-acting, either. His feelings are murderous. So the confrontation within the man between the restraint upbringing and basic nature have made him and his overwhelmingly strong aggressive feelings, results in the hilarious action we witness. Perhaps most startling instant is when, having missed the professor the first time, he says aloud, "Bang!"—himself, as it were, the pistol that will not shoot straight. Vanya's responses here seem an enactment of an "inner strength of opposites" that is very strong indeed.

What makes Vanya so effective a character is that he projects his contradictions with such force.[2] When played well, he affects audiences more viscerally than intellectually. His mother's persistent needling is one of the factors that makes his character so familiar. "Maman"—so well-read and intellectual, so myopic—constantly throws the professor

---

[1]   One of the several recent film versions of the play, entitled *Country Life,* has him witnessing Astrov and Elena having sexual intercourse in the barn—action which is not far off the mark, really, in terms of Vanya's violent reaction.

[2]   Most interpreters see Vanya, despite his contradictions, as finally ineffectual. See, for example, Ieva Vitins, "Uncle Vanya's Predicament," *Slavic and East European Review* 22 (1978): 454–463; and Maurice Valency, *The Breaking String* 181–203.

and his supposed achievements up to her son, prompting responses that have the ring of adolescence. She has the capacity to misjudge her son in such immediate yet universal ways that we can believe in the force of his blow-up. At the same time we always have the sense that Vanya is *Uncle*, the most mature character in the play. It is consistent with the character Chekhov has created in this play that he grittily allows himself to be talked out of the suicide his predecessor in *The Wood Demon* committed. His final restraint in this regard sets him apart from Ivanov and Konstantin. We also get a strong impression of the triumph of his uncleness over his immaturity in the play's final scenic image, where, at his abacus and still much troubled by what has happened, he is with Sonya's aid restoring order to the estate.

Serebryakov

Is the professor really the pretentious fool Vanya makes him out to be? The answer is an emphatic, yes—accompanied by an only slightly less emphatic, no. Since it is chiefly academics (in the humanities) who write about Chekhov, it is natural for them (us!) to recognize Serebryakov as one of their own, in spite of the century of separation. The game is not that different. He had to fight for the respect and admiration of his peers and students. In order to create the right image and style, he appears utterly self-assured about the extent of his learning and the rightness of his positions. We learn most of what we do about his professional past from what Vanya says, and although perhaps what he says is a little exaggerated, there is no reason to assume Vanya is wrong. Especially galling to Vanya is the professor's apparent dismissal of the probability that not a soul besides an occasional impressionable student will read his work.

> And what self-importance! What pretentiousness! He has retired, and not a single living soul knows who he is. … And look at him; he struts like a demigod! (177)

What Vanya ignores, of course, is that having given most of his life over to scholarship, the professor is naturally disinclined to recognize that his life has been a waste.

Then there is the matter of impressing the other sex—ever in fashion among academic males and Vanya's particular gripe about the professor. Serebryakov, we may assume, having always sought to awe his attractive female students, after his wife (Vanya's sister) died married a particularly awed (and particularly attractive) one. In the play, we witness both husband and wife paying the price. But Vanya's resentment that he was not around to woo Elena earlier is not so justified as his judgment of the professor's scholarly achievements. First, he'd never have impressed Elena because he spoke no "wisdom" from a podium; and second, had he succeeded in attracting a woman like Elena, he'd have had the same trouble the professor is having. With regard to women, he and Serebryakov are not that different. With all the attraction May has for November—they are at opposite ends of the year.

The professor's contradictory nature is revealed, however, in an unforeseen practicality. In no way so romantic about the estate as the others, and in anticipation of the bourgeois Lopahin's attitude toward the estate in *The Cherry Orchard,* Serebryakov is the only one to realize the advantages for them all in selling the estate while they can get a good price for it. What here galls Vanya, who has worked so hard on the estate over the years, in part to support the professor, is that Serebryakov's proposal is unthinking with regard to Vanya and Sonya. But the proposal does make sense at a time when the old estates are breaking up, and an increasingly impoverished landed aristocracy must scratch for means. That he does not think about where Vanya and Sonya will live after the sale does not negate this point.

All of which is to say that the pompous professor is more hard-headed than the others. But he is also and will ever be the hypochondriac and whiner his disillusioned wife and family must put up with. Perhaps the most important component of this selfish academic's contradictory nature is his childishness. The one figure who can comfort him, as he drives everyone else mad with his complaints, is the old nurse, who instinctively recognizes that he needs, not the soporific "valerian drops" the doctor keeps wanting to give him, but the comforts of a motherly breast. Our essential sense of the professor's contradictory nature is that of a posturing pretender, who is also shrewd, and a child who needs maternal ministrations.

Astrov

Probably the most attractive figure in the play (as both Sonya and Elena will vigorously attest), Astrov is both defeated by, and redeemed by, the violent oppositions in his nature. Based on the figure of Krushchov in Chekhov's earlier *The Wood Demon,*[3] who has given up medicine to devote his life to extremely idealistic environmentalism, Astrov is, unlike Krushchov, the very image of what the good country doctor should be—dedicated, self-denying, sensitive to the needs of those around him.

---

[3]   For an insightful discussion of the relationshhip between *Uncle Vanya* and its predecessor, see Harvey Pitcher, "A Study in Evolution: From *The Wood Demon* to *Uncle Vanya,"* in *The Chekhov Plays* 69–112.

But that he is in fact over-sensitive leads to his one crippling quality; he cannot deal with the guilt he associates with his real or imagined deficiencies as a doctor, and so has turned to excessive drink.

Astrov also demonstrates that he is a dedicated friend. I am thinking of his relationship with Vanya, which is in no way contradictory, in spite of their rivalry regarding Elena. Astrov's going from drinking companion earlier in the play to cold counselor in the last act is totally consistent with his affection for Vanya, since by forcing Vanya to return the morphine he has stolen from the doctor's bag, he may prevent the suicide that is the fate of Vanya's original in *The Wood Demon*. Astrov and Vanya are natural friends, both compassionate and intelligent in the midst of the rough ignorance and sloth of provincial Russia.

But there is an essential contradiction in Astrov's love of the forests and abhorrence of the encroachment of man on nature. Unlike the obsessive environmentalism of Krushchov in *The Wood Demon*, Astrov's is more the informed avocation of a genuine idealist. But Astrov also takes refuge in that avocation, using it as an escape from the country doctor's exhaustion and fear of failure. He pushes his ideas in his encounters with Elena out of a double motivation: the real desire to protect the countryside and the somewhat immature demands of his ego. His elaborate charts illustrating the decline of the forests over the years are both useful instructional devices and the treasured achievements of the adolescent who has created something very personal that he wishes to be praised for—especially by an object of his affections.

Astrov's feeling for Elena in itself is uncomplicated. Despite the rather rash liberties it takes with Chekhov's plot, the film version I earlier referred to (see note 1), which has the doctor having sex with Elena in the barn (and her agreeing to it), gets at what Chekhov could never get at so explicitly in the 1890s: the overwhelming (and ephemeral) force of sexual attraction. The tone of Astrov's pursuit of Elena, his proposal that they meet secretly at a later time, is essentially that of Trigorin's pursuit of Nina in *The Sea Gull*. The very over-heatedness of Astrov's pursuit calls into question the assumption that Astrov does not and can never love Sonya. Like Nina's feelings for Konstantin, which are temporarily derailed by Trigorin's appearance, Astrov's for Sonya have been temporarily derailed by his passion for Elena. Astrov himself makes the point to Sonya that what he feels for Elena is "not love" (198). He even tells Elena that had she not appeared, he might have come to love Sonya. And who really can say that his feelings for her might not again grow stronger over the long loneliness of his life to come? He is attracted to two women, even if the nature of the two attractions is different, and that to Sonya is perhaps better for the long haul. He is here, as in the other ways discussed, divided, the inner strength of the opposites in his nature in this case having partly to do with chemistry.

To conclude a discussion of Astrov, one might again draw upon *The Wood Demon,* the title of which is the name used for the fallen-away doctor, Krushchov, of that play—who, incidentally, throughout loves Sonya, not Elena. In deepening the character of his doctor in *Uncle Vanya,* Chekhov seems to have combined him with the figure of the rake, Fyodor Ivanovich, of the earlier play—who, while rebuffed, tries to make love to Elena in much the same terms as does Astrov here. In short, Chekhov adds to the oppositions in the character of the doctor a libidinous element that helps make the humanitarian, alcoholic, idealistic, guilt-ridden, somewhat self-absorbed, still actively practicing physician into one of the richest characterizations in the canon.

Elena

It is perhaps hardest of all to deal with a character like Elena, who while being indolent and bored as her adoring Vanya accuses her of being, is in some ways the most long-suffering figure in the play. Her beauty and sexuality are certainly her most important attributes. But while she does nothing to counter that attraction, she is also persecuted by it, primarily in her relations with Vanya and Astrov. It is said of beautiful young women that they are always aware of their beauty and its effect on others. But how do they deal with their beauty as it relates to those other aspects of their persons which they share with the rest of us, the insecurities and inconsistencies which are the human lot? Her beauty seems to blot out those qualities for others, leaving her feeling isolated. She must maintain it as a protective screen—though of course it can also be a means of aggression.

We must try to understand Elena's relationships with the four other major characters in the light of all the contradictory aspects of her being in the play. For the others, all these relationships turn on her beauty, a fact she both cherishes and detests. Her relationship with the professor is the least complicated. She tells of having been awed by his teaching as he was awed by her beauty. She does not fully explain what prompted her to become what we might call his 'trophy wife', but again we are sufficiently familiar with such marriages in and out of academe as not to feel pressed to inquire further. But from what we see of Elena and the professor in the play, Chekhov is certainly illustrating the poor judgment on both sides involved in such a marriage. She is bored by his constant complaints, and most tired; he, no longer in need of a beautiful wife, wants a nursemaid. Elena, aware of her obligations as a wife, is quite torn. Their departure together at the end signifies a most unhappy conclusion for Elena, and perhaps for him as well.

Elena and Vanya also conform to a classic pattern—the beautiful young wife pursued by the older man who is convinced he could have won her earlier, had fate provided the opportunity. It is hard to say whether Vanya really loves her—he certainly thinks he does—or whether his interest is merely something to alleviate the boredom of his life. Certainly his feelings about the professor have something to do with his feelings toward her. Only at one point is she really affected by what he says to her, and that is when he tells her to "let yourself go for once in your life," (203) but that advice affects her attitude toward Astrov, not toward Vanya. She is, plain and simple, embarrassed by his attentions. But not so plain and simple, she contributes to the self-torment that dominates his existence after her arrival and culminates in his assault on the professor.

Elena's response to Astrov should be more complex, but I wonder if it really is. Clearly it is a divided response. On the one hand, she is most attracted to him; on the other, she is determined not to be an adulterous wife (except in the one film version referred to in note 1). But that kind of divided response reveals not so much complexity of character as the age-old challenge of body chemistry to acceptable behavior. One cannot tell what might follow from the third-act kiss she allows Astrov had Vanya not appeared, but when the episode is over, all Elena wants is for the professor to take her away as quickly as possible.

Chekhov's real probing of Elena takes place in her complex relationship to Sonya: the situation in which a beautiful stepmother is almost the contemporary of the not-so-beautiful stepdaughter. Of primary interest here is that they are genuinely rather than artificially drawn to each other—in spite of the jealousy and hostility that has dominated their relationship earlier. Both need a female friend—and, unexpectedly perhaps, both seem ready to be one. Their drinking "bruderschaft" is the key indication of their sincerity.

But the opposition in Elena's attitude toward Sonya is revealed following Sonya's confession of her love for Astrov. Elena's willingness to speak to the doctor on Sonya's behalf demonstrates this opposition. She is genuinely interested in Sonya's feelings and does not want her to be hurt. At the same time, she is genuinely interested in Astrov herself and would like Sonya out of the way. Both these opposing motives are strong, and it is impossible to separate one from the other. Astrov later suspects that Elena has simply connived, but in fact she does have the girl's interests at heart—along with her own very different ones.

But what if Astrov acknowledged an interest in Sonya? That is the chance Elena takes, sensing that it is a slim one. Does this make her treacherous? That depends on from which side of Elena's feelings one looks at the situation. She is like the politician who does good things for people out of truly altruistic feelings but also because it will win votes. She may herself recognize this opposition but is overwhelmed by the onslaught of erotic feelings that lead to the kiss.

Sonya

But far more complex than Elena's are the conflicting feelings in Sonya. The emotionally strongest character in the play, Sonya, in allowing Elena to approach Astrov on her behalf, reveals a corroding weakness with regard to her ability to attract a man—an area where Elena is anything but weak. There is nothing unique about Sonya in this regard. But the contradiction resides in the juxtaposition of this weakness with her great emotional sensitivity—the comparable Varya in *The Cherry Orchard*, for example, seems less sensitive—and with her very real strength in other ways. She is the central pillar upon which the estate and the life within it rests. She understands her father (the professor), though unlike Marina can do little to help him. She understands her uncle (Vanya), and does a great deal to help him. (The very title of the plays focuses the centrality of their relationship.) She also even understands Astrov, whose drinking she almost begins to bring under control. She seems rather tearful in emotional crises, as in her reactions to Vanya's assault on the professor in Act Three, but being tearful in her case should not be mistaken for being out of control. (It is Elena who seems that in demanding to be taken away immediately.) Rather, in the fourth act, Sonya appreciates the very real psychological trouble Vanya is in following his outbreak. It is she who persuades her uncle to return the morphine he has stolen from the doctor's bag. Perhaps the biggest question surrounding Sonya at the end of the play is why she would make such an impassioned statement about the afterlife in the face of her and Vanya's feelings of defeat:

> We shall go on living, Uncle Vanya, We shall live through a long, long chain of days and endless evenings; we shall patiently bear the trials fate sends us; we'll work for others, now and in out old age, without even knowing rest, and when the time comes, we shall die submissively; and there, beyond the grave, we shall say that we have suffered, that we have wept, and have known bitterness, and God will have pity on us; and you and I, Uncle, dear Uncle, shall behold a life that is bright, beautiful, and fine. We shall rejoice and look back on our present troubles with tenderness, with a smile—and we shall rest ... We shall hear the angels, and see the heavens

all sparkling like jewels; we shall see all earthly evil, all our sufferings, drowned in a mercy that will fill the whole world, and our life will grow peaceful, gentle, sweet as a caress. I have faith, I have faith. … (230–231)

It is easy enough to say what this speech does not represent; it does not represent Chekhov's affirmation of an orthodox Christian view of the afterlife. But it does represent how Chekhov understands the reactions of this particular character—in her strength, and perhaps in her weakness as well. Her strength is certainly seen in her statement about living through the long chain of days and evenings, and being patient before the trials life sends them, working for others, and dying "submissively" (probably the greatest strength needed to do that). But is then her statement about the heavens sparkling and hearing the angels a sign of an opposing weakness? It sounds like what this character might say, but is it weakness? I wonder if Chekhov might have intended it to be at first but that his affection for his idea of Sonya prompted his characterization to get out of hand.

The speech comes to be one of the most powerful statements of the play. I think it is Chekhov's hymn of praise, not to God and his angels, but to this character—who is able to see these things in a way he cannot. Vanya's tears at Sonya's speech represent not an acceptance of Sonya's vision of heaven so much as a release from the burden of thinking only in negative terms about life. The important thing is Sonya's statement about bearing it. Sonya's thoughts about an afterlife that goes beyond human comprehension is important in relation to the human ability to bear life. Sonya's final speech may represent the quintessence of Chekhov's understanding of the contradictory nature of human existence, an understanding not that different from Strindberg's in plunging a heavenly creature into the vicissitudes of life in *A Dream Play.*

The Other Characters

To say the three remaining characters—Telyegin (the neighbor who is called "Waffles" because of his pock-marked face), Marina (the Nurse), and Maria (Maman)—are more one-dimensional than multi-dimensional is not to take away from the sharpness of their definition as dramatic, and in this case, comic, characterizations. Telegin comes closest to being a complex figure, though his original, the protector figure Dyadin in *The Wood Demon*, is more complex. But Telyegin never really goes beyond the figure we encounter early in the play, a sweet-natured (if not quite lovable) hanger-on. Marina, as has already been observed, is all good nurse—to everyone—and a point of steadiness amid the tumult that prevails around her. Maman fell in love with books when she was an adolescent, and never looked up. The most impenetrable character in the entire canon, she exists primarily to infuriate her son while myopically admiring the professor, whose intellectual pretensions she refuses to see as anything but true wisdom. She and Telegin help make the play feel like the comedy Chekhov intended it to be.

For many *Uncle Vanya* is the preferred Chekhovian play precisely because of its rather more gently humorous tone than that of the other plays, a tone given it in part by its secondary figures. But its true Chekhovian nature lies where that of the other plays resides, in the "inner strength" of its major characters achieved by their multitude of contradictory attitudes and emotions, and that nature is mostly successfully synthesized in the characters of uncle and niece.[4]

---

[4]   In remarks that do not directly address *Uncle Vanya* as such, John Gassner in the early 1960s discusses Chekhov's plays in terms which complement what I say about the play: "Chekhov ... transcended the superficiality that often adhered to optimistic literature and at the same time besets pessimistic profundity. ... He was, so to speak, Olympian and yet also companionable. It is chiefly by bearing these polarities in mind, and remembering especially the plain yet somehow elusive fact that there was ever sympathy in his comedy and some degree of comedy in his sympathy, that we may hope to bring his plays authentically to the stage." See "The Duality of Chekhov," in *Chekhov: A Collection of Critical Essays,* R. L. Jackson 175–183. (Quote is from 183.)

The Three Sisters

While the Chekhov plays I have just discussed probe the oppositions within their major characters deeply, *The Three Sisters* probes the oppositions within its people more deeply still. The internal balances that keep its characters functioning are more delicate even than in the earlier Chekhov plays, and its implications border more closely on the tragic. It has been for twentieth century audiences in the west his hardest play to "take," his hardest not to be affected by, his hardest for performers to interpret.

True to the complexity about everything else in this play is Chekhov's treatment of the pattern of the visit that sets things aboil: i.e., the *status quo* versus what disrupts the *status quo*. The *status quo* is represented by just two characters in this play: Andrei's *enamorata* and later wife, Natalya Ivanovna (Natasha), and Masha's husband, the schoolmaster Kuligin. To these should be added the shadowy but all-important Protopopov, Natasha's undoubted lover and Andrei's boss, who never appears in the play but is certainly important to it. They, or at least their forbears, were mainstays of the "provincial town" in which the action takes place before the army, including the late General Prozorov and his family, arrived eleven years earlier. And that image of a *status quo* is a good deal less appetizing than are the images representing the *status quo* in *Uncle Vanya* and *The Sea Gull*. In those two plays the *status quo* is represented by some interesting, unusual, and relatively moral people. In *The Three Sisters*, it is represented by the vacuous and the vicious; and the particular sadness of the play's ending is the thought, with the departure of the army, of Masha and Andrei stranded among the likes of Natasha and Protopopov.

But the army has had its day in the provincial town, and its stay has generated the characters and their problems that I shall be looking at. Of melodrama there is very little. There are the love stories of Masha and Vershinin, and Irina and the Baron. But the former is bound to come to nought because both are married to others, and the latter cannot be really happily resolved because Irina cannot love the Baron, even though she finally does entertain the notion of marriage—just before the Baron's demise. The focus in neither case is upon a happy resolution, which would be a key focus were this traditional melodrama. I suppose there may be a degree of suspense about whether they will "go to Moscow," but no one in the play and few viewing it really believe they ever will go. It is again the oppositions and contradictions within the characters that hold our chief interest, and I shall approach those in the fashion of my other discussions—though the number of important characters is large and some will have to receive less attention than I would like.

The Sisters and Natasha

The plays begins and ends with the sisters, and although they are quite different from one another, each with inner contradictions of her own, the play's title and their frequent appearances together on stage invites one to look at them together. They came to the town as young girls, Olga the oldest no more than a teenager, Irina the youngest not yet ten, and the town's effect on them is most evident. Sensing their cultural superiority to their surroundings, they have sought to affect those surroundings positively, especially to educate and to refine. But they have quickly learned that reading foreign languages, one of the signs of the culture they represent, strikes most of the townspeople as having, in Masha's words, "a sixth finger." Olga tries to be grimly hopeful because as a teacher she is supposed to be hopeful, and Irina the youngest clings to her ideals until they are dashed by her introduction to society's coarseness as an employee of the telegraph office. But the Masha we meet in the play has been made cynical by having had to be a small-town schoolmaster's wife. She is the most caustic of the three, and her fate verges on the tragic. Her one attempt to seize a kind of happiness is her love affair with Vershinin, which she knows is doomed from the start.

I begin by looking at Natasha, since, because she and the sisters are so critically different from each other, an understanding of her is key to our understanding of them. The most memorable instance of this difference is the confrontation between Olga and Natasha in the third act, when all tempers have frayed as a result of the fire that has raged through the town. The confrontation is precipitated by Olga's sympathy for old Anfisa, who has been nurse to the three girls from childhood. Anfisa, exhausted by the work she has had to do in relation to the fire and fearful she will be "sent away" because she is so old, is near collapse, prompting Olga to insist she sit down. Natasha, also exhausted, suddenly sees Anfisa seated and blows up, literally chasing the 80-year-old woman from the room. In her shallowness, Natasha is concerned only with the appearance of a sitting servant, even if that servant is infirm and exhausted. Early in their subsequent exchange, Natasha thinks she will be nice to Olga, asking her forgiveness for her abusive treatment of the old woman. But what develops is something radically

different from "nice." Olga begins by trying to explain her reaction to
Natasha's abuse of Anfisa:

OLGA.

You must understand, my dear ... perhaps we were brought up in a peculiar
way, but I cannot bear that. Such an attitude oppresses me, I feel ill, simply
sick at heart.

NATASHA.

Forgive me, forgive me. ... (*Kisses her.*)

OLGA.

Any rudeness, even the slightest, even a tactless word upsets me. ...

NATASHA.

I often talk too much, that's true, but you must agree that she could just as
well live in the country.

OLGA.

She has been with us for thirty years.

NATASHA.

But now she can't work any more. Either I don't understand, or you don't
want to understand me. She is incapable of working, she just sleeps or sits.

OLGA.

Then let her sit.

NATASHA.

What do you mean, let her sit? She's a servant, isn't she? (*Through tears:*) I
don't understand you, Olya. I have a nurse. I have a wet nurse, we have a
maid and a cook ... what do we keep that old woman for? (*The fire alarm is
heard offstage.*)

OLGA.

I have aged ten years tonight.

NATASHA.

We must come to an understanding, Olya. You are at school—I am at home:
you're doing the teaching—I'm doing the housekeeping. And if I say
anything about the servants, then I know what I'm talking about; I-know-
what-I'm-talking-about. And by tomorrow that old thief, that old hag
(*stamping her foot*) that old witch, will be gone! Don't you dare cross me!
Don't you dare! ... (281–282)

What began as a mildly disagreeable confrontation between sisters-in-
law ends in a violent outburst. All of Olga's deeply offended compassion, yet also inherently polite hesitancy, is swept aside by Natasha's
spreading wildfire. (The offstage fire alarm at this point is brilliant.) All
that Natasha has always resented about the sisters' breeding, their
gentilesse, their confidence in the rightness of their views, suddenly
brings about a conflagration that must have the ultimate effect of

figuratively burning the sisters out of their home, their way of life. The town and its hypocritical mores will get its own back.

Everything about Natasha here says what she is. She is simply what the unfortunate Andrei will later call a "small, blind, sort of thick-skinned animal." Natasha's description of Solyony earlier as "rude" and "ill-bred" actually fits Natasha herself far better than Solyony, who may be rude but is certainly not ill-bred. And her on-going affair with Protopopov is of a piece with the rest. She is in a way refreshing after the complexity of all the others, a sort of counterpart to Shakespeare's Goneril—pragmatism, lover, and all. She has been repeatedly put in her place by the sisters, who question her manners and her taste in clothes. More implicitly insulting still, they feel she would be a good match for their detested Protopopov. Nevertheless, Chekhov never permits us to really sympathize with her. Unlike the successful bourgeois Lopahin in *The Cherry Orchard*, who stands in a similar relationship to the family in that play as Natasha does to the Prozorovs, she elicits nothing but our contempt—no complications or contradictions attached.

But, again, all this is not really about Natasha; it is about the sisters. Her insensitivity bordering on cruelty is ever certain and clear-headed; their gentility is often ineffectual and is self-defeating. Gilman sees characterization in this play, and all of Chekhov, in terms that seem particularly applicable to the sisters. The playwright, he says,

> never gives us careful, narrow typologies, strict divisions of human nature, but instances of varying consciousness, appetite, and behavior.[1]

In distinct ways, each sister is torn between a need and determination to do something with their lives and a debilitating sensitivity which renders that need all but meaningless. Olga must battle the mind-numbing work of teaching, Irina the ignorant rudeness of the telegraph office (to which she painfully realizes she has succumbed in her response to the woman who has lost her son), Masha the demands placed upon her as a schoolmaster's wife. Masha makes most explicit what they all feel, stating at one point that the "coarseness" of those around them, the army excepted, "upsets and offends" her. Yet they try to plow through that coarseness to a point where they sometimes appear to be simply be-wildered. Olga retreats from her conflict by trying to avoid the spectre of becoming the new headmistress, Irina by leaving the job she has been so excited about obtaining, and Masha by taking up with Vershinin.

Obviously not types, the sisters, though chiefly Olga and Masha, respond more even than the other characters this book deals with out of

---

[1]   *Chekhov's Plays* 162.

such a variety of feelings and motives that it is next to possible to make generalizations about them.[2] Olga is dead tired, very desirous of having a husband, disapproving of Masha's love-affair, motherly advisor, rather snobbish, unshakably loving toward her sisters, full of a sense of responsibility toward those she is close to, a bit humorless, a bit of a prude, as pleasure-loving as the others when the officers come to enjoy themselves, somehow out of touch with the real world (as she appears to be in confronting Natasha), yet a first-rate administrator. She is also the one with the strength to hold the three together at the end.

Masha, unlike Olga, is tough, and brilliantly caustic. Told in Act 2 that Nastasha has determined that the partying must cease because little Bobik "is not well," she says to Irina, "It's not Bobik that's sick, but she herself ... here! (*Taps her forehead.*) Common creature!"(273–274).[3] A snob, perhaps—a touch of snobbery might seem a limitation in all three sisters—but Masha's statement is on the mark, especially when we see Natasha go out to ride in a troika with Protopopov a short time later. And Masha again reveals her tough wit in Act 3, the "fire" act, when after Natasha crosses the crowded stage without speaking to anyone, Masha responds: "She goes about looking as though it were she who started the fire" (290). In terms of what the family is going through, this remark has a kind of Shavian incisiveness. It is notable that Natasha never directly challenges Masha—as she does the other two. She would be no match for the articulate Masha, whose wit shows particularly in such unexpected responses. But along with her winning toughness, Masha is one of the most self-victimizing character in the play. She made her own bed when she married Kuligin, and now she is doing so again by falling in love with Vershinin. Herein lies the essential contradiction in her nature. In fact, "making their own beds" is what the characters we feel closest to in the play—Masha, Andrei, Chebutyukin—do repeatedly.

In Gilman's terms, what we see of all three sisters throughout are "instances of varying consciousness, appetite, and behavior." It is impossible to separate out the competing functions of their extremely complex natures. They are as fully wrought as anyone in the play.

---

[2] Pitcher (7,124–125) calls attention to the contradictions that characterize the responses of all three sisters.

[3] The late 1970s television version (BBC/Time-Life Classic Theatre) starring Janet Suzman as Masha, Eileen Atkins as Olga, and Anthony Hopkins as Andrei, has Masha say "bourgeoise" instead of "common creature," which is I suspect may be more what she means.

Chebutykin

John Styan is one of the best analyzers of Chekhov's plays because he
goes through each play scene by scene, in the fashion of a director,
examining the characters individually and in relation to one another and
to the situations they are in. Styan attempts to see in specific terms what
Gilman describes in general terms when Gilman says, in the passage
quoted above, that individual characters in the plays are composed of
"instances of varying consciousness." And many of Styan's assessments
I agree with—notably that *The Three Sisters*, in its final juxtaposition of
the words of Olga ("if we only knew") and the Doctor's cynically
absurd song refrain ("Tarara boomdeay"), concludes with a message of
"resignation and endurance."[4] But where I disagree with Styan, I
disagree strongly, and never more strongly than with his assessment of
the doctor. To him Chebutykin is the epitome of self-pitying useless-
ness, inured by his own failures in life to seeing everything as futile and
meaningless—the ultimate nihilist, whose nihilism is perhaps worse in
the final analysis than Natasha's selfishness. To me the doctor is the
play's deepest and most feeling character, whose vital contradictions,
whose awareness of those contradictions, and whose compassion make
him, despite his cynicism, into the play's chief figure.

I shall begin by looking at Chebutykin in Act 3, the "fire" act. Here,
in the face of his obvious responsibilities as a doctor to help the injured,
he has gotten drunk in his room (drinking heavily it appears for the first
time in two years). He appears on stage tearfully lamenting his failure as
a doctor, then accidentally or on purpose breaking a valuable ceramic
clock that belonged to the sisters' late mother, with whom the doctor
was in love. Should we condemn Chebutykin for his behavior in this
scene? My answer is a resounding "Yes!" once more followed by an
equally resounding "No!" He is obviously a wretch for being so
neglectful of his duties as a physician. But he is also, through all the
alcohol and sleeplessness, painfully aware of what he has done. He is
also haunted here by his earlier failure in regard to a patient he feels he
let die, precisely as the also drunken Astrov is unable to get over his
guilt about the remembered death of a patient in *Uncle Vanya*. The
culpability of either doctor is something we cannot know, but we do get
a sense of their terrible, unerasable guilt in these situations.

---

[4]   Styan 236. See also Gilman 195–196; Pitcher 153–156; Maurice Valency, *The
       Breaking String* 243–244; and Richard Sheldon, "Cathartic Disillusionment in *The
       Three Sisters*," in *Russian Literature and American Critics: In Honor of Deming B.
       Brown*, ed., Kenneth N. Brostrom. Ann Arbor: *Papers in Slavic Philology* 4, 1984.
       All treat the balance between the doctor's and Olga's outlooks at the end and the
       theme of endurance in the face of doubt.

Most important in this scene is the degree of Chebutykin's suffering. Is he wallowing in self-pity? Of course. But he is also totally aware of his wallowing, and suffering the more for that additional awareness. We cannot forgive him, but we can most certainly empathize with him; we drag up shame and suffering for our own inadequacies through his suffering. And it is that unforgivability along with that suffering awareness that makes his contradictions so vital.

The doctor shows the true substance of his contradictory nature in the way, in spite of his glaring failures, he serves others throughout this play. Chebutykin is everything his denigrators say about him, while he is also, along with Olga, the positive force in this play. He is irresponsible, doesn't pay his rent, loafs about the house, and speaks disjointedly. What is more, he blatantly uses Irina in particular to keep alive the romantic ideal of their mother, whom he loved but who probably did not return his affections. Witness his inappropriately giving Irina a silver samovar, typically the gift of a suitor to his beloved, on her name day. And yet, to the sisters he is a mainstay, particularly in the absence of their father. This is most evident in the final act, where they seek from him some reassurance concerning the Baron's death; and whereas some may see the reassurance he gives as useless in the light of his stated cynicism, he is nevertheless supportive when they most need him, like the befuddled Sorin in *The Sea Gull*, who stays by the troubled Konstantin to the end. It is a matter of physical presence and implied gesture as much as anything the doctor says. The emptiness and desolation that life will be for the Prozorovs after the army leaves is really the emptiness and desolation that will be their lot after *he* leaves, even if the sisters fail to quite acknowledge this fact. Will life be more empty because Solyony leaves? Hardly. Vershinin's departure is crushing to Masha, but his relationship with the other sisters, and with Andrei, is marginal. He is too concerned about himself. In that often chaotic way Chekhov's characters show their concern for others, Chebutykin is throughout the play concerned about the sisters; and laugh at him as they might, their constant turning to him reveals that they know it.

The most important relationship in revealing the strength of this unusual doctor is that with Andrei, which quite contradicts, while it does not deny, the selfish irresponsibility he demonstrates during the fire. They go out gambling together, in the course of which Andrei ultimately loses a huge amount of money, enough to force him to mortgage the house, which he does to Masha's particular dismay, without consulting his sisters. Has Chebutykin thus been complicit in Andrei's downfall? Perhaps, but at the same time he alone is aware of the brother's isolation and despair. Late in the second act, as Andrei and the doctor prepare to go out on one of the first gambling escapades, Chebutykin, knowing from his own experience what must be Andrei's fate as Natasha's husband, makes the observation that "loneliness is a terrible thing." Like the similarly dissolute doctor, Relling in *The Wild Duck*, he is more precisely aware than anyone else of the needs of others. So, when he goes out gambling with Andrei, it is to give him much-needed companionship, and a brief escape from his wife. The morality of the situation the doctor cares little about, but the pain Andrei endures, and will continue to endure, he cares a great deal about. This is very much borne out in his fourth-act advice to Andrei to "take up a walking stick, and be off ... walk out, leave, without looking back. And the farther you go the better." (302) If the morality of this advice is questionable, the psychology of it, from what we have seen of Natasha in action, is very sound indeed.

As for Chebutykin's often criticized participation in the duel in which the Baron is killed, I think it should be clear to anyone familiar with pre-twentieth-century military codes of behavior that, especially as an army doctor, he has absolutely no alternative. And the degree to which he is upset about the duel is often overlooked. His seemingly unfeeling remark, "but one Baron more or less—what does it matter?" (301) is spoken in a spirit of deep and terrible irony. When he says, after reporting the results of the duel, "I'm worn out," I believe him entirely; and when he adds again "As if it mattered!" I get the feeling it matters a great deal. He is as shattered at the end of the play as the sisters, though he reacts in significantly different terms. And he does stand with them at the end, as no one else does.

The contradictions between the doctor's irresponsibility and his concern, between his irony and his tenderness—vital contradictions of which he is always aware—elicit conflicting responses to what he says and does. But seen in the overall context of this study, he is second only to O'Neill's equally cynical Jamie Tyrone in the strength inherent in those contradictions.[5]

---

[5]   I recall my reactions to this scene amazingly well from the Katharine Cornell (Masha)–Judith Anderson (Olga)–Ruth Gordon (Natasha) production I was taken to at the age of 12 (1940). Should one trust the reactions of a 12-year-old? I don't know, but it is safe to say they are honest. The actor who played the doctor was a short, volatile figure who aroused great feeling in me, and if I was terribly depressed by him, I nevertheless felt what today I would call an overpowering empathy. Other performers of the role I have seen since—in particular, Joss Ackland in the late 1970s television version alluded to above—have enlarged upon and made me better understand that initial feeling. Ackland and this production in general strike me as superior to the more static American Film Theater production of the early 1970s

Vershinin

Like the doctor, Vershinin appears to have rather gross defects. He talks too much, is an impractical dreamer, and is rather short on the kind of responsibility he owes to those close to him—notably his wife and children, and even to Masha in the end. Yet along with these defects, he is also a deeply feeling individual, who, a little like the doctor, is tormented by his deficiencies. He pursues Masha, but from the beginning Masha gives every indication of wanting to be pursued. And while Masha's excuse is a boring husband, his is a highly neurotic wife, who, like the invisible Protopopov, never appears in the play. I have long felt that if Vershinin had spent a little more time with his wife, he might have been able to understand her better, but that does not seem to concern the playwright so much as the terrible fix she puts him in by repeatedly attempting suicide, which significantly she never succeeds in bringing off. His concern about his children is obvious, but he also appears not to spend much time with them, either. In his relationship with his wife, he almost seems another Ivanov, except that his wife, unlike Ivanov's, elicits no sympathy.

Also like Ivanov, Vershinin loves words, which is both what attracts us to him and at the same time makes him seem somewhat ridiculous. When he goes on about how wonderful life in the future will be, he resembles Astrov talking about his forests. But what makes him sympathetic is his love for Masha, which is genuine and something she has desperately sought for and deserves. The love counters the dullness of the country town with a kind of richness which would otherwise not be there. Regardless of how others are wronged by it, we feel grateful for their love. If that love is wrong, as Olga feels, what could be right? Going for Sunday walks with the faculty and the headmaster with Kuligin in her case, or perpetually tending to the moods of a hysteric in his? If Chekhov seems at times suspicious of irresistible romantic love—e.g., Elena's sexual attraction to Astrov—he here presents it as both life-destroying and life-affirming. Vershinin's love for Masha is a gift which having had she must always cherish. It is a little like the sense we get of Chebutykin's love for the sisters' mother, which has sustained him even as it has destroyed him.

To further complicate Vershinin's contradictory nature, he is, along with his long-windedness, also a dedicated officer, whose men hold him in high regard. Exhausted and very much concerned with his daughters,

starring Laurence Olivier as the doctor, Joan Plowright as Masha, Alan Bates as Vershinin, and Derek Jacobi as Andrei.

he is nevertheless energized by a sense of mutual purpose and loyalty successfully fighting the fire has generated.

> If it weren't for the soldiers, the whole town would have burnt down. Brave boys! (*Rubs his hands with pleasure.*) Salt of the earth! Ah, what a fine lot! (283)

But the need for companionship his family cannot provide, and a pervasive fear of loneliness that prompted visits like those to the Prozorovs in the first place, has clearly pushed Vershinin toward adultery with Masha. It is also what prompts him late in Act 3 to invite Kuligin (of all people) to go out with him for a drink, which the increasingly jealous schoolmaster coldly refuses. Separation from Masha, which his obligations as a husband and father plus loyalty to his brigade clearly necessitate, will make him almost as great a sufferer as Masha chiefly because of his fear of isolation. But in the final analysis the relationship has meant more to her than it has to him.

I can only say in concluding a discussion of Vershinin's contradictory nature, that he seems strong and trivial at the same time. In his first visit to the Prozorovs he seems pleasant, talkative, and somewhat vain. He is prone to a flirtation with Masha yet that it can ever be anything more than a flirtation is rendered questionable by his necessary loyalty to his wife, which like his relationship with Masha can be viewed in two ways. He is strong in being loyal to his wife, but I do not get the sense that the wife is really more than an embarrassment. Similarly, with Masha at the end, I get the feeling he can bear the separation because, while he feels a deep need for her, he at the same time views their tearful farewell as also something of an embarrassment. The only area where his ego and his sense of responsibility does not seem divide him is in his relationship with his men.

The Baron

Tuzenbach is intelligent, sensible, and courageous, yet he has the poorest self-image of any character the play. He understands music, has a strong sense of his responsibilities, and is the center of the good will represented by the army officers in the Prozorov home. Arguing with Vershinin, he gives as good as he gets, and his view that people one hundred years in the future will be exactly as they are "today" seems more convincing than Vershinin's idealistic optimism. While his responses in these debates are just about as long as Vershinin's, they somehow do not seem to be so long-winded.

At times Tuzenbach seems quite sure of himself, at other times woefully, if not tragically, unsure. He seems steady in proclaiming his love for Irina in the first act, and consistent in maintaining his commitment. Yet when Irina seems ready to finally accept the marriage, he cannot believe that she really does. Perhaps Olga really needs to give her speech to Irina in Act 3 about marrying (quoted below) to him in the end. While I do not believe he intentionally invites Solyony's bullet, his finally having enough of Solyony's taunts (referred to as the cause of the duel), when he knows the latter's reputation as a marksman, tells me he knows and accepts the fate that awaits him. His entering into the duel is thus a point of honor while at the same time reflection of his insecurity. It is as though Tuzenbach feels with society that marriage without inevitably short-lived physical attractiveness cannot work, while ironically Irina with Olga's help is coming to sense that it can.

What Chekhov appears to be saying about the contradictory nature of romantic love in *The Sea Gull* and *Uncle Vanya* is made most manifest in the relationship of Irina and the Baron. There is no Trigorin or Elena to blind Irina to Tuzenbach's worth, as Nina and Astrov are blinded. Irina is blinded by her dreams alone, dreams that are entirely tied up with her desire to go to Moscow. (It is significant that no relationship that we can call romantic works in the plays.) Romantic love by its very nature is the love we cannot have. But Chekhov fervently believes in love and makes his characters wither without it. More even than Nina and Konstantin and Sonya and Astrov, Irina and the Baron are suited to each other to such an extent that the chances are good they will be, if not happy (no one is that in Chekhov), then at least able to get along well with one another, perhaps even be fulfilled on a permanent basis. Olga makes this idea as explicit as it ever gets in the plays in advising Irina to accept the Baron:

> After all, you respect him, you value him highly. ... It's true he's not good-looking, but he's so honest, so pure. ... You see, one doesn't marry for love, but to do one's duty. At least that's what I think, and I would marry without love. I'd marry anyone who asked me, so long as he was a decent man. ... [W]hen Baron Nikolai Lvovich left the army and came to see us in his civilian clothes, he seemed to me so homely that I actually began to cry. ... He said: "Why are you crying?" How could I tell him! But if it were God's will that he should marry you, I'd be happy. That, you see, would be a different matter, quite different. (290)

We are thrown off when Olga uses words and phrases like "duty" and "God's will," but we must take her words as we do Sonya's at the end of *Uncle Vanya*, not as the way we might put it but expressive in her more conventional terms of ideas we are meant to accept in our own terms. And accept them Irina finally does, though clinging still to the idea of

Moscow. Significantly, she says nothing further about Moscow following the Baron's death.

Can the Baron's death be considered tragic? Can short, ugly people
be tragic heroes? It depends how one responds to the play, but the
Aristotelian elements are there. In his vitally contradictory nature we see
in the Baron an almost great man who falls, and his fall works in us a
tragic catharsis of a sort. That the play is less than tragedy, however, is
not because the Baron cannot be a genuinely heroic figure, but because
it is primarily about the sisters, and not finally about the Baron.

Solyony

A discussion of Solyony really should not appear in a discussion of
characters with inner contradictions because while he wishes he had a
contradictory nature, he does not. He wants to be the murderer with the
soul of a poet, but he is just a murderer. I think Coleridge's description
of Shakespeare's Iago as a "motiveless malignity" fits Solyony. Despite
his pursuit of Irina and his obsession with the Baron, I do not see erotic
attraction toward either sex as part of his nature, as I do not find that
nature, in spite of his probable loneliness, deep in any way. He embodies the basest kind of hostility the flesh is heir to (as the twentieth
century certainly attested to), and given the chance to act out that
hostility, he does so, masking that essential bestiality with scent and
romantic notions. If there is another character in the play he is really
like, it is Natasha—though obviously in killing the Baron (even if he
meant to "just wing him"), he goes her more than one better.

Kuligin

On the other hand, Masha's seemingly foolish husband does have a
contradictory nature. He is unquestionably the boring country schoolmaster, with trite Latin phrases always at hand. His presenting Irina his
own history of his school on her name day, when he had given her the
same gift a year earlier, is appallingly obtuse, and he compounds this
folly by presenting the book in turn to Vershinin, who has all he can do
to keep from laughing at him. And his habit of grading everyone on
their behavior, as he would his students, while intended humorously, is
irritating. He has not encouraged Masha to continue her piano playing,
which Tuzenbach assures us is excellent, and has insisted she perform
all the *pro forma* duties of the schoolmaster's wife, including the
aforementioned Sunday walks with the faculty followed by insufferable
suppers at the headmaster's home. He at first seems so insensitive to her
needs that one wonders why, at the impressionable age of 18—even

though "he seemed ... terribly learned, clever, and important" (261)—
she could have accepted him as her husband. One can better understand
Elena's acceptance of the professor at a similar age.

But accept him she did, and in the event, the decision may not have
been so bad as it seems. She has, she says, "grown used to him," and
what she has grown used to, she implies (261), is a man distinctly less
coarse than others in the town. We see her during the period of her
passion for Vershinin, a passion fed by her boredom and need for the
refinement she cannot have. But Kuligin's love for her is genuine, in
spite of the fact he protests it far too much, and he does appear to
understand her feelings at Vershinin's departure in Act 4. His claim that
he is happy, "no matter what" (309), suggests that he has been fully
aware of her adultery, and that awareness is a forgiving one. His putting
on the funny beard and moustache at the point of her near-hysterical
sorrow, is intended to, and actually seems to, amuse her. And he is
gentle with her as he observes her reaction to the Baron's death. In
short, this fool is "not altogether fool."

Andrei

Which brings me to the last, and most unfortunate, of the play's major
characters. It seems clear that, more than the sisters, Andrei is the victim
of a domineering father. Withdrawn from the start, and having first
escaped from a prescribed military career into music and scholarship, he
falls away into marriage to a local bourgeoise and then to membership
on the town council as the *summum bonum* of his career. As the one
most likely to have returned to Moscow to further his education, he is
the only one to say nothing about going to Moscow. He is shy, in need
of mothering, easily dominated by stronger personalities: his sisters, his
wife, his council superior the ever-present but never appearing
Protopopov (who undoubtedly has cuckolded him).

But what deepens Andrei's personality is his total awareness of what
he has become and, like the doctor, his final honesty about himself. Try
as he will, he cannot keep up a front, particularly with his sisters. In
Act 3, he tries to defend his decision to become a town official and even
more to defend his wife, but these defenses collapse. He has also
mortgaged the house to pay his gambling debts without telling his
sisters, which he is at pains to explain, but to no avail. So he returns to
Natasha:

> They won't listen. Natasha is a superior, honest person. (*Paces the stage in
> silence, then stops.*) When I married, I thought we should be happy ... all of
> us, happy ... but, my God! (*Weeps.*) My dear sisters, my darling sisters,
> don't believe me, don't believe me. ... (293)

The repeated phrase "don't believe me" encapsulates a great deal. It describes better than anything lengthier could the opposing forces working within Andrei, the pain he is in because, try as he does, he cannot lie to himself. And this pattern is repeated in his fourth-act conversation with Chebutykin, where this time he speaks of Natasha in directly negative terms:

> A wife is a wife. She's honest, good ... well, kind, but for all that, there's something in her that reduces her to the level of a small, blind, sort of thick-skinned animal. In any case, she's not a human being. I am speaking to you as to a friend, the only person to whom I can open my heart. I love Natasha, it's true, but sometimes she seems to be extremely vulgar, and then I feel lost, and I don't understand why, for what reason, I love her so, or at least, did love her. ... (301–302)

Which, of course, prompts the doctor's advice that he walk out.

The essential contradiction in Andrei's nature is that he is both able (which includes his sense of obligation to others) and weak. He genuinely loves Natasha, but he just as genuinely sees through her and hates her, not only for her betrayal of him, but, like his sisters, because of her vulgarity. Andrei is the most unfortunate because he is in a trap, which the others, with the possible exception of Masha, are not, quite. Conventional decency, plus his own shyness, prevents him from walking out; yet life with Natasha will not be anything other than increasing deception and vulgarity—without Chebutykin to provide relief from time to time. We see him last struggling with himself much as he has been struggling throughout the play. And while in the sisters' struggles we find some meaning (if not hope), in Andrei's we find little.

The Three Sisters is Chekhov's most complex play because the major characters' dimensions seem greater and because with its unusually large number of such characters the movement of feeling within and among the characters is often surprising and unpredictable. It is a large canvas which deserves far more examination than I can give in a work such as this. But as in the other plays, the inner strength of the major characterizations is revealed in the many and varied oppositions within their natures.

The Cherry Orchard

The pattern of visitors intruding upon a *status quo* works to perfection in *The Cherry Orchard*. Ranevskaya and her entourage return home from Paris for a visit of some months, during which their estate is sold at auction for its failure to pay off a mortgage and pay current taxes. With her are her daughter Anya, the daughter's governess Charlotta-Ivanovna, and a rude servant named Yasha. In Paris she has left a lover, who has sucked her dry of money but to whom she returns at the end. The dominant figures at home, the *status quo* group, are her brother Gayev, her adopted daughter Varya (who serves as housekeeper), Gayev's ancient valet Firs, and the servant-girl Dunyaska. They are joined, most of the time it seems, by the clumsy clerk Yepikhodov, their impoverished neighbor Semyonov-Pishchik (who is suddenly made financially secure in Act 4 by the discovery of a "precious substance" in the soil on his estate), and their friend Lopakhin, a wealthy merchant who as a child was a serf on the estate. The visitors are joined by Trofimov, a perpetual student who is wooing Anya. At the end they all must leave the estate because Lopahkin has bought it in order to build *dachas* (vacation cottages) on it.

The play is constructed with great economy and its characters marvelously delineated, but it is the least of Chekhov's four major plays for my purposes. I say this because fewer of the characters avoid being the types Gilman describes.[1] Several of them, however, are distinguished by the glaring contradictions within their natures, and those are the figures on whom I shall concentrate. They are Lopakhin and Ranevskaya, the secondary figures Yepikhodov and Charlotta-Ivanovna, and, to an extent, Ranevskaya's brother Gayev. I leave out one important figure in the play, the student Petya Trofimov, for reasons I shall suggest later in this discussion.

---

[1]   See p. 136, n. 1. Gilman suggests that the characters in Chekhov's plays are never types, but in this play I believe several are: e.g. Anya, Varya, Yasha, Firs. These are all marvelously drawn figures but still, I think, more types than not types.

Lopakhin

I begin with Lopakhin because he is for me the most interesting figure in the play. It is almost as though Chekhov wished to make amends for the way he characterized Natasha, who takes over the family home in *The Three Sisters* much as Lopakhin does in this play. Both are members of the rising bourgeoisie, and both have in the past suffered humiliation at the hands of the aristocratic families they finally come to dominate. The differences are that Lopakhin is considerate whereas Natasha is cruel, intelligent whereas Natasha is wily but essentially stupid, and capable of love while Natasha loves only herself.

Lopakhin is rife with contradictions, focusing on his compassionate and understanding nature set against his bourgeois rapacity. I am tempted to say that unlike Natasha he is not destructive. And from the point of view of intention to hurt others he is not really, even if at the end he has given orders to chop down the cherry orchard, the symbol of all the family has stood for, and as a developer he will break up the estate. These are things he has hinted he might do since early in the first act when he suggested that the family might "save" the estate by such means. Is this to say Lopakhin is a hypocrite? By no means. His loyalty toward the family is intact throughout. It is just that another part of his basic nature, one part of which is that loyalty, is the desire to make money. Essential to his character is that the two contradictory feelings stand juxtaposed within him, neither as it were commenting on the other.

I have seen this play more often than I have seen any other Chekhov play. I have seen it performed in Russian three times, twice in New York by the visiting Moscow Art Theater, and once by the Maly Theater of Moscow on tour in then Leningrad. The Maly Theater production (which we saw in 1984), obviously influenced by Communist views, made Lopakhin into a cartoon figure of the capitalist. He was flamboyantly dressed, flung giant rouble notes around, and toward Ranevskaya seemed fawning and insincere. Yet nearly twenty years earlier, the Moscow Art Theater production we saw in New York was easily the most sensitive production of any that I have seen (perhaps because that was permissible as a result of the "thaw" in East-West relations of that period). What struck me most about that earlier production, aside from the genuine beauty of the sets, which were based on photographs I have seen of the original Stanislavski production, was that Lopakhin and Gayev seemed almost indistinguishable in dress and manner. They were both dressed in fashionable Scottish tweeds, and I remember thinking that this was how Lopakhin, as an aspiring bourgeois who was once a serf, might well be dressed. But it was Lopakhin's ease and seeming, though never affected, gentility that I particularly remember. That caught the Lopakhin of my imagination. His kindness and consideration always stood out in sharp contrast to his rapacity. Both facets of his personality were genuine, each contradicting the other.

A more complex reflection of Lopakhin's contradictory sides comes in his relations with the step-daughter Varya, who everyone expects him to marry. Clearly Lopakhin and Varya are suited to each other. They have known each other for a long time and, despite their argumentative banter, seem compatible. But the torrent of feeling in him aroused by the visit of Ranevskaya, whom he used to adore from afar, upsets what even for him has seemed a natural affiliation with Varya. His relationship with the great lady of the estate is not unlike that of Strindberg's Jean with Miss Julie, though Lopakhin is hardly the sexual aggressor Jean is. Lopakhin's affections are divided—he loves Varya in one way, Ranevskaya in another. His impossible love for the latter dissipates the possibility of a marriage proposal to the former at the very moment everyone, including Varya, expects him to make such a proposal. So that at the end he leaves to winter in Kharkov, leaving everyone stunned. But the question remains, as it does with Astrov and Sonya, is that the end of the matter? I wonder, especially as the great lady will be returning to her lover in Paris while Varya will be working somewhere locally. But who knows?

The most powerful image of Lopakhin in the play is in Act 3, following his purchase of the estate at the auction. In no way has his feeling for the family diminished, yet he revels in what he has accomplished:

> If my father and grandfather could only rise from their graves and see all that has happened, how their Yermolai, their beaten, half-literate Yermolai, who used to run about barefoot in winter, how that same Yermolai has bought an estate, the most beautiful estate in the whole world! I bought the estate where my father and grandfather were slaves, where they weren't even allowed in the kitchen. (366)

Herein lies one of the most notable contradictions in all Chekhov drama, because what Lopahkin plans to do with this "most beautiful estate in the whole world" is to chop down its legendary cherry orchard and tear down its fine neo-classical home to build the dachas. This highly sensitive man is insensitive to the sounds of the axe in Act 4 and has to be told to instruct the loggers to wait until after the family leaves. And as with the estate, so with the family. Love Ranevskaya as he does, his actions nevertheless mean her permanent banishment; there will never be another such visit as this one. She is in effect chopped down along with the trees, though his feeling for her remains unchanged. And this contradiction in his behavior toward her is treated without irony—as the natural outgrowth of his divided personality.

Ranevskaya

Lopakhin's contradictions stand in contrast to those of the plays' central woman character, Lyubov Andreyevna Ranevskaya. She is the play's most difficult figure to assess, harder to portray even than Arkadina in *The Sea Gull*, with whom she has some similarities. Of the several productions of the plays I have seen, I have never seen her played memorably—at least in the positive sense. In the 1984 Mali Theater production she was memorably hysterical, but I can think of no interpretation I have seen that struck me as right (unless it was that of Judi Dench in an otherwise only so-so television production of the early 1980s). She must be young enough to generate erotic interest, but she must also be on the edge of being a matron. And the contradictions in her nature, which I look at in the following paragraphs, must be at the same time subtle and extreme.

On one side, and obviously unlike Lopakhin, Lyubov Andreyevna is maddeningly impractical. She herself points out that she could never handle her money. Hardly able to make ends meet, she nevertheless gives a 20-rouble gold piece to a beggar at her door, which infuriates the ever-practical Varya. And when their equally impoverished neighbor Pishchik asks her for a loan to pay the interest on his mortgage, she casually tells her brother to give him the money, though it is patently obvious they do not have it. And as for the mortgage on their own estate, she will not come to terms with the inevitable result of not paying it.

On the other hand, Lyubov Andreyevna is anything but impractical when it comes to human feeling. Her gesture of giving the twenty roubles to the beggar is a case in point. Impractical as she seems to Varya, the active part of her charitable nature is what is demonstrated, in spite of the consequences. But still more of a case in point is that the one thing that made life in the least bearable for Lopakhin when he was a child was the comfort she as a lovely adolescent gave him after he had been beaten by his father, comfort which has made her the romantic ideal of his imagination—his "Moscow," as it were.

Lyubov Andreyevna loves everyone with a convincing sincerity. But she has special affection for the student Trofimov—in part because he had been tutor to her dead son, and in part because he is 27 and dreadfully earnest. She also finds him an agreeable suitor for her daughter Anya (if only he will finish his degree). That in large part her feeling for

Trofimov is that of a mother for a troublesome son is suggested by the
similarity of their chief exchange, in Act 3, and the conversation
between Arkadina and Konstantin in *The Sea Gull*, which begins
amicably, becomes hostile on the subject of Trigorin, then returns to
affection as guilt over their hostile reactions sets in.[2] The "Trigorin" in
this case is Lyubov's sick lover in Paris, who sends her telegrams
begging her to come back to him. Lyubov and Trofimov have begun
expressing their mutual admiration for one another, but things change
radically when the subject of the lover comes up:

LYUBOV ANDREYEVNA.

.... I love him, love him ... It's a millstone round my neck. I'm sinking to
the bottom with it, but I love that stone. I cannot live without it. (*Presses
Trofimov's hand.*) Don't think badly of me, Petya, and don't say anything to
me, don't say anything. ...

TROFIMOV (*Through tears*).

For God's sake, forgive my frankness: you know that he robbed you!

LYUBOV ANDREYEVNA.

No, no, no, you mustn't say such things! (*Covers her ears.*)

TROFIMOV.

But he's a scoundrel! You're the only one who doesn't know! He's a petty
scoundrel, a nonentity—

LYUBOV ANDREYEVNA (*angry, but controlling herself.*) .

You are twenty-six or twenty-seven years old, but you're still a schoolboy!
...

TROFIMOV.

... [*Angrily)* Yes, yes! It's not purity with you, it's simple prudery, you're a
ridiculous crank, a freak—(358–359)

Shortly afterward, the offended Trofimov rushes from the room and
promptly falls down a flight of stairs. But the next we see of them, not
many lines later, the two are seen waltzing across the stage together.

The mixture of contradictory feelings in Lyubov implied in this
exchange is volatile.[3] And the culmination in the waltz expresses, more
than any words could, the quick resolution of their hostility in mutual
affection. Everything we have come to know about Lyubov Andreyevna
throughout the play is embodied in this scene: her great impracticality,
her torrential feelings, the centrality in her of love in all its forms, her

---

[2]   I have previously discussed this exchange in the article referred to on p. 1170, n. 3.

[3]   For a more extended assessment of Ranevskaya which more or less harmonizes with
       my own approach, see Pitcher 174–178.

capacity to forgive. These things must all be at work in her as we see her on stage, and no performer I have yet seen in the role has achieved that.

Yepikhodov

So much for the play's major characters. But among the minor ones, one of the most interesting characters in Chekhov's plays begins as a stock farcical figure of an inept young man. A clerk who works for Lopakhin, he is so clumsy that he sows destruction in his path. He first comes in wearing squeaky boots and dropping the flowers he has picked to greet the new arrivals with. Lopakhin, irritated with him, tells him to leave, whereupon he knocks over a chair on the way out. He is called "Two-and-twenty Troubles"—a translated phrase for which there is no adequate equivalent in English, though we certainly know the type from old and not so old movie farces (e.g., Harold Lloyd, Buster Keaton, and especially the early Woody Allen). No character in the plays seems so clearly intended to make us laugh, and make us laugh he certainly does.

Yet Chekhov makes this stock figure wildly contradictory. We see this clearly at the opening of Act 2, where he is discovered playing the guitar, rather well it seems, and trying to impress the maid-servant Dunyasha, who is being more successfully pursued by the rake Yasha. Very much in the style of our Woody Allen, he speaks in rashly philosophical, rather insanely comic terms:

> I am a cultivated man, I read all sorts of remarkable books, but I am in no way able to make out my own inclinations, what it is I really want, whether, strictly speaking, to live or to shoot myself; nevertheless, I always carry a revolver with me. Here it is. (*Shows revolver.*) ... Strictly speaking, all else aside, I must state regarding myself that fate treats me unmercifully, as a storm does a small ship. If, let us assume, I am mistaken, then why, to mention a single instance, do I wake up this morning, and there on my chest see a spider of terrifying magnitude? ... And likewise, I take up some kvas to quench my thirst, and there see something in the highest degree unseemly, like a cockroach. (338)

Then, when it becomes clear Dunyasha is rejecting him, he adds darkly, "Now I know what to do with my revolver."

What is going on here? Yepikhodov is still the clown but now the philosopher clown, which his falling over his own feet would not have led us to expect. I believe him when he says he is a "cultivated man" who has read "all sorts of remarkable books," which again his first appearance would not have led us to expect. Yasha calls him a "stupid fellow" after Yepikhodov has left the stage, but he is quite obviously not that. Eccentric he may be, but not stupid. It is the bizarre quality of the last speech, with its spider and cockroach, intended perhaps to shock the impressionable Dunyasha, that gives Yepihodov a surrealistic quality. One would have to say he is not your typical clerk. He is never really explored further in the play, but we are at the very least left with the impression of a young man who is full of contradictions. And in view of Yasha's subsequent treatment of Dunyasha, whom Yasha in short order rapidly beds (it is implied) and betrays, she might be a lot better off with Yepikhodov, however eccentric.

Charlotta Ivanovna

Still more eccentric is Anya's rifle-toting governess. Like those of Yepikhodov, many of her responses may be for effect, but she never ceases to surprise. And therein lies the core of her contradictory personality. Her perfectly attuned governess qualities are regularly countered by her unanticipated responses. Contrary to what one might expect, Charlotta is the one person in the play to be genuinely impressed by Yepikhodov, whom she calls "a very clever man" who "women must be mad about." And earlier in the play, when Lopakhin offers routinely to kiss her hand, she pulls her hand away, with the startling response: "If I permit you to kiss my hand you'll be wanting to kiss my elbow next, then my shoulder."

Charlotta is a performer, a stage magician, who does card tricks, and sleight of hand; she can make Anya and Varya miraculously appear. Women magicians are rather rare in our time and must have been rarer still in Chekhov's. And for an apparently prim governess to be a performing magician not only verges on the uncanny but makes her far more interesting than we are first led to expect. Plainly she is a quite talented woman, for whom there is no place in society other than to be a governess. Her most revealing speech comes at the start of Act 2:

> I haven't got a real passport. I don't know how old I am, but it always seems to me that I'm quite young. When I was a little girl, my father and mother used to travel from one fair to another giving performances—very good ones. ... Then when Papa and Mama died, a German lady took me to live with her and began teaching me. Good. I grew up and became a governess. But where I come from and who I am I do not know. ... Who my parents were—perhaps they weren't even married—I don't know. (*Takes a cucumber out of her pocket and eats it.*) I don't know anything. (*Pause*) One wants so much to talk, but there isn't anyone to talk to ... I have no one. (337)

It might be the conventional thing to say of Charlotta that she uses drollness as a cover for her terrible loneliness, but I get the feeling that while she is indeed sad and alone, as the conclusion to the quoted passage makes clear, she is also naturally gifted in other directions, many of them probably learned from her parents in the music halls, but by this time entirely part of her nature. She is naturally an entertainer; in our time perhaps she would have been a stand-up comic as well as a stage magician. The quoted speech is not so much an appeal for sympathy, though she certainly evokes our sympathy, as a statement of fact, and with her act of taking out the cucumber and eating it, she never stops being the comic, even here. Charlotta is a good match for Yepikhodov. Taken together, the vitality of their contradictions may be seen as the chief source of the comedy Chekhov intended for this play.

Gayev

In sharp contrast to figures like Yepikhodov and Charlotta is the aristocrat Leonid Andreyevich Gayev. While unquestionably a type figure of the impoverished aristocrat about to lose his land because of his debts, Gayev has some of the self-awareness that gives vitality to the contradictory figure of Sorin in *The Sea Gull*. Like Sorin, he has stayed at home to oversee the estate while his sister has gone off to make her life in the city, and like Sorin he has been an affectionate uncle. More even than Sorin, however, Gayev has trouble keeping his mind on present affairs, allowing himself to wander into psychological retreats, demonstrated by his imaginary billiards game and his certainty that the estate can never be sold out from under him. One side of his nature is illustrated by his affection for an old bookcase, which represents for him all the best things his class stands for:

> Dear, honored bookcase, I salute thy existence, which for over one hundred years has served the glorious ideals of goodness and justice; thy silent appeal to fruitful endeavor, unflagging in the course of a hundred years, tearfully sustaining through generations of our family, courage and faith in a better future, and fostering in us ideals of goodness and social consciousness. ... (327–328)

But Gayev is aware of his here-demonstrated tendency to "talk too much," and he is ashamed of his urge to lose himself in the past:

> Really, it's awful! My God! God help me! And today I made a speech to the bookcase ... so stupid! And it was only when I had finished that I realized it was stupid. (334)

It is this kind of realization of his contradictions that enlarges Gayev as a character and takes him to the edge of the kind of complexity Sorin and the doctor in *The Three Sisters* represent. But he never quite enters that realm. He has few such realizations in the play. A memorable image of him is that late in Act 3 returning home after the estate has been sold with tears in his eyes but with a bag of expensive delicatessen purchases in his arms. And the crowning touch is when we learn in the last act that he has been appointed to the board of a bank—probably because of his status as an aristocrat. Finally, he is more a comic type than a genuinely complex figure.

The Other Characters

As for the others, they strike me as all well-drawn types: the perpetual student (Trofimov), the embittered step-daughter (Varya), the delightful ingenue (Anya), the nattering neighbor (Pishchik), the philandering valet (Yasha), the giggling maid-servant (Dunyasha), and the aged butler (Firs). Taken together, they make up the rich texture of the country estate in decline which is this play. And the interplay of all the characters is even more important here than in the other plays. We have already looked at an instance of that interplay in the violent disagreement followed by a waltz involving Trofimov and Lyubov. In addition, Gayev persistently indulges his habit of looking down on Lopakhin (commenting on his cheap cologne), which is one reason why their similarity of appearance in the 1965 Moscow Art Theater production in New York was so telling. In turn, Lopakhin repeatedly attacks Trofimov for not knowing the meaning of real work. And Firs cannot get over treating Gayev as a little boy, always telling him how to dress, for example. And then there is the happily-resolved love story of Trofimov. But except for the Trofimov-Lyubov exchange, these things are ancillary to the purposes of this book.

Also ancillary, if quite important, is the oft-discussed historical significance of the play: Francis Fergusson's "poetry of change" idea.[4] Even more than *The Three Sisters, The Cherry Orchard* is a superb dramatic representation of the passing of the old landed aristocrats and the rise of the bourgeoisie. Chekhov could not have foreseen what lay ahead for the newly successful Lopakhins, of course, but the years of that character's joy in his increasing wealth were to be numbered. The second of the Russian productions I saw (1984) tried to picture Trofimov as a heroic proto-Communist. If that is viable, our Petya will have to learn how to really work—since Lenin would have had little patience for lazy aging students in the new regime. I am not sure even Trofimov's declarations about work, and his happy running off with Anya would have resulted in his being the happy party worker. Trofimov's youth and sincerity call attention to him rather than his inner

---

[4]   See Francis Fergusson, "The Plot of *The Cherry Orchard*" in *The Idea of a Theatre* (Princeton UP, 1949) 161–177.

contradictions. Except in his argument with Lyubov discussed earlier, which really focuses on her more than it does on him, Petya's attitudes do not shift much.

Then there is Firs, who more than any of the others the embodiment of the old order in the play. His abandonment, locked into the estate at the end, is one of the most potent images in the play—as is his recall of the all-but-forgotten recipe for cherry preserves, which with the orchard itself falls victim to the axe. The "poetry" that Fergusson identifies remains probably the most important single aspect of the play. That vital contradictions are not central to all its figures does not take away from the greatness of *The Cherry Orchard*. It balances satire of its comic types and issues regarding social change with focus on the oppositions within its central figures in a blend that makes it possibly the most stage-worthy and enjoyable than any of the plays, if not perhaps the deepest.

In sum, if I were asked which of the four playwrights dealt with in this book is "the best"—the closest to Shakespeare, let us say, for want of a better way to put it—it would be Chekhov. And I say this because of the range and depth of his characterizations, and because of the "inner strength" given his most memorable figures by the contradictions within their natures. O'Neill, the playwright on whom I have done most of my work in recent years, lies ahead in this study, but I do not consider O'Neill, Ibsen, or Strindberg, quite as good as Chekhov in doing what they all do so well.

O'NEILL

More Stately Mansions

The three playwrights I have previously dealt with may or may not have been consciously aware that they were making their strongest characterizations emerge from those figures' inner contradictions. Strindberg probably was, but it is hard to say with Ibsen and Chekhov. Eugene O'Neill, on the other hand, was very much consciously aware of the importance of such contradictions in his major characters, even in his earlier plays. That he was conscious of what Eisen calls the inner strength of opposites in characters is evident, for example, in his use of masks in *The Great God Brown*, the interior monologues in *Strange Interlude*, and his splitting a main character into two characters representing two opposing sides of that character in *Days Without End*. But he expanded the idea and employed it more effectively as his art matured. Certain statements made by Simon Harford in *More Stately Mansions* show O'Neill taking the idea a stage further.

In particular, a perfectly legible passage O'Neill excised from the typescript of the play makes the new stage clear.[1] In that passage the character Simon Harford in describing the contradictory nature of all the play's central characters, develops a theory about how contradictions within the characters affect relationships between the characters. Simon is speaking to his mother Abigail (later named Deborah) about feeling isolated by Abigail's unexpected alliance with Simon's wife Sara:

> You—or, at least, one of your two selves—believes it was you who accomplished that [separation], in order to prove you still [have] the power to drive me from my dreams. And one of Sara's two selves, I am sure, secretly prides itself that she did it and thus proved her independence and supremacy in her home. ... But, in my opinion, all these arrogances are delusions—of our vanities, and it was, as a matter of fact, accomplished through an alliance, a secret, unconscious partnership between corresponding selves within the three of us. A self in each that hates its opposite and summons its natural allies within others to help it destroy its enemy. In short, it's another manifestation of that duel to the death between opposites ..., the self that longs for freedom and the self that clings to its slavery. ...

---

[1]   The typescript is in the Beinecke Library at Yale University.

These selves within the self change...in the process of Time—appear to
merge and become each other. ...[2]

The passage assumes that there are opposing sides in each character's
personality but goes on to explore the idea of sides of the characters
"merging" with compatible sides in others. Thus the emphasis shifts
from individual characters to pairs or trios of characters. And this shift
in emphasis is borne out not only in this play but in better-known plays
to follow: in the character pairings at the tables in *The Iceman Cometh*,
in the explosive exchanges between James and Jamie, Edmund and
Mary, James and Edmund, and Edmund and Jamie in *Long Day's
Journey Into Night*; and in the long nights together of Jim Tyrone and
Josie Hogan in *A Moon for the Misbegotten* and of Erie Smith and the
Night Clerk in *Hughie*. These pairs may begin in violent disagreement,
then they come together and gradually appear to merge, then forcefully
separate again. The compatible sides in the nature of each join forces, as
Simon describes the pair doing in his quoted speech, before their
incompatible opposing sides again force the characters apart. It is a
pattern like that Chekhov uses with Arkadina and Konstantin in *The Sea
Gull*, and Ranevskaya and Petya Trofimov in *The Cherry Orchard*, but
O'Neill takes the idea further in his late plays. My discussion of O'Neill
will focus on plays beginning with *More Stately Mansions* and ending
with the one-act *Hughie*.[3]

More Stately Mansions

This play, which begins in the early 1830s and ends in 1842, was central
to O'Neill's conception of the eleven-play cycle (mostly destroyed by
him) bearing the overall title "A Tale of Possessors Self-Dispossessed."
It was central because it focuses on the marriage of Sara and Simon
Harford, who are among the "possessors" in question. The play deals
primarily with the struggle for Simon Harford's soul between his wife
(daughter of the late Con Melody the Irish innkeeper with aristocratic
pretensions of *A Touch of the Poet*), and his mother Deborah, last in a
line of elite Bostonians going back well into the eighteenth century
(whose lives and careers are dealt with in the early plays of the cycle).
Simon, a Thoreau-like idealist in *A Touch of the Poet*, having now

---

[2]   Quoted in my "At Home with the Harfords," *Eugene O'Neill Review* 20: 105–106.

[3]   My discussion of O'Neill is an extension of the following published articles, listed in
     the order in which the plays they deal with will be taken up: "At Home With the
     Harfords," *Eugene O'Neill Review* 20 (1996): 102–109; "The Stature of *Long Day's
     Journey Into Night*," *The Cambridge Companion to Eugene O'Neill*, (Cambridge
     University Press), 1998: 206–216; and the articles listed on p. 18, n. 10.

forgotten his idealism, is making steady strides as a successful business-man. Upon the death of his once-rich but recently near-bankrupt father, and through the offices of his fantasizing mother, he comes into his father's vast textile company, which he expands into shipping, banking and ultimately railroading, becoming a prototype of the nineteenth-century robber baron. Simon, along with Sara and their four boys, move into the Harford mansion, which they will share with his still-dreaming, still-scheming mother.

Like his father before him, Simon becomes greedier as the business expands, and to make it expand yet more borrows heavily, gambling large amounts on the future. But spending more and more time in his office, Simon comes to resent becoming isolated from his family, as he sees wife and mother apparently getting along quite well without him. In an effort to regain possession of his wife, he offers her a job as his personal secretary, a job which will involve her taking over the company piece by piece by granting him sexual favors, whore-like, in the office in return for the pieces acquired. And in an effort to regain his mother's affection, he sets about regularly visiting her in her garden, recreating the relationship they had when he was a child. In this process Sara gives up her role as nurturing mother to become instead a ruthless (and shameless) businesswoman, while Deborah gives up her role of loving grandmother to return to her narcissistic fantasies. Leaving behind their amity as mothers and nurturers, the two women return to the intensely jealous rivalry that had dominated their relationship before the younger Harfords moved into Deborah's home.

The last two acts deal with Simon's disintegration under this new state of affairs. Far from re-establishing his role in family life, he plots with Sara to destroy Deborah and with Deborah to destroy Sara. But in the end he is himself all but destroyed. In the course of the last act, Deborah appears to have won the battle for Simon's soul. Followed by the now-childlike and near-mad Simon, she is about to withdraw into a little summer house in her garden, which she calls her "temple of liberty," where her paranoid fantasies had almost driven her into mad-ness before. But in an apparent reversal of intention, Deborah, who has been inviting Simon to follow her, suddenly pushes him down the steps leading into the summer house as he attempts to follow her. As a result, Simon suffers a blow to the head which results in a case of long-term amnesia. Not the possessive wife, but the possessive mother appears at the last moment to save Simon from a disastrous fate.

The play, like the whole of the cycle, was intended as a dramatic representation of the bankruptcy of the American spirit, and vital contra-dictions in all three major characters are part of that representation.

O'Neill implies here that there can be no faith between people, no lasting trust, because the fact that we have opposing sides to our natures can only result in repeated betrayal. Love Simon as they may, one-half of both Sara and Deborah Harford hates him, and when that half in each gets together with the corresponding half in the other, they will go all-out to destroy him. Similarly. Simon's feeling for both wife and mother have a virulently destructive side which ultimately cannot be denied. Yet, in spite of O'Neill's self-proclaimed bankruptcy-of-the-American-spirit idea, the hostility among and between these figures is repeatedly offset by their mutual, and genuine, love.

Throughout the play, as in earlier O'Neill plays, the characters reveal the contradictory sides of their feelings through interior monologue. We are at times back in the world of *Strange Interlude.* Thus we have Sara on the subject of Deborah:

> I'll say this for her, she's never tried to interfere. (*Then cynically*) Maybe it's because Simon's father never gave her the chance. (*Then honestly*) No, that's not fair. I ought to feel grateful to her. It was the two thousand dollars she sent Simon after we were married gave us our start. (*Resentfully*) Not but what we didn't pay her back every penny as soon as we'd saved it. (306)[4]

And Deborah from the start is aware of and impatient with her "insane interminable dialogues with self" (316):

> Age? I am only forty-five. I am still beautiful. You harp on age as though I were a withered old hag! ([Self-]*mocking again*) Oh, not yet, Deborah! But now that the great change is upon you, it would be wise, I think, to discipline your mind to accept this fate of inevitable decay with equanimity. (*She gives a little shiver of repulsion—determinedly*) No! I will not think of it! I still have years before me. (*She ... sits down—sneeringly*) And what will you do with these years, Deborah? (315)

And she continues in this vein later in the play, as she impatiently awaits Simon in the garden:

> How dare he humiliate me like this! a common, vulgar, money-grubbing trader like his father!—... You better beware, Simon!—if you think I will bear your insults without retaliating!—(*then trying pitifully to reassure herself*) No, no, I must not blame him—he has been detained at the mill by something unforeseen—(*with angry scorn*) Ah, how can you make excuses—lie to yourself when you know the truth—he deliberately forgot you—he is even now lying in the arms of that slut, laughing with her to think of the pitiable spectacle you make waiting in vain! (*In a fury*) Ah, if I

---

[4]   All quotations from O'Neill plays are from *Eugene O'Neill: Complete Plays, 1932–1943,* edited by Travis Bogard (The Library of America, n.d.).

were sure of that. I would have no more scruples!—I would make him go into the summerhouse instead of protecting him from his insane desire—that would revenge me for all his insults! ... . No!—I could not—he is my beloved son who has returned to me—and he will come here soon—he loves me. ... (504)

All three major characters go interminably through such internal reversals, and Simon several times refers to his "two selves" in endless competition:

... I no longer have the power to discipline my will to keep myself united—another self rebels —secedes—as if at last I must become two selves from now on—division and confusion—a war—a duel to the death. ... (393)

More than any play yet examined, this play explores its characters' contradictions. But as I stated at the beginning, what the play adds, consciously on O'Neill's part (as evidenced in Simon's deleted observations quoted at the start), is the idea of selves merging with compatible selves in others. This pattern can best be explored by a close examination of Act 3, scene 3 (448–476), the scene in which Simon's statement about character-merging, quoted at the beginning of this chapter, takes place. The three characters are sitting together in the evening apparently at peace with one another but "thinking" private thoughts that are anything but peaceful. Their interior monologues contain the usual antiphony of self-satisfied thoughts countered by fearful thoughts, smug assurance and hostility countered by insecurity and guilt. Each woman thinks she has won the battle to control Simon, but then is unsure, suspecting the other of one or another form of treachery. Similarly, Simon gloats that he has both women under his control, then becomes unsure whether that is in fact the case, and concomitantly whether he really wishes that his life should be so taken up with his women. At times, first one, then the other, begins to speak aloud, but always with their real thoughts carefully masked. Each keeps trying to read the others' thoughts, always falling back into their own.

Gradually, however, the hostile thoughts between Sara and Deborah subside, and each begins thinking of their former camaraderie—particularly in connection with the children—that Simon's moves have deprived them of. What Simon fears most begins to take place; their characters start to merge. First, Sara joins Deborah on the sofa, where they had sat together on previous evenings:

SARA.

(*Turns to Deborah with impulsive frankness*) I want to beg your forgiveness,
Mother—about the children. It was mean of me to let myself be made
jealous, and not to trust you.

DEBORAH.

(*Takes her hand—gently*) I understand. One cannot help being jealous. It is
part of the curse of love.

SARA.

(*With a quick resentful look at Simon*) Yes, you do feel cursed by it when it
becomes too greedy.

DEBORAH.

(*Patting Sara's hand*) Thank goodness we've understood each other and
what might have developed into a stupid quarrel is all forgotten now, isn't
it?

SARA.

Yes, and I'm happy to be here beside you again, feeling your trust and
friendship—(458)

At first Simon is relieved by their renewed friendship, but quickly once
again feels isolated by it. Together, speaking almost as one, the women
begin to express their hostility toward him, "their expressions [having]
changed to revengeful gloating cruelty."(461) Then, typically, they
switch back to tenderness about him, but it is "maternal tenderness";
they both speak as one about him as if he were a misbehaving child:

DEBORAH.

(*Their arms around each other's waist, they advance on Simon with
mocking, enticing smiles...*) We must humor his manly pride, Sara. Anything
to keep peace in our home! (*She laughs.*)

SARA.

(*Laughingly*) Yes. Anything to give him his way, as long as it's our way!
(*...They group together in back of him, Deborah at left-rear and Sara at
right-rear of his chair...*)

SIMON.

.... I cannot keep them separate—they will not remain divided—they unite
in spite of me. (465–466)

But even as they gain total control over him, Sara and Deborah, once
again in their private thoughts, begin to separate again, becoming
increasingly suspicious and hostile. Grouped "together in back of him,"
they seem literally to have become one, yet once they have mastered
him, the inevitable return of the split between them occurs. O'Neill does
not want their mutual warmth to prevail, since he is implying that no
harmony between people is permanent. Yet, at the same time, little of

the harmony he creates feels hypocritical. O'Neill clearly wants us to feel the harmony is genuine—while it lasts.

What I am saying here is important in regard to *More Stately Mansions*, but more important still in regard to the succeeding plays, especially *The Iceman Cometh* (which immediately follows *Mansions* in the O'Neill canon). In *Iceman,* during encounters involving three characters in close quarters, two begin attacking one another, then are drawn together by mutual need for companionship and reassurance, then begin attacking the third, more isolated, character, then end up attacking one another again.

But a new idea underlies the divisions in the characters' feelings in *More Stately Mansions*: that each opposing side of those feelings seems subject to a division of its own. Quoting from my earlier work:

> At the heart of these scenes is the thought that whatever any character does or says is only one-half of what they are at any particular moment. Simon's sexuality (not his sexual fantasies) is one-half sexual desire and one-half greed. And the ... 'little boy' half when he is with his mother is one-half genuine desire for love, of which he was earlier deprived, and one-half a compulsive need for withdrawal, like his mother's. Similarly, Sara's whore/tycoon half is one-half sensible and one-half grasping, and her wife-motherly-half is one-half supportive and one-half possessive. By the same token, Deborah's withdrawing half is one-half imaginatively creative and one-half selfish, and her grandmotherly half is one-half supportive and one-half possessive (here like Sara). ... Each half of each response is separate and true, and each half is itself subject to bisection.[5]

And thus, of course, Sara's and Deborah's harmony in 3.3 is itself one-half genuine affection and mutual need and one-half aggressive desire to control Simon. This further division in the nature of characters' feelings becomes more important as we assess the motivations of a character like Mary Tyrone.

O'Neill in this play implies that all the bifurcations and bifurcations within bifurcation are evidence that: 1) the true nature of a human responses can never be single, and 2) that human beings' motives are never to be trusted. Bad motives always intermingle with good motives. But a concomitant idea, not probably intended by O'Neill in this play but increasingly important in succeeding plays, is that the good motives will *always* be there—intermingled with the bad to be sure—but nonetheless there. One must recall here Strindberg's phrase from *Easter*: "He was a false friend, but a friend nonetheless."[6] Altruistic responses

---

[5]   *New Language of Kinship* 120–121.
[6]   See discussion on pp. 75–85.

are themselves a mixture of altruism and self-interest, inseparable. Even hypocrisy has within it that which is sincerely meant.

What I have been saying about *More Stately Mansions* makes the play seem pretty schematized, and indeed one of the play's weaknesses that it is overly schematized, as well as terribly wordy in places. But the schematization reveals O'Neill's basic design for the play, and he probably would have revised it into something less schematized (and wordy), as he did with *A Touch of the Poet*, had he not decided to destroy it. This schematized effect is particularly evident in Act 3, scene 3, the scene involving Sara, Deborah, and Simon discussed earlier, where each character too systematically reveals constantly shifting emotions through their interior monologues. There is a "clockwork" quality to the scene, if not the entire play, which O'Neill happily was to correct in later plays. But the pattern of emotional relationships in those great later plays is established in this play, and this scene in particular.

The other great weakness of the play is that found in all his early and middle plays: an over-dependence on melodrama in action and dia-logue.[7] This excess is especially evident in the play's final act, where Deborah wins her battle with Sara for Simon's soul, only to push him away suddenly and violently as she enters for a final time her little temple of freedom, or madness—thereby either looking out for Simon's best interests or wishing no company in her final suicidal withdrawal. The whole effect is Wagnerian at best, banal at worst—but most revealing of O'Neill's state of mind when he wrote the play, as I have suggested elsewhere.[8]

Certainly not a great play, or even a particularly good one in the state in which we have it, *More Stately Mansions* is an important one to our understanding of O'Neill's creation of his last great plays. The opposi-tions within the major characters gives them more force and depth as characters than the otherwise melodramatic nature of their situations and utterances might suggest. Their vital contradictions transform them from the banal into figures Anton Chekhov in particular might be at home with.

---

[7]   From quite different points of view, this over-dependence has been examined in Virgil Geddes, *The Melodramadness of Eugene O'Neill* (Norwood PA, The Norwood Press, 1977); Jean Chothia, *Forging a Language;* and Matthew H. Wikander, "O'Neill and the Cult of Sincerity," in *The Cambridge Companion to Eugene O'Neill* 217–235.

[8]   *New Language of Kinship:* 116–125.

The Iceman Cometh

More than any other play discussed in this book, with the possible exception of Strindberg's *A Dream Play*, *The Iceman Cometh* is rooted in central contradictions about life revealed in the contradictions at the core of each individual in it and in the relationships they have with one another. But the play at first does not seem to involve the contradictory at all. Its characters are at rock-bottom. While they try to hide from themselves and the essential meaninglessness of their lives, they cannot, at least for long. There is, as Larry Slade, the *raissonneur* of the play, says, nowhere to go from here. And the conclusion that Larry finally reaches (though he claims to have reached it much earlier) and invites his audience to reach, is that there is no possible way to rationalize life, to give it permanent meaning, to explain the emptiness that apparently surrounds us in a limitless universe, to affirm that moral behavior and moral systems have any purpose whatsoever. The play's characters all blame themselves for something in their pasts which has made them betray themselves and those closest to them, but their betrayals, the play implies, are inconsequential in the great non-scheme of things. The only firm reality is death, and as Larry says, quoting philosopher Nietzsche and poet Heine in a seemingly endless variety of ways: "The best of all were never to have been born!" (Heine) *Hope*, the idea of it, not the character, is the ultimate whore of the play. It makes men mad.

The way to come at this play, as I have at different times observed, is to work toward its vision through that of the other great dramatic testament to nihilism in the twentieth century, Beckett's *Waiting for Godot*, written somewhat later than *Iceman* but unquestionably the product of the same kind of intellectual despair, treated in an essentially similar manner.[1] The erring, guilt-ridden, morally bankrupt pair of protagonists of Beckett's play are in the same end-of-the-line situation as the denizens of Harry Hope's saloon—awaiting fulfillment of a pipe dream that can never be realized. That pipe dream may have to do with a saving god, as Beckett's title seems to imply, or simply the intellectual or blindly believed conception of anything saving: that is, explanatory, redeeming, re-assuring, or simply having a point. The protagonists in

---

[1]   See my *New Language of Kinship* 145–147; and Normand Berlin, "The Beckettian O'Neill," *Modern Drama* 31 (March 1988): 28–34.

Beckett's play, along with a second pair of characters who join them, struggle against a fate which is inevitable: i.e., they will never find a first cause, they will never have ultimate knowledge. There may be evanescent buds of seeming hope along the way, but they are illusory. The only thing they all can do is wait.

But the key word in all the statements of hopelessness about both plays is *they*, and herein lies the central contradiction. What the characters in both plays do during their infinite waits is relate to one another, relate in sometimes highly aggressive ways, and in mutually nurturing ways. In *Waiting for Godot*, they engage in what one of the central pair calls "canters," evanescent discussions involving questionings, recollections, musings on a wide variety of disparate subjects ranging from the geography of France, to the location of lost boots, to playing at being someone else—all leading to frustration, then despair. But the despair is inevitably followed by one character's physically comforting the other, a brief period of happiness, then a return to the discussions leading nowhere, and finally back to the state they were in at the beginning of the play, when they state that "Nothing is to be done," and doing nothing. At the end one character says "Let's go," and they stay where they are.

O'Neill's and Beckett's plays have similar visions and their playwrights employ similar means to dramatize those visions. As Beckett's play begins with the characters in despair and ends in their going nowhere, O'Neill's begins with one of its two central characters, Larry Slade, staring in front of him, and ends with him staring in front of him: from nothing to be done to not going anywhere—which in view of Larry's statement near the end that he has finally become a true convert to death must mean deciding to commit suicide, but not doing so. Intellectually speaking both plays are nihilistic.

But what takes place throughout much of both plays is what Estragon in *Godot* calls "blathering," and the blathering suggests something other than nihilism. As I have several times observed, my early 1980s book on O'Neill is based on a phrase O'Neill used to describe Strindberg's *Dance of Death*, which O'Neill says contains a "new language of kinship."[2] What O'Neill refers to is a process whereby people in close relationships naturally move from mutual hostility to mutual affection and back again, based on both their needs of the moment and their enveloping fear of isolation. The only certainty about feelings within characters in O'Neill's late plays, and about feelings those characters set off in one another, is that they reverse themselves. And these contradictions, rather than what the characters are feeling, or saying, are for

---

[2]   See p. 70, n. 7.

O'Neill what give substance to human existence. In both plays, the wait "for Godot," or the fulfillment of the pipe dream, while seemingly the main issue, is really not the issue at all. Rather, the canters, and the range of emotions from despair to happiness and back again that those canters career through, are the issue, the stuff of life being lived.

The canters, the "blathering," of one pair of characters in *Iceman* illustrates this idea best. At one table sit the disgraced Captain Lewis, late of the British army in South Africa, and the similarly disgraced Boer officer Wetjoen. In his description of these characters earlier in the play, Larry tells us that "they met when they came here to work at the Boer War spectacle at the St. Louis Fair and they've been bosom pals ever since."(584) And as pals do, they alternately fight and commiserate with one another. In their hostile moments, they attack, refighting the Boer War, which was still fresh in everyone's memory in the year (1912) in which the play is set:

LEWIS.

(*Smiling amiably*) As for you, my balmy Boer that walks like a man, I say again it was a grave error in our foreign policy ever to set you free. ... We should have taken you to the London zoo and incarcerated you in the baboon's cage. With a sign: Spectators may distinguish the true baboon by his blue behind.

WETJOEN.

(*Grins*) Gott! To dink, ten better Limey officers, at least, I shoot clean in the mittle of forehead ... and you I miss! I neffer forgive myself! (589)

They are smiling during this particular exchange, which makes it part of the usual kind of barroom banter. But later in the play, when they are sober and trying under Hickey's guidance to live out their pipe dreams of rehabilitation, the banter turns violent. Now they go after one another's notorious weaknesses:

LEWIS.

(*Grows rigid—his voice trembling with repressed anger.*) There was a rumor in South Africa that a certain Boer officer—if you call the leaders of a rabble of farmers officers—to retreat and not stand and fight. ... . [A] suspicion grew afterwards into a conviction among the Boers that the officer's caution was prompted by a desire to make his personal escape. His countrymen felt extremely savage about it, and his family disowned him. ... .

WETJOEN.

(*With guilty rage*) All lies! You Gottamned Limey—(*trying to control himself and copy Lewis's manner*) I also haf heard rumors of a Limey officer who, after the war, lost all his money gambling vhen he vas tronk. But they found out it vas regiment money, too, he lost—

LEWIS.

(*Loses his control and starts for him*) You bloody Dutch scum!

ROCKY.

(*Leans over the bar and stops Lewis with a straight-arm swipe to the chest*) Cut it out! (*At the same moment Chuck grabs Wetjoen and yanks him back*)

WETJOEN.

(*Struggling*) Let him come! Let him come! I saw them come before. ...and I kill them vith my rifle so easy! (*Vindictively*) Listen to me, you Cecil! Often vhen I am tronk and kidding you I say I am sorry I missed you, but now, py Gott, I am sober, and I don't joke, and I say it! (663–64)

But the hostilities, light-hearted or serious, give way to a harmony which, even if precipitated by drink and the return of pipe dreams, is as real as the mutual rage. At some earlier moment of harmony, Lewis had apparently invited Wetjoen to join him on a trip to England, and they return to that theme. The following exchange suggests the kind of merging that O'Neill conceived in Simon Harford's deleted passage:[3]

LEWIS.

(... *dreamily to Wetjoen*) I'm sorry we had to postpone our trip again this April, Piet. ... We'll make it next year, even if we have to work and earn our passage, eh? You'll stay with me at the old place as long as you like ... England in April. I want you to see that, Piet. The old veldt has its points I'll admit, but it isn't home—especially home in April.

WETJOEN.

(*Blinks drowsily at him—dreamily*) Ja, Cecil. I know how beautiful it must be, from all you tell me many times. I vill enjoy it. But I shall enjoy more ven I am home, too. The veldt, ja! You could put England on it, and it would look like a farmers small garden.. Py Gott, there is space to be free, the air like vine is, you don't need booze to be drunk! (594)

Their being drunk, of course, has a lot to do with their mood. Could they merge without it? Possibly not. Yet if one calls to mind Edmund Tyrone's invoking of Baudelaire in *Long Day's Journey*, one gets a sense of what O'Neill is driving at in this play:

Be always drunken. If you would not feel the horrible burden of Time weighing on your shoulders and crushing you to the earth, be drunken continuously. ... Drunken with what? With wine, with poetry, or with virtue, as you will. ... But be drunken. (796–797)

The only protection from the abyss which Hickey's insistence that the men (and women) face themselves at all times brings them to is one or another form of drunkenness—which Larry sees as the only basis for a

---

[3]   See previous chapter, p. 159–160.

human sense of self-worth. One must keep in mind that this play presents human beings in Bedrock Bar, the Bottom of the Sea Rathskeller—in Yeats's "foul and rag bone shop of the heart."[4] For Lewis and Wetjoen, in their merged state, O'Neill implies (following Baudelaire's statement), the drunken state, in one form or another, is the saving state. Lewis and Wetjoen merge in the drunkenness of mutual good will—along with the drunkenness engendered by the alcohol. Both, however, are subject to the morning after.

In this play O'Neill first gives us the character pairings as a vision of the contradictions that govern human relationships. Lewis and Wetjoen are like Sara and Deborah Harford (and like Beckett's pairs) in their oscillations between hostility and amity and back again. And so too for a time are other pairs: the Runyonesque Pat McGloin and Ed Mosher, the bartender/pimps Rocky Pioggi and Chuck Morello, the streetwalkers Pearl and Margie. But O'Neill goes beyond the pairings. Accompanying each pair at their tables are more isolated characters, who only half succeed in merging with the others: the innkeeper Harry Hope, who sits with McGloin and Mosher; Joe Mott, the Black who alternates between the Rocky-Chuck pair and the Lewis-Wetjoen pair; Jimmy Tomorrow, the dead-beat journalist who tries to be affiliated with Lewis and Wetjoen; Cora, whose intelligence and marital aspirations separate her from the other whores but who is at times one with them. Then there are the more desperately isolated figures, who can never merge with anyone, who sit alone at the other tables: Willie Oban, the youngest of the characters and also the most educated and articulate (besides Larry Slade); and Hugo Kalmar, the old anarchist bomb-thrower, who is the one most lost in alcoholic reverie.

But finally, the pairs, the hangers on, and even the more desperate solo players yield to the group, where general hostility alternates with general elation. The most important scenic images[5] of the play are those of people going after one another tooth and nail countered by those of people celebrating with one another in universal mergings.[6] The first act, following Larry's introductory descriptions of the group for Parritt (and us), is one of morning hangover irritation giving way, as Harry allows the booze gradually to flow, to good will reflected in the jests and

---

[4]   Quoted by Jean Chothia in describing what O'Neill achieves in his late plays. See "Trying to Write the Family Play," *The Cambridge Companion to Eugene O'Neill* 193.

[5]   I base my use of this phrase on Timo Tiusanen, *O'Neill's Scenic Images* (Princeton UP, 1968).

[6]   These scenic images were beautifully realized in the 1999 New York production of the play featuring Kevin Spacey as Hickey.

winking at others complaints. Each is on to the pipe dreams of the others; each allows his own pipe dreams to improve his mood. Harry is the big provider, his morning grouch giving way to the calculated reminders by others of his own pipe dreams about his love for his long-dead wife and his insistence that he will shortly take his long-intended walk around the ward. All this is prelude, of course, to the long-awaited arrival of Hickey, whose jokes, general good will and forgiveness, and free whiskey will provide the big merging. He seems the Godot of the play arrived. His earlier visits have regularly made it appear that the wait may be over. The derelicts will "for a time" be freed from having to live in "hope." So it has always been, and so it will be again—but not until the end of the play.

What Hickey brings this time is a new booze, a booze that will not work. It is the booze of release through confession, the admission that pipe dreams regarding both past and future are just that, pipe dreams. He assures them that they will be able for the first time to really live at peace with themselves—as he is for the first time, he thinks, living at peace with himself. He has become drunk with something like Baudelaire's virtue, and it seems to be carrying him along so well that he is sure it will work for the others. The climax of the play comes, of course, when he realizes it will not work for them, and has not worked for him. Admitting that their pipe dreams are purely illusory fills the others with such despair that even the whiskey, which has always been along with their pipe dreams protection against despair, loses its kick. The question for Hickey, and for us, throughout the last part of the play is why Hickey's idea doesn't work. Why does facing reality make life worse instead of better?

This was a tremendous question for me when I first encountered the play at the Ted Mann/Jose Quintero/Jason Robards production of the mid-1950s. At the time, I was in my late twenties and thoroughly immersed in the pipe dream of salvation through self-revelation, deeply influenced by ideas I associated with Freudian psychology. Freed, I felt, from fears from my past, the last thing I needed at the time was to have my new security dashed. But that was what this production did to me. I was all with Hickey as he came to Harry Hope's with the message: Save yourself by breaking through your fears. Take action where you are most afraid to take action. Against all logic, I fully expected the romantic conclusion: that each of the crew would go out and face his or her demons. Harry Hope would take his walk; McGloin and Mosher would be re-established in their old professions; Lewis and Wetjoen would go back home to the forgiving arms of friends and relatives; Jimmy would go back to work for a newspaper; Willie would begin his career as an attorney; Joe would again be a force in the Black community; and Chuck and Cora would marry and live happily ever after. My own pipe dreams were so pervasive that I was shocked that Hickey never expected any of these things to happen, that he only intended these people to finally be at peace with being the deadbeat alcoholics they had become. I had never really thought in such terms.

The response to the shock and dilemma of my youth is not simple. It would be easy enough to say I was naive, that these figures are beyond rehabilitation. They are beyond it, but there is a sense in which their pipe dreams have validity. Each character's past allows for the possibility of a basic contradiction. It is not just that, as Larry, following Ibsen's Relling, says, "The lie of the pipe dream is what gives life to the whole misbegotten mad lot of us."(569–570) It is that the *lie* of the pipe dream is not necessarily a lie. The past lives of all the derelicts is governed by contradictions. Did Jimmy's wife leave him because he was an alcoholic, or did he become an alcoholic because his wife left him (the pipe dream)? Did Larry betray Rosa, or did she reject him (the pipe dream)? Did Harry hate his nagging wife, or does he genuinely revere her memory (the pipe dream)? Was McGloin a victimizer or a victim (the pipe dream) in a corrupt political system? Was Hugo a would-be aristocrat or a genuine revolutionary (the pipe dream)? In short, were these figures the antagonists or protagonists of their privately-conceived melodramatic past histories?[7] Since in each case, both are possible, we can only acknowledge the contradictions. Both explanations may be true. Thus, to say the present is determined by past failure is inaccurate, because in fact the past is indeterminate (as Gina Ehdahl knew). So in one sense Hickey is right in considering Larry's encouraging the bums in their pipe dreams the wrong kind of pity.

But Larry is right from another, all-important, perspective. Regardless of the indeterminacy of their past experiences, the characters we see in the present are shot. As Josie Hogan must come to realize in *A Moon for the Misbegotten* that Jim Tyrone is beyond saving because his drink has all but killed him, so, physically and mentally, the residents of Harry Hope's saloon are beyond saving. Understanding that the past is contradictory will not help them. They can now only be protected from the abyss by their drink.

But that does not resolve the issue for Hickey, who still does not recognize the contradiction involved in his own recent cataclysmic experience, or for Larry, who has always acknowledged the primacy of

---

[7] See my "The Transcendence of Melodrama in *The Iceman Cometh.*" (See p. 18, n. 10).

the contradictory in all things. For Hickey, it is easy to conclude that his claim to have loved his wife is a lie. His whole last-act confession builds up to the great explosion: "Well, you know what you can do with your pipe dream now, you damned bitch!" Certainly his repeated promises to her that he would reform were part of a pipe dream, and the guilt over his not reforming built up the tremendous amount of hostility in him that led finally to his violent act. But in fact, Hickey did love his wife, and his final confession in the play is totally honest when he says that he did. He means it when he says, following his confession of the murder: "Why I loved Evelyn better than anything in life!" He means it just as much as he means it when he calls her a damned bitch. One statement may contradict the other—but both are equally true.

An understanding of Hickey comes best through an understanding of Jamie Tyrone in *Long Day's Journey*, to whom he is closely related.[8] Like his predecessor Hickey, Jamie has always been the life of the party, like Hickey he has deep compassion for people in emotional need (*viz.*, his relation with the whore Fat Violet), and like Hickey he is savagely guilt-ridden, specifically in relation to the woman he has wronged. That in Jamie's case the woman is his mother does not alter the parallel. Nor does the fact that Jamie does not murder his mother: his reference to Mary as "hop head" indicates aggressiveness in the extreme. Jamie talks about a "dead part" of him, the part that has turned his noted ebullience into sardonic aggressiveness toward mother, brother, father, and most notably himself. But he also has a *live* part of him, the part that resides in the things mentioned first: the wit, the compassion, the genuine desire for forgiveness. And this part vitally contradicts the dead part.

And so with Jamie's spiritual ancestor Hickey. When people react to his calling his dead wife a damned bitch, there is the temptation to conclude that this is the real Hickey: a murderous hypocrite whose over-whelming aggressions finally drive him to murder. But murder of whom? The one he loves, of course. (O'Neill uses that famous idea from Oscar Wilde's "Reading Gaol" on more than one occasion.) Hickey's whole long confession in the final act stresses repeatedly the long-standing sincerity of that love, and there is no reason to doubt him. This is one thing he would not lie about. O'Neill brings us to the core of Hickey's contradictory nature as we encounter both the live part of him and the dead part of him in this play—the live part most evident in the joy and release he brings the derelicts. Unfortunately, the live part failed to control him at a crucial instant, and he allowed himself to give way to violence. So when Hickey says, after he recalls referring to his murdered

---

[8]   By this time the similarity has been acknowledged by most biographers and critics.

wife as a damned bitch, which he certainly means, that he loved Evelyn better than anything in life, he also means that, too. The chief *anagnorisis* of the play occurs at the instant he realizes what he has just called his wife.[9] At that moment he recognizes the radical contradiction that has underlain all his reactions. But it is also at this moment that he realizes that the others (Larry excepted) cannot comprehend that recognition. He not only accepts the necessity of his own death but realizes that he now genuinely must save the others. His declaration that he was insane when he murdered his wife is his final gift to them, a gift that grows not out of his insanity, but out of his recognition. Like Jamie he comes to understand that his true nature is rooted in contradiction. And he realizes that while the others' lives have been built out of experiences comparable to his own,[10] that realization cannot come to them—battered, weakened, and in most cases severely limited as they are. So he gives them back their booze—and their sustaining pipe dreams—by declaring his insanity at the time of the murder. He becomes their savior as he denies being their savior.

Finally, we must return to Larry Slade, whom Kurt Eisen correctly calls the play's center of understanding. As quintessentially revealed by Robert Ryan in the American Film Theater production of the early 1970s, Larry's vital contradiction is glaringly obvious. He has become an extremely hard-bitten cynic about life, declaring that he no longer cares about anything or anybody, yet he very definitely is what Jimmy Tomorrow calls "the kindest man among us." He instinctively lives the role of the tired old priest that O'Neill hints at in his first description of him.[11] He listens, he cajoles, he encourages, he reassures. And this role he seems likely to continue in until his much wished-for death, which one suspects is some time off yet. He is well ahead of the others on the subject of contradictions, declaring that he was born to be one of those who has to see all sides of a question, and he seems instinctively to know that what seems genuine aggression among his fellow deadbeats, toward one another and toward him, will inevitably be countered by equally genuine affection.

The real problem in understanding Larry is implicit in his relations with Don Parritt, the son of the woman he once loved and whom he either betrayed or was betrayed by, which is the kind of question inherent in the contradictory interpretations of the past we get concern-

---

[9]   See Stephen Black,"Tragic Anagnorisis in *The Iceman Cometh*," in *Perspectives on O'Neill*, edited by Shyamal Bagchee (U of Victoria, B.C.) 17–32.

[10] See my "The Transcendence of Melodrama in *Long Day's Journey into Night.*"

[11] See Edward L. Shaughnessy, *Eugene O'Neill in Ireland* (Westport, CT: The Greenwoood Press) 24–26.

ing all the derelicts. Like Hickey, he is caught between over-whelming rage and overwhelming guilt, in Larry's case both toward Rosa and toward her son. That he might be the boy's father is intriguing, Rosa Parritt having believed in free love, but not finally that important. What is important is that his proclaimed indifference to the boy is a fake. He is profoundly moved by the boy's story and still more moved by Parritt's ultimate suicide. That story, he says, makes him a *true* convert to death.

Parritt's story is that of a young man who has committed the greatest crime of all. He has betrayed his mother. He has turned her in to the police, for money, along with her fellow bomb-throwing anarchists in what is referred to in the play only as "the Movement." And to make matters worse, he has spent the money he got for it on whores. While he did not actually murder his mother, her incarceration he knows is like death to her. In response to what he has done, Parritt is suffering from guilt the depth of which is so great that it can only be alleviated by his death.

Yet there are aspects to Parritt's character that set him off from Hickey and the others, who also feel guilt. For one thing, he comes without the capacity for laughter into a play that is half dominated by camaraderie and laughter. He can make no contact with the others and does not want to make contact, even with Larry, really, from whom he only seeks not companionship but a kind of absolution, and thus he condemns himself to live in isolation, the worst hell of all for an O'Neill character. Further, despite his desire to "parrot" Hickey, Parritt's protests that he loved his mother, and later that he hated her, are strangely unmoving. We are given no specifics of that love, or that hate really, whereas one of the most telling features of Hickey's long confession from the start is the very specific nature of both his love and his hate for his wife. Stated another way, Parritt is a man without vital contradictions. In contrast to Hickey, the man of most vital contradictions, Parritt is rather an image of raw, unalloyed guilt. He is impossible to fully understand outside the context of O'Neill's own past,[12] but even without that context it is clear that he cannot be comforted by pipe dreams or alcohol, and he can never go through the reversals in his feelings that can allow him the "kinship" that saves the other figures in the play, Larry included. He can parrot others in their confessions, but he cannot convincingly confess. A reprise of O'Neill's self-isolated Orin Mannon in *Mourning Becomes Electra*, who with his

---

[12] I discuss the autobiographical nature of Parritt's story as it applies to O'Neill himself and his brother Jamie in my *New Language of Kinship* 136–140. See also Stephen Black, *Eugene O'Neill: Beyond Mourning and Tragedy* (Yale UP, 1999) 422–424.

sister drove his mother to suicide, Parritt can find no consolation but in death.

Nevertheless, Parritt needs one human contact. He needs Larry to acknowledge and finally lead him. Like Strindberg's Julie, he must be instructed by someone close to do what he knows he must do. He must bring Larry out of his "grandstand" to tell him his crime is unredeemable. And what this does to Larry seems, along with Hickey's *anagnorisis*, one of the great crises of the play. Larry must find that the right kind of pity in this instance is the opposite of the right kind of pity for the others. Larry must stop being the forgiving priest and become the punishing judge, a role that goes entirely against his nature.

Following Parritt's leap from the fire escape, and Hickey's arrest, Larry says he has become the only real convert to death Hickey has made. But his mentioning Hickey is misleading. Hickey's confession has disturbed him, of course, but it is the need to tell a young man who may conceivably be his son to take his own life that has converted him. It is so difficult to reconcile this conversion to the rest of the play that Larry's line about being converted to death was omitted in the 1999 New York production of the play referred to earlier. Elsewhere, I have sought to rationalize Larry's statement in a variety of ways, none of them very clear. But one thing is clear: it is not a suicidal statement. Contrary to one critic's interpretation of this line,[13] Larry makes no move to follow Parritt up to that fire escape, and his posture at the close of the play makes it highly doubtful he ever will. Stephen Black suggests that Larry has awakened to both life and death.[14] Larry will still have the genius to see all sides of a question and will still be embittered by that genius. He will continue to hate the human race yet have a compassion for the human that exceeds everyone's.

No O'Neill play seems so fittingly concluded as this one, with the saturnalia in which each character sings his or her favorite song full volume in glorious disharmony, while Larry sits staring silently in front of him. If Hickey is absent, his spirit is very much there and one gets the feeling it will always be, like Shakespeare's spirit of Caesar. The next morning will of course be the morning after, with all its attendant hauntings and assorted miseries, but the power of eternal renewal is the power alive on stage as this play concludes; and as that idea catches on, as it did so well in the 1999 Kevin Spacey production, the play may increas-

---

[13]   Reviewing the original production of the play, Mary McCarthy was convinced that Larry intends to emulate Parritt and throw himself off the fire escape at the earliest possible moment. See her "Dry Ice," *Partisan Review* 13 (1946): 577–579.

[14]   "Tragic Anagnorsis in *The Iceman Cometh*" 31.

ingly be seen as one of O'Neill's most life-affirming works—rather than as purely lugubrious, as it has been considered over the past half century.[15] Close to twenty years ago I wrote: "*The Iceman Cometh* is ... about the possibilities of human kinship in the face of enervating twentieth-century nihilism."[16] This is a view that I believe is coming to be understood.

---

[15]   See Ben Brantley's and Vincent Canby's reviews of this production, *NY Times*, 4/9/99 and 4/18/99.

[16]   *New Language of Kinship* 146.

Long Day's Journey into Night
and *Hughie*

Long Day's Journey into Night

Since *Long Day's Journey into Night,* is, like *The Iceman Cometh,* so commonly regarded as despairing, much needs to be said in favor of the vitality that makes the play for me both hopeful *and* despairing. The supposed pessimism governing the play is usually based on its dealing with what many today call a *dysfunctional* family. I reject that term in dealing with the play primarily because it is borrowed from the world of the psychological social worker and connotes the clinical, an approach the audience might feel external to rather than included in. The term makes me think of quasi-professionals nodding sagely to one another rather than as an audience which feels itself deeply involved in the experience depicted. Those who feel themselves sufficiently separate from this play as to use the term dysfunctional to describe the family central to it should put the text away or leave the theater, and pick up an article on family life in *Psychology Today.* Seeing this play as an exploration of a dysfunctional family is like seeing *King Lear* as a case study in geriatrics. People who think of this play in such terms are saying, in effect, this play is not about me, not about my father's truculence and miserliness, not about my mother's periods of withdrawal and denial, not about my children's lack of direction. Because of my control of my own life, this is a work I can be aloof from, that I can assess objectively. In fact, it is a play that cannot be assessed objectively. It can only be successfully assessed subjectively.

Long Day's Journey is about a family that is as dysfunctional as most families with adult children are—especially when under trying emotional circumstances. To say that the members of this family speak feelings that most families leave unexpressed is undoubtedly true, but that does not leave this family less functional than most, but more, just because much is spoken in this play that most families leave unspoken. In this play just one member, the drug-addicted mother who is the subject of so much of the family's unease, keeps her true feelings unspoken, except when under the influence of her drug. Her husband and sons actually function very well, function in much the same way the derelicts in *Iceman* function—by alternately attacking and comforting one another. And while most families do not have drug-addicted mothers at their center, most families have some problem which can seemingly never be remedied. Rather than speaking of the Tyrones as a dysfunctional family, perhaps we should begin speaking of them more as a family with a serious problem, but possessing the gift of speaking about that problem more freely than most would under similar circumstances.

While some of the dialogue of *Long Day's Journey* sounds melodramatic, the play is also far from melodrama.[1] Little real interest is generated by whether Mary has reverted to her addiction or whether Edmund has contracted tuberculosis, questions which would be the centers of interest in the play were it melodrama. It is clear almost from the beginning that Mary has fallen back and that Edmund has the disease. Rather, the interest derives from how Mary's and Edmund's conditions affect them and the other two members of the family. Joseph Golden sees it this way:

> Here is a play that derives its ultimate power *not* from plot ... but from a process of character revelation that is awesome in its grinding inevitability, not from the usual sordid probes into the subterranean streams of humans compulsively tearing away from one another, but from a compassionate insight into profoundly lost humans groping blindly, sometimes viciously, often pathetically, *toward* one another; not by melodramatic swirls and eruptions, but by a tightly compressed, well-controlled development of human interrelationships.[2]

Golden is correct in saying the play does not derive its power from plot (for which I would substitute the term melodrama), but from O'Neill's development of the human interrelationships. And those interrelationships are rooted in this play, as in the other plays I look at in this volume, in contradictions within its individual characters.

Contradictions abound in this play: from the play's title and setting to the personalities of its four characters. The meaning of none of its central images is as fixed as it may seem to be in the minds of the men as they think about the drug-addicted Mary. The fog, for example, has comforting as well as threatening connotations in the play. Edmund and Mary both tell us of being reassured by it. And the ambiguous sea that figures in so many of O'Neill's earlier plays, connotes opposing ideas:

---

[1]   See my essay "The Transcendence of Melodrama in *Long Day's Journey into Night.*" See p. 18, n. 10.

[2]   *The Death of Tinker Bell: The American Theatre in the Twentieth Century* (Syracuse UP, 1967) 44–45.

all the way from the panic of isolation in an absurd universe to the reassurance afforded us by the Emersonian idea expressed by Edmund in the play that at moments one can sense the eternal connections between human beings and nature. Other details have similar contradictory connotations: the placement, as Jean Chothia has observed,[3] of the books by late nineteenth century pessimistic writers and philosophers on one side of the stage and the plays of Shakespeare on the other, the mockery of the sons and the moral certainty of the father figured in the first set of books offsetting and offset by the second. One thinks too of Mary's complaint about James's having provided her with a second-hand Packard—used, to be sure, but still a Packard—of her complaints about the cheap way in which the house has been furnished, which has led many scene designers to place a lot of wicker and pine tables on the stage, but others to catch the counter-implication that her complaints may be a sign of her desolate feelings. Most recent productions represent the furniture as quite handsome—more masculine than she might like, perhaps, but not shoddy. Similarly, there are the land deals James has allowed himself to be "stuck with." In spite of the contempt the other three have for these deals, James seems to be accumulating a fairly substantial estate. What Mary and her sons say about James on the subject of money is true but at the same time not true.

But more important are the contradictions within the characters. Is James the "stinking old miser" Edmund accuses him of being at the point at which the seriousness of his illness has just been confirmed and the decision must be made where Edmund will go to for treatment? While James has tentatively decided on a cheaper, state-supported institution, following Edmund's outburst on the subject, he says he never intended Edmund to go to any sanatorium he did not want to go to. Is he lying? I think what O'Neill gets across here, as elsewhere, is that human motives in such circumstances are complex. James sincerely wants the best for his son, but James, because of what he tells us of his childhood, always lives in the shadow of the "poor house." It is as incorrect to say that the first motives govern his responses as it is to say the second do. What he says at a given moment is a response to one set of motives; what he says directly following may be a response to an opposing set of motives. One must guard against the acceptance of anything he says as the final word. The swings back and forth are ongoing. When James says that Edmund can go to whatever sanatorium he wishes, he adds the famous qualification—"within reason"—which takes them back to

---

[3]   In "Trying to Write the Family Play," *The Cambridge Companion to Eugene O'Neill* 196–197.

where they began. Jamie savagely points out that his father is motivated by the "Irish peasant" notion that consumption must be fatal, so why waste the money. But James is also motivated by both a genuine love for his son and a desire for respectability, which counter Jamie's accusation, although the accusation is also legitimate. James is governed (and tortured) by his contradictions, which are finally more integral to his nature than any opinion he may express at a particular moment.

Turning to Mary Tyrone, contradictions in her responses run right through her characterization, contradictions which may be exaggerated by her drug but which are also integral to *her* nature. They are focused first in her famous line, too often taken to signify O'Neill's assertion of life's futility: "The past is the present, isn't it? It's the future, too." But what takes the play beyond such a simple construction is the way Mary's clear definition of the past is played off against multiple other possible interpretations of the past. The play fights the simple blacks and whites of melodrama. She is "weak," her family members say, unable to show the "willpower" to conquer her addiction. But is Mary's succumbing to her drug altogether the result of weakness? She also wanted to be a concert pianist, and there is evidence she had some ability. Was her addiction the result of fearful dependency upon others, or evidence of a strong artistic sensibility frustrated by a talented woman's probable rejection in a man's world? Was it the result of having been attracted at an early age into the role of wife and mother, when her natural inclinations lay elsewhere? Might not her so-called weakness reveal a kind of inner strength, a determination to struggle against the inevitable? I am not claiming it was, of course, but only trying to suggest possible contradictions in her nature associated with a past which is, according to her, the present and the future, too.

More to the point are her responses within the dialogue. In one episode—an exchange late in Act 2, just before her men leave her to go downtown—Mary (in a relatively unnarcotized condition) reveals much about herself.[4] She zig-zags among contradictory feelings associated with Edmund's health, her rage at Doc Hardy for preaching "will power," her husband's niggardliness, her fear of being left alone, her genuine concern that she is hurting her son, and her denials, which always represent the nadir of her efforts to overcome her fears. And out of these marked shifts in feeling comes a moment of startling clarity:

> How could you believe me—when I can't believe myself? I've become such a liar. I never lied about anything once upon a time. Now I have to lie,

---

[4]   See my "The Stature of *Long Day's Journey into Night*," *The Cambridge Companion to Eugene O'Neill* 206–216.

especially to myself. But how can you understand, when I don't myself. I've never understood anything about it, except that one day long ago I found I could no longer call my soul my own. (769–770)

But Mary's clarity here leads inevitably to a new theme. The Blessed Virgin Mary will one day forgive her, she says, and she will once again be "sure" of herself, even when she hears herself "scream with agony." O'Neill seems to present Mary's religion as the one possible means for her recovery (as it may well have been for O'Neill's mother), but when Mary lowers "her voice to a strange tone of whispered confidence," that religion sounds like a new version of her drug. So her clearest moment is followed by still another contradiction. And the passage ends with her once again in denial:

> ... She [the Virgin Mary] will believe in me, and with Her help it will be so easy. ... (*Then as Edmund remains hopelessly silent, she adds sadly*) Of course, you can't believe that. ... Now I think of it, you might as well go uptown. I forgot I'm taking a drive. I have to go to the drugstore. (770)

The more famous scene focusing on Mary is that opening Act 3, which contains many of the same contradictory elements just looked at, except that in Act 3 Mary has come more fully under the influence of her morphine, the drug coloring and distorting her several contradictory recollections of the past, making them at times feel more like ravings. And in her final appearance during the last scene of the play, the contradictions, along with anything resembling the real world, disappear, and her lines suggest a seamless pattern of fantasized memory. The drug obscures the contradictions in her nature, and the loss of contradiction in what she says makes her more truly pitiful than at any other point in the play. The central contradiction of that final scene resides not in Mary, but in the men, who must recognize in their wife-mother the source of both their love and their hate. She becomes the great life-giver/life-destroyer by whom they are both uplifted and devastated.

What needs to be said more specifically about the vitality of this play rests primarily on two related factors: 1) the character of Jamie,[5] than whom there are few characters in literature more vitally contradictory, and 2) the sense of merging one gets from this family during its rhythmically recurrent harmonious moments.

Quoting from what I have previously written about Jamie, he is

> the holy sinner of this play, the epitome of its view of the human condition as innately contradictory. On the negative side Jamie is its most corrupt

---

[5] It is noteworthy that among the play's four major figures, Edmund, the representation of the playwright himself at an earlier age, is the only one not deeply contradictory in his attitudes.

figure. Not only is his alcoholism pernicious, but along with it come other aspects of his corruption: the sardonic tongue, the malicious sexual behavior, the indolence, the gambling and general financial profligacy, and his dependence on the support of his father. So sardonic does he become ... that he refers to Mary as a 'hop-head.'... But on the all-important other hand, Jamie Tyrone is the one truly humane figure in the play—and while this idea may seem incomprehensible to some, it contributes much to the kind of stature the play possesses." In Jamie we are aware of "the deepest kind of emotional suffering accompanied by the recognition and under-standing of that suffering by the sufferer. When Jamie says early in the play that he knows how his father feels about Mary's condition, he speaks out of an empathy which is his unique gift. Along with the large capacity of his own suffering, he can feel the suffering of others—even Mary's.

The way to understand Jamie best is to consider

his rendition of his visit to the bordello, where he chose as his sexual companion 'Fat Violet,' the whore who is about to be let go because none of the customers want her. Though speaking sarcastically (which is his wont), Jamie's description of his time with her as a 'Christian act' is in fact just that. He felt sorry for Vi, he says—sorry for her when his purpose in going to the brothel was to make him forget his sorrow for himself." But then, he says, he stayed and had sex with her to make her feel better about herself, an act which "may be seen as the one act of completely selfless giving in the play.[6]

Jamie Tyrone is like no other character discussed in this book so much as Chekhov's doctor in *The Three Sisters*. A vital contradiction in drama is a contradiction that enhances our sense of a character's humanity. It is not simply that at critical moments the character is inconsistent in word or behavior. It is that the force of the contradiction is such that we recognize the character's individuality more deeply than we would if the character were not contradictory. We are more, not less, convinced of the love Arkadina has for Konstantin by her radical reversals in feeling toward him. And so with Julie's responses to Jean, or Hjalmar's to his wife and daughter. Of none of these relationships would it be correct to say that because of the outbursts of animosity that the affection they demonstrate is false or put on. The outbursts are part of the emotional rhythm of their relationships. The claims that pull them away from each other are as strong as those binding them together. Conflicting claims are part of the human condition.

And what holds for the characters just mentioned holds especially for the doctor and Jamie. Like the doctor, Jamie sees, especially when

---

[6]   The quoted passages in this paragraph are taken from my "Stature" essay (see note 4 above), 214–215.

drunk, appallingly exaggerated images of his failures, and gives full vent to his self-hatred. The doctor is not vindictive toward anyone the way Jamie is when Jamie blames Edmund for being born and taunts him as "Mama's baby, Papa's pet!" The doctor's abuse is more restricted to himself in his famous drunken scene. But he does break a valuable ceramic clock that belonged to the sisters' mother, and his failure to assist at the fire is certainly comparable to Jamie's periodically vicious cynicism when it is turned outward. At the same time, like the doctor Jamie is capable of giving to others in the ways he alone is sensitive enough to recognize they most need. Jamie gives to his brother the way the doctor gives to Andrei; he gives him vital emotional support at a critical moment.

What distinguishes O'Neill in these late plays from the other playwrights is what I, following Simon Harford in *More Stately Mansions*, have called character merging, and that merging comes to be most evident through the character of Jamie Tyrone in this play, and his stand-in Erie Smith in *Hughie* (who I look at briefly at the conclusion of this chapter.) The idea of character merging, comes in the form of sudden bursts of mutual sympathy between characters who are in the midst of sometimes fierce disagreement, to which they return following the bursts of mutual sympathy. The agreeable sides of the contradictory responses in each character join forces for a brief time.

We first get such a burst during the family's responses to Edmund's story of Shaughnessy's pigs—later to be repeated in the action surrounding Hogan's pigs in *A Moon for the Misbegotten*. The mutual laughter of the family to the story shows them at their most harmonious in the play, all of them pleased at Shaughnessy's humiliation of the "Standard Oil millionaire." But the harmony is broken by James's recurrent anger both at his sons and at Shaughnessy for getting him in trouble with his rich and powerful neighbor.

JAMES.

(*Admiringly before he thinks*) The damned old scoundrel! By God, you can't beat him! (*He laughs—then stops abruptly and scowls.*) The dirty blackguard! He'll get me in serious trouble yet. I hope you told him I'd be mad as hell—

EDMUND.

I told him you'd be tickled to death over the great Irish victory, and so you are. Stop faking, Papa.

JAMES.

Well, I'm not tickled to death.

MARY.

(*Teasingly*) You are, too, James, You're simply delighted. (726)

The emphasis here is on James's countering mood, but the harmony is certainly present, especially in that it involves Mary, who is nowhere else so in tune with the others. And in that harmony is represented the merging of feelings that tells us they are very much a family, in spite of all that is to follow.

The volatile contradictions in brother Jamie makes the idea especially evident later in the first act, where Jamie and his father testily discuss all the play's themes before going out to work on the hedge. Their merging amid the quarreling is focused on two themes: Mary's addiction and Edmund's illness. James repeatedly attacks Jamie for his dilatoriness, drinking and financial dependency, while Jamie repeatedly attacks James for his niggardliness accompanied by his uncontrollable buying of "bum property." There is a flash of mutual sympathy with the first mention of whether Edmund is infected. They argue over Doc Hardy's medical abilities, but come together for an instant as the seriousness of Edmund's condition becomes apparent:

JAMIE.

... You talked to him when you went uptown yesterday, didn't you?

TYRONE.

He couldn't say anything for sure yet. He's to phone me today before Edmund goes to see him.

JAMIE.

(*Slowly*) He thinks it's consumption, doesn't he, Papa?

TYRONE.

(*Reluctantly*) He said it might be.

JAMIE.

(*Moved, his love for his brother coming out*) Poor kid! God damn it! (*But then Jamie's anger again breaks out.*) It might never have happened if you'd sent him to a real doctor when he first got sick. (729)

Their closeness is clear, but the rhythm of accusation and counter-accusation begins anew. There is about six parts antagonism to one part mutual sympathy is this episode, but if played correctly, the one part will balance the six parts. This is especially true when the conversation turns to Mary. Here the responses of the two seem to merge into a single response—again, just for a moment. James muses on how well Mary has seemed since her return from the sanatorium.

TYRONE.

... It's been heaven to me. This home has been a home again. But I needn't tell you, Jamie. (*His son looks at him, for the first time with an understanding sympathy. It is as if suddenly a deep bond of common feeling existed between them in which their antagonisms could be forgotten.*)

JAMIE.

(*Almost gently*). I've felt the same way, Papa. (734)

But again, James's suspicions of Jamie are once again aroused merely because Jamie has said Mary "seems" all right, and the re-criminations return ever more virulently.

I keep thinking in writing this of Prince Hal's famous image in Shakespeare's *1 Henry IV* when he imagines himself imitating the sun "breaking through the foul and ugly mists" that "seemed to strangle" it. The breaking through of the sun suggests the feeling created in this play when characters merge amid the foul and ugly mists of recrimination. The instances of such mergings are few and far between but the more impressive for being so. We hear them in scenes involving James and Mary, especially when they momentarily express their genuine love for one another, and between Mary and Edmund—in exchanges like the one I discussed earlier, in each case the harmony being broken by one of Mary's denials. And they are quite audible in the first of the two long exchanges in the final act, that involving James and Edmund, in their heated discussion of what kind of sanatorium Edmund will go to, and especially in their autobiographical monologues. In the second instance, each character, though primarily listening to the other, seems to grow increasingly a part of the other character's experience. Edmund, prepared to be bored by his father's oft-repeated story of his childhood, this time can honestly say that he knows his father "a lot better now"; while James, despite his repeated attacks on Edmund's literary paragons, genuinely hears in Edmund's monologue about his life at sea "the makings of a poet."

But the instances of character-merging seem most feelingly instigated by the self-condemning Jamie. It is Jamie who first responds sympathetically to the mention of Edmund's illness, as it is Jamie who is described empathizing with his father regarding Mary. And it is Jamie who feels and identifies his mergings with Edmund during their all-important late-night conversation. As their attacks upon one another in this episode are virulent, so are their comings together the deepest of any in the play. It is of course often the virulence that prompts the emotional reunion. These sharp twists and shifts, tightly intertwined in the dialogue, are most recognizable in their intensity, especially when Mary is their subject:

JAMIE.

(*In a cruel, sneering tone with hatred in it*) Where's the hop head? Gone to sleep? (*Edmund jerks as if he's been struck. There is a tense silence. Edmund's face looks stricken and sick. Then in a burst of rage he springs from his chair.*)

EDMUND.

You dirty bastard! (*He punches his brother in the face, a blow that glances off his cheekbone. For a second Jamie reacts pugnaciously and half rises from his chair to do battle, but suddenly he seems to sober up to a shocked realization of what he has said and he sinks back limply.*)

JAMIE.

(*Miserably*) Thanks, Kid. I certainly had that coming. Don't know what made me—booze talking—You know me, Kid. (818)

They become especially close here, because of Edmund's physical violence and immediate regret, and Jamie's strong appeal to their mutual hurt:

I've known about Mama so much longer than you. Never forget the first time I got wise. Caught her in the act with a hypo. Christ, I'd never dreamed before that any women but whores took dope. (*He pauses.*) And then this stuff of you getting consumption. It's got me licked. We've been more than brothers. You're the only pal I've ever had. I love your guts. (818)

And that Jamie will within a few minutes say he hates Edmund's guts takes away not a whit from the sincerity of the love and the sense of merging conveyed here. And despite what he says, it is not the alcohol that prompts these protestations of both affection and hostility so much as it is the rhythm of Jamie's feelings heard *in extremis.*

The main thing that sets Jamie apart from the others is his awareness of the critical contradictions in his nature and his ability to articulate that awareness. In his "big" confession of the scene, he begins with the insight that Hickey only comes to at the end of his confession: that (with Wilde) he hates the one he loves even at the instant of his most unconditional love, and that the hate is always to be feared. It is the hate that prompted Hickey to kill his wife, and that Jamie warns Edmund against:

Want to warn you—against me. ... I've been a rotten bad influence. And worst of it is, I did it on purpose. ... Did it on purpose to make a bum of you. Or part of me did. A big part. That part that's been dead so long. That hates life. ... What I wanted to say is, I'd like to see you become the greatest success in the world. But you'd better be on your guard. Because I'll do my damnedest to make you fail. ... Think it over when you're away from me in the sanatorium. ... And when you come back, look out for me. I'll be waiting to welcome you with that "my old pal" stuff, and give you the glad hand, and at the first good chance I get stab you in the back. (820–821)

This is O'Neill's deepest insight of the late plays, and it goes back to Strindberg's in *Easter*, when Elis tells of the man who was a "faithless" friend to his father while at the same time a true friend. In this confession Jamie merges with his brother because he puts himself wholly in his brother's place, feeling with Edmund's prospective feelings as well as his own. He prompts us to feel Edmund's predicted delight in his brother's welcome, a delight so profound that Edmund will not be ready for the inevitable attack. In effect, Jamie at this moment of most selfless bonding is warning Edmund to distrust their mergings. Jamie knows well that he is Edmund's "old pal," knows it so well that he is at pains here to warn him of the extremes to which the "dead part" of his nature can lead him. I have heard Jamie's attitude here described as his "hypocrisy." It is the very opposite of hypocrisy. It suggests a merging of the two deeper than anything that has gone before. In trying to save his brother he knowingly tears apart the attachment to his brother that is "all I've got left." In his own life, as Stephen Black most recently has told us, O'Neill was trying in this play and especially its sequel to make amends to his brother for having many years before accepted—indeed in part caused—the separation.[7]

Long Day's Journey into Night puts before us the extremes that Jamie represents as the live part and the dead part of human existence like no other O'Neill play—or, for that matter, any play looked at in this study. Nowhere else are the recriminations so grim and insistent, but nowhere is the sense of mutual support gone so deep (unless it be when Jim and Josie come together in *A Moon for the Misbegotten*). The stasis reached at the end of the play is a dark one. It has been a journey into the dark night of human relationships. But it has also been about the fleetingly restorative power that only such relationships can have, unless one has become self-protectively narcotized. Like the alternatives suggested by what Chebutykin says vis-a-vis what Olga says at the end of *The Three Sisters*, the final scenic image of the narcotized Mary *vis-à-vis* the surrounding presence of her three men is that of a kind of death-in-life and life ongoing.

Hughie

I think I might best close this discussion of *Long Day's Journey* with a brief look at this play's immediate successor in the O'Neill canon, the one-act *Hughie*, with which it shares, despite the many differences in the characters and the setting, something essential in common. Erie Smith, the small-time gangster and central figure of the play, is the very opposite of Jamie Tyrone in cultural background and intellect. He lacks Jamie's wit, and he has none of Jamie's instinctive concern for others revealed in Jamie's attitude toward Fat Violet. But the two are similarly

---

[7]   See Black, *Eugene O'Neill: Beyond Mourning and Tragedy* 298, 465–469.

open, voluble, and vitally contradictory; and when Jamie says of Edmund, "You're all I've got left," we are hearing the same feelings Erie had for his lost friend, the earlier night clerk, Hughie. Erie feels as isolated by the loss of Hughie as Jamie feels he will be once he has cut himself adrift by his confession that he means to harm his brother, whom he loves. What Erie seeks from Hughes, the new night clerk, is of the same order as what Jamie has always had with his brother: a capacity for an emotional merging focused on some particular subject, in the case of Jamie and Edmund their attitudes toward women, or drink, or their father, or finally their mother. In the case of Erie and Hughes, it is a merging focused on the crap shoot, which both know is fixed by Erie, but which gives both a sense of order and reassurance in the seemingly eternal night of the play—the night of Erie's fears and Hughes's chaotic imaginings.

In other words, through the parallels between Jamie and Edmund, and Erie and the night clerk, *Hughie* is a fitting sequel to *Long Day's Journey*. The other, more important sequel, however, is the play I shall discuss in the following, concluding section of this study.

A Moon for the Misbegotten

A Moon for the Misbegotten is a play about alcohol, sex, love, and death. Jim Tyrone, the figure we have until now known as Jamie (and in other manifestations as Hickey and Erie), is both O'Neill's tribute to his dead brother, to whom the play is in part a plea for forgiveness, and the dramatic embodiment of O'Neill's final coming to grips with his two-decades long struggle with death, as Stephen Black has brilliantly recognized.[1] It is what I have elsewhere called an elegiac play, an autumnal play, its final mood encapsulated in Jim's quote from Keats's "Ode to a Nightingale":

> Now more than ever seems it rich to die,
> To cease upon the midnight with no pain,
> In such an ecstasy.

It is hard to imagine O'Neill's having written anything after it, despite his ideas and notes for subsequent plays discussed by Virginia Floyd.[2]

The play's plot, which seems more complicated than it is, pits melodrama against tragedy. The secondary plot line, established at length up until the middle of the second act, is a version of the old "farmer's daughter" story of seduction and prospective blackmail—in short, a comic melodrama. In order to entrap a wealthy suitor (Jim) into marrying his daughter, a scheming farmer (Phil) plans to "discover" the suitor in bed with his daughter (Josie). Closely involved with this secondary melodrama, and equally comic, is the story of whether Jim plans to sell the land on which Phil and his daughter are tenants to the millionaire Harder at a huge profit, even though he has promised it to the Hogans for a minimal amount. This element of the plot must be played for farcical effect, especially the action surrounding the humiliation of Harder at the hands of the poor Irish tenant farmer and his "over size" daughter. These plot elements are intended to have the effect of situation comedy, or comic melodrama. They have everything to do with farce and bald deception and very little to do with any kind of deeper exploration of the characters involved.

---

[1]   See Black, *Eugene O'Neill: Beyond Mourning and Tragedy* 298, 465–469.

[2]   See *Eugene O'Neill at Work* (NY: Frederick Ungar, 1981).

The primary plot line, however, or what becomes the primary plot line midway through the play, abruptly sweeps the secondary plot line, the comic melodrama, aside. At the moment Josie realizes that Jim has never had any intention of selling the land to Harder and that Phil's scheme is really only intended to get his daughter married, the emphasis shifts radically to the main subject of the play: the psychological agonies and emerging, though short-lived, mutual love of Josie Hogan and Jim Tyrone. In this play, O'Neill toys with a popular audience's expectations, knowing that such an audience willy-nilly expects melodrama, then pulls the rug out from under it.[3] The play, like life itself he seems to imply, is not really about the intrigues and deceptions that are the stuff of most popular entertainment but about the struggle toward self-revelation. It is finally, as I have said, also a play about the coming to grips with death. Josie comes to realize that Jim's drink has in fact already killed him, that her midnight encounter with her lover is in fact an encounter with death, but a death that "ceases upon the midnight with no pain." Like Phil, the playwright tricks his audience, and while some audiences have felt betrayed, having hoped for a comic melodrama with a happy ending, others have experienced a kind of catharsis from the play rivaling that in Shakespearean and ancient Greek tragedy.

All this I have already discussed in earlier writings previously mentioned. What I have not looked at is the degree to which contradictions central to the major characters make us become so deeply involved with them. I shall begin with the least of the three, Phil Hogan, who follows in a long tradition of tricksters and comic manipulators in folk drama going back to the middle ages, and before that to Roman comedy. Part leprechaun, reminiscent of Ibsen's troll king, Phil sets all the play's secondary action in motion. He quite literally entices Jim to the farm with the promise of drink and entertainment, trusting his daughter will do the same with the promise of sex. Of the play's primary action—that involving the mutual confessions of Jim and Josie—he knows nothing at the start, though he is very much affected by it in the end.

But the end makes us finally question whether Phil is in fact the leprechaun he pretends to be at the start. His motivation is ambiguous. Late in the play he protests that it was his daughter's prospective happiness in marrying the man she loved, and Jim's in marrying her, that prompted his scheming rather than the promise of personal wealth:

---

[3] I treat this theme in my essay "The Transcendence of Melodrama in *A Touch of the Poet* and *A Moon for the Misbegotten*." (See p. 18, n. 10.) Eric Bentley states that the play is a "well-made melodrama in which the expectations of melodrama are disappointed." See "Eugene O'Neill's Pieta," in *The Dramatic Event* (NY: Horizon Books, 1954) 31.

But it wasn't his money, Josie. I did see it was the last chance—the only one left to bring the two of you to stop your damned pretending, and face the truth that you loved each other. I wanted you to find happiness—by hook or crook, one way or another, what did I care how? I wanted to save him, and I hoped he'd see that only your love could—It was his talk of the beauty he saw in you that made me hope—And I knew he'd never go to bed with you even if you'd let him unless he married you. And if I gave a thought to his money at all, that was the least of it, and why shouldn't I want to have you live in ease and comfort for a change, like you deserve, instead of in this shanty on a lousy farm, slaving for me. (944)

How should we take what Phil says? The easy answer, the answer which would fittingly conclude a comic melodrama in which the schemer is revealed to have a heart of gold, would be to accept what he says at face value. He has underneath his scheming been thinking of his daughter's happiness all along. But he does include that suspicious phrase, "If I gave a thought to his money at all, that was the least of it!" Earlier in the final act, just after Phil discovers Josie holding the sleeping Jim's head on her breast and protests that it has just been her happiness that he meant to bring about, Josie accuses him of lying, saying he would "swear on a Bible while you were stealing it," and there is no reason to assume he is not lying in the quoted speech. His saying Jim's money was the least of it could be part of the same Irish palaver he has been using throughout to deceive both Jim and Josie. If this were a vaudeville act, we might imagine him winking at the audience as he says this. Of course he wants to get his hands on Jim's money, and not just for his daughter's happiness. How can one know that now his scheming has stopped and his role of sentimental father has taken over?

The answer is, of course, that one cannot know, any more than one can know that Phil is and will always be a scheming Irishman. There is no denying he loves his daughter and sincerely wishes for her happiness—and, as he adds, Jim's as well. Can a loving father also be a self-interested schemer? Of course he can. It is in the very nature of the beast Phil Hogan is that contradictions govern his essential nature. Thinking back to his pretending to come home drunk, taking a swing a Jim, even to when he goads Harder, we can never decide what he is really out to achieve. We never know, as Phil never knows, which motives are governing him, if it can be said that one or the other set of motives dominates what he says at any given moment. We find ourselves tilting one way, then the other, in assessing him, and there is no final way to tilt. He is literally both sides of him at once. Seeing Phil in these terms de-sentimentalizes a play O'Neill never intended to be sentimental. The broad strokes with which the playwright must draw the

Irishman allow the two sides of the glaringly recognizable contradiction in Phil's nature to be seen as inseparable from each other.

Phil's vital contradiction sets the standard for the play, but Phil is the least complex of the play's three characters. The contradictions within Jim and Josie are more complex. Josie's basic contradiction, which at first seems simple, is far from simple. It resides in the idea of her being a virginal whore. We come to know that Josie is literally a virgin, but through much of the play we are asked to believe her "whorish" pose. She is given to what Jim calls the "smut stuff," possessed of what one critic calls a "mythic sexual appetite,"[4] and thus capable of an uninhibited directness and an unashamed use of her body. These qualities early take the form of sexually inviting gestures but later will take the form of a physical giving and forgiving that is wholly genuine. In *Desire Under the Elms,* O'Neill refers to his heroine's mixture of "lust and mother love" in regard to her lover, and it is this mixture—certainly in the earlier twentieth century, if not today, indicative of a glaring contradiction—that O'Neill has in mind in his characterization of Josie Hogan.

Aside from her literal virginity, Josie is "virginal" in her attitudes throughout. She is prone to believe what people tell her, essentially unaware of the potential duplicity that may be practiced against her. Even her whorish pose has an element of the virginal about it. She takes things and people at face value, especially her father, whom she believes she dominates but really is dominated by—until the end. O'Neill wants us to see her as Jim does, when he is not possessed of his demons: as "real and healthy and clean and fine and warm and strong and kind." (915)

Josie Hogan is O'Neill's ideal woman because of the essential contradiction between her innocence and her brazenness. If the biographies are correct, the younger O'Neill could never be at ease with "nice girls" so much as with the tarts and street-walkers his brother first brought him into contact with (treated in the Sheaffer, Gelbs, and Black biographies). They gave him an emotional release more important than the sexual release he sought from them. He was never afraid of baring his soul to them. And in a variety of ways he created characters in whom he tried to approximate the whores and whore-like women he'd come in contact with in life: Anna in *Anna Christie*, Cybel in *The Great God Brown*, even the described Fat Violet of *Long Day's Journey*. But none of them embodied the various facets of personality he saw as his ideal until

---

[4]   Edward Shaughnessy, *Down the Nights and Down the Days* (U of Notre Dame P, 1996) 182.

Josie. Because like it or not today, he persisted in what his up-bringing dictated about a virtuous woman's virginity before marriage. Phil, for example, is certain Jim will never sleep with Josie without marrying her. Yet at the same time, the whore's utter abandon enchanted him. It meant he could be anything he wanted with her, as he could not with other women. And so he had to feel about his ideal the way he felt about a whore—even down to being crudely sexually aroused—while at the same time feeling as he would about a virgin. This necessity for Jim generates the characterization of Josie Hogan.

O'Neill makes it all work, of course, by giving Josie her own set of problems—which only Jim really understands. Rather than making this solely Jim's play, O'Neill makes it Jim's and Josie's play. Both are the misbegotten of the title, and if Josie's haunts are more remediable than Jim's, they are no less painful than his. Her size has been the source of constant grief to her. To compensate, meaning to attract the masculine attention most young women seek, she plays the whore. It is an act that has become part of her nature. And that means she must be played so that crudely whore-like language and gestures seem part of her nature. Not all actors playing the role fully bring this out—not even the incomparable Colleen Dewhurst, who defined the role for audiences of the last quarter of the twentieth century through her interpretation of it on stage and television. Josie must appear genuinely vulgar with her "smut stuff," so much so that Jim in his alcoholic fit of awful remembrance can briefly but convincingly confuse her with the "whore on the train." She must at times actually seem as though she were the "blonde pig who looked more like a whore than twenty-five whores."(931) Only then can we begin to sense the vital nature of Josie's contradiction. That she has slapped her would-be lovers "groggy" as they make their advances is not really the point. It is that she is capable of making them make the advances even while they know what will be the result. She has got to be the whore at the same time that contradictorily she will always be the virgin. And the shame that results from her being the whore is what Jim alone recognizes as the true nature of her suffering. It is a shame that he also recognizes as parallel to his own.

No psychologist or priest ever brought a sufferer to face his or her suffering the way Jim snaps Josie out of her whore "pipe dream." All the "live" part of him is revealed here, as much as in Jamie's attempt to save his brother in *Long Day's Journey*:

TYRONE.
... What a bluff you are, Josie. (*Teasingly*) You and your lovers, Messalina—when you never—

JOSIE.

(*With a faint spark of her old defiance*) You're a liar.

TYRONE.

"Pride is the sin by which the angels fell." Are you going to keep that up—with me?

JOSIE.

(*Feebly*) You think I've never because no one would—because I'm a great ugly cow—

TYRONE.

(*Gently*) Nuts! You could have had any one of them. You kidded them till you were sure they wanted you. That was all you wanted. And then you slapped them groggy when they asked for more. But you had to keep convincing yourself—

JOSIE.

(*Tormentedly*) Don't, Jim.

TYRONE.

You can take the truth, Josie—from me. Because you and I belong to the same club. We can kid the world but we can't fool ourselves, like most people, no matter what we do—nor escape ourselves no matter where we run away. Whether it's the bottom of a bottle, or a South Sea Island, we'd find our own ghosts there waiting to greet us—"sleepless with pale commemorative eyes," as Rossetti wrote. (923)

Josie's subsequent admission that she is a virgin, aside from parodying the old take in melodrama of the "fallen" woman confessing she is *not* a virgin, signifies the point at which the play finally stops being the comic melodrama and focuses its major attention on Jim. But it is important not to overlook Josie's reactions following Jim's confession. The unrestrained comfort and forgiveness she gives him has the same unashamed, uninhibited quality of her whore-like attitudes earlier in the play. Part of the vital contradiction that is central to Josie is in the much argued-over Pieta image,[5] the all-out, unrestrained giving to her dying hero. There is a quality of abandon in her even as she nurtures her sin-sick lover.

Vital contradictions are finally most central to the play's dying hero, Jim Tyrone. To begin with, we are introduced to a figure who is on the one hand the embodiment of sleaze, a Broadway bad-guy but a step removed from Erie Smith. Quite apart from the incessant drinking and whoring, we are introduced at the start to a figure

---

[5]   See Bentley 30-33. See also Rolf Scheibler, *The Late Plays of Eugene O'Neill* (Berne: Francke Verlag, 1970) 85–96.

dressed in an expensive, dark-brown suit, tight-fitting and drawn in at the waist, dark-brown, made-to-order shoes and silk socks, a white shirt, silk handkerchief in breast pocket, a dark tie. This get-up suggests that he follows a style set by well-groomed Broadway gamblers who would like to be mistaken for Wall Street brokers. (875)

But also at the start we get a striking counter-impression. He addresses Phil in Latin, and Latin that suggests he has advanced knowledge of the language, this accompanied by a translation fully in keeping with the image of a Broadway sport:

TYRONE.

"*Fortunate senex, ergo, tua rura manebunt,*
et tibi magna satis, quamvis lapis omnia nudus."

HOGAN.

... That was Latin. I know it by ear. What the hell—insult does it mean?

TYRONE.

Translated very freely into Irish English, something like this. ... "Ain't you the lucky old bastard to have this beautiful farm, if it is full of nude rocks." (875)

This of course anticipates the vaudeville routine Jim and Phil will shortly commence dealing with Jim's desire for a drink. What is captured is the image of an Erie Smith who can quote Latin, a Damon Runyonesque figure who can also quote Milton and Dante Gabriel Rossetti with ease. Small-time Broadway gamblers also do not normally possess Jim's biting wit. What we get here is a set of contradictions, coming immediately upon his first appearance, suggesting the vitality essential to his nature. Similar contradictions, of course, helped define the personality of Jim's more youthful embodiment in *Long Day's Journey*.

The contradictions in Jim manifest themselves in a variety of ways. Along with the erudition and the wit set against Jim's somewhat sleazy appearance is the genuinely giving nature set against his rapacity, suggested later in the play by his description of his experience on the train and his attempt to rape Josie. That rapacity is first suggested in his relationship with Phil. The vaudeville routine between them, which exists primarily for its humor, expresses two opposing ideas. Jim has come to cadge that drink, no doubt about it, but he also wants to give Phil the pleasure he knows the old man will get from the encounter. It would be easy enough to say, as people usually do in assessing literary characters, that what Jim really wants is the drink, or what Jim really want is to provide the entertainment, but both motives exist alongside each other and at the same time—like Phil's grasping desire for Jim's money and Phil's fatherly desire for his daughter's happiness. And the same goes for Jim's attitudes toward Josie, which will constitute his major reason for coming. He has come for her body, but her body in two contradictory ways: for near-violent sexual release, and for the peace that will let him die in peace.

We get deeper when we actually encounter Jim's much-proclaimed corrupt sexuality. There is something Dostoyevskian about this aspect of Jim's personality. Not exactly a rapist, as are some of Dostoyevski's vitally contradictory figures,[6] Jim, in spite of his inebriation, always, as he says, knows what he is doing. His lust for Josie when he attacks her is precisely the lust he has for his "dainty little whores" and had for the "blonde pig" on the train. O'Neill intends it to be as offensive as Josie's pose, and the one who is most offended is Jim himself. Here in his drunkenness he most resembles the drunken doctor breaking the treasured ceramic clock in *The Three Sisters*, tormented by his sense of personal degradation into greater personal degradation. Like the doctor's "getting back" at the sisters' mother by getting drunk, not assisting at the fire, and breaking the clock, Jim's sexual aggressiveness is an enactment of his revenge against his mother for betraying him by dying and earlier for depriving him of her attention during her drug-addicted states (not mentioned in this play but obviously there once we know the Tyrone story).

For Jim, the passion for sex that gets back at his mother resides alongside the contradictory passion that seeks all-out maternal forgiveness. The same untrammeled lust that prompts the attack, part of which is prompted by her "beautiful breasts," exists in tandem with his overwhelming need (a kind of lust, too) for comfort and forgiveness, also directly associated with those breasts. But the revenge he takes against his mother is nothing to the revenge he has taken upon himself, a revenge which effectively already has had the result of death-through-drink not so slowly approaching. Jim must be played as physically incurable, in the last stages of an alcoholism that has already destroyed the "membranes of his throat" referred to comically in his vaudeville routine with Phil in what may be a hint as to his actual condition. Jason Robards caught that condition on stage (though not on television) by showing symptoms in his coughing suggestive of the last stages of tuberculosis. So along with the lust, it is with the knowledge of approaching death that Jim has come to Josie.

---

[6]   I have in mind Svidrigaylov in *Crime and Punishment* and Stavrogin in *The Possessed*.

I have skirted Jim's confession itself, his great agon, in part because I have discussed it before,[7] and in part because neither quotation nor descriptive assessment of it can ever equal the experiencing of it when performed adequately. (I have unfortunately several times seen it performed inadequately.) The set of realizations of what he has done must approach the set of realizations Oedipus goes through before tearing out his eyes. He must convincingly demonstrate his awareness of the monumental contradiction between his love and his behavior. It exceeds even Hickey's sudden awareness resulting from his outburst: "You know what you can do with your pipe dream now, you damned bitch!" It is akin to Mr. Kurtz's famous "The horror, the horror!" in Conrad's *Heart of Darkness*. And from that terrible awareness Jim has come to seek some kind of relief before his inevitable death.

Finally, there is the question of the constant and radical shifts in feeling between the two central characters. In dealing with this idea in my kinship book, I was anticipated by the Swiss critic Rolf Scheibler,[8] who first recognized the "cyclical structure" of the dialogue between the two, the "musical possibilities" of which remind him of Ibsen, Strindberg, and Chekhov (Scheibler 73, n. 24). In each of what he identifies as the "five scenes" of their relationship, Scheibler finds "peace and battle" alternating, each of the "battles more fierce, the moments of peace longer drawn-out. ..." (68) And later, he adds: "The scenes follow a rhythm of alternating tension and relaxation. ..." (71) Scheibler's most important point may be that the moments of peace become increasingly "drawn-out." Scheibler's insights lead me again to the question of character "merging." The swings between the tension and the peace, between the hostility and the comings together in the rhythm of kinship, are apparent enough. Far less pronounced than the hostility expressed in the other late plays, the natural hostility between Jim and Josie is seen at first in his more or less puritanical aggressiveness and her defensiveness, later in his sexual aggressiveness and her disgust. Josie has not really *seen* this bleakest side of him until, egged on by her belief that he is going to sell the farm to Harder, she gives him the full temptation. The countering comings together are expressed in their mutual need for and desire to help one another. Recognition is the key idea here, not the melodramatic recognition Josie experiences in regard to Phil's deception, but Jim's instinctual recognition of what Josie is hiding and Josie's instinctual final recognition of what Jim needs. The climax of the play is Jim's confession followed by his night at Josie's breast, that image

---

[7]   It has been the centerpiece of my two previous published discussions of the play, one in my *Kinship* book, and the other in the essay mentioned in note 3 above.

[8]   See *The Late Plays of Eugene O'Neill*, 57–101.

which so offended Eric Bentley because to him it smacks of infantilism and, implicitly, sentimentality.[9] To see Jim's needs as infantile is one thing. The presumed deprivation of his mother's love at crucial points in his childhood has rendered him infantile, and that is hardly a flaw in a dramatic characterization. The suggestion of sentimentality is another. I wonder whether those who consider it sentimental simply find it hard to take. If it is sentimental it is presumably shallow, and it is anything but shallow. Josie's willingness to nurture him comes as a result of her finally *getting the point,* of her recognition of his real need for absolution before he dies. And if we too get the point from the convincingly all-out nature of his confession, we just might be genuinely affected. What we see enacted is the active part of what is called forgiveness.

Rather than seeing Josie's holding Jim as a Pietà image, one might better see it as like the image of Isolde holding the dead Tristan to her breast while singing her famous "Liebestod" in Wagner's opera. Like the opera, *A Moon for the Misbegotten* is a story of love and death. The same tough critics might object to this, too, of course. But death is death, and it is either accompanied by a sense of support or by despair (an idea that the recent play *Wit* by Margaret Edson also effectively dramatizes). And the deepest support comes from those who love most unconditionally. Josie gives Jim that deepest support, and if he does not die at once, she knows he will die soon—in his sleep, she hopes, a sleep that will finally be less troubled because of what she has given. The merging of Jim and Josie is their shared love—a love that is sexual, psychological, and existential—and in the end, that merging is completed by the knowledge of his death. It is Josie's acceptance of Jim's death, which Stephen Black recognizes as figuring O'Neill's acceptance of his brother's and parents' deaths, that gives closure to the play, if not indeed to O'Neill's artistic career, and makes it go beyond the other late plays.

What makes Jim's confession and especially Josie's forgiveness so large is that they take us to the core contradiction of human existence—that between life as cold and meaningless and life as secure and wondrous. These contradictory views exist in twain in these plays, neither ever totally offsetting the possibility of the other. The live part can outdo the dead part, but only (recalling Mary's final phrase in *Long*

---

9   Bentley (33) sees the play as a case of "neurotic fantasy unorganized into art." See also Matthew Wikander, "O'Neill and the Cult of Sincerity," *The Cambridge Companion to Eugene O'Neill* 217–235, especially where Wikander (228) quotes Mary McCarthy's comment on the image: "The defeat of all human plans and contrivances is suddenly shaped in the picture of the titaness sitting staring at a stage moon with a shriveled male infant drunkenly asleep at her side."

Day's Journey) "for a time." If Jim had gone back to his speakeasy to die his death to the sounds of drunken laughter, we say the former would have prevailed. If he stays, as he does, and accepts Josie's nurturing forgiveness and conquers his Brooklyn Boys, we say the latter has prevailed. But that latter only contradicts the former; it does not erase it. Josie's forgiving embrace takes Jim back to feelings that precede the separations implied by birth and weaning, and those are the most reassuring of feelings. But the bleakness of separation and the reality of guilt are always present, essentials of human maturation. Contradiction is what has been experienced—neither the defeat of despair nor the triumph of hope. There are no real *liebestods* or returns to the Cross (*a la* the conclusion of *Days Without End)* in the late O'Neill. We end still in the posture of Larry Slade staring in front of him. Erie's managed crap games will continue, the bums at Harry Hope's will stumble from saturnalia to saturnalia, and Josie will return to her games with Phil. Like Beckett's Estragon and Vladimir, we go but do not go. *A Moon for the Misbegotten* is not about defeat because of what the communion of the lovers achieves, but equally true of this play is a line in a recent play by Edward Albee: "We can't take glory because it shows us the abyss."[10]

---

[10]   Quoted in Ben Brantley's review of a New York production of Albee's *Play about the Baby*, *NY Times*, 2/2/2001, Section E-2:1.

Conclusion

What I call vital contradictions are split in this study between underlying ideas in the plays and qualities inherent in the characters. Characters almost always embody ideas, of course, but sometimes contradictions within the characters are less important and sometimes more important. In *The Wild Duck, Easter,* and *A Dream Play,* contradictory ideas take precedence over contradictions within individual characters. The contradiction between the necessity for factual truth or the necessity for "vital lies" is the finally unresolvable issue in *The Wild Duck,* as are issues centering around the value of human existence itself in *Easter* and *A Dream Play.* Vital contradictions within Hjalmar Ekdahl, Elis Heyst, and Strindberg's various quasi-allegorical figures in *A Dream Play* give dramatic interest to scenes in which they appear, but the ideas the playwright want us to think about as we leave the theater are more important than the characters.[1] And the same may be said about *The Iceman Cometh,* in spite of its emphasis on contradictions within the individuals, especially Hickey. The play's final spokesman is not Hickey but Larry, the play's intellectual center, and Larry is an evaluator of ideas who will always see all sides of all questions.

By far the greater number of plays looked at take their lead, however, from *Peer Gynt.* Vital contradictions integral to the characterizations of Hedda Gabler; Julie and Jean; most of Chekhov's major figures; Simon, Deborah and Sara Harford; the four members of the Tyrone family; Erie Smith; and Jim, Josie, and Phil are what chiefly focus our interest in their plays. Our sense of the humanity of these figures achieved through their contradictions is what we chiefly take away from these works and is why the acting of these roles is particularly important. Whereas I have seen successful productions of *The Wild Duck* in which the acting has been only fair but the ideas underlying the play came through vividly, it would be impossible to conceive a successful or even adequate production of *Hedda Gabler, Uncle Vanya,* or *A Moon for the Misbegotten* in which the contradictions within the central figures were not extremely well realized. I have

---

[1]   I had the good fortune to see a production of *A Dream Play* by the Stadstheatr of Stockholm at the Brooklyn Academy of Music in December 2000. Done in a surrealistic manner, this production emphasized the contradictory ideas that are the basis of the play.

seen one production of the last named of these plays in which Josie's contradictions were well realized but not at all Jim's, and it was not one of the better productions I have seen of this play.[2]

The concluding ideas in my discussion of O'Neill take me back to Ibsen and *Peer Gynt.* Like Peer the major characters and situations in the plays looked at throughout this study await the Button Molder's final judgment—a judgment that can never come. Peer will never know whether his life has had significance because it both has and has not had significance, depending on one's perspective at the moment of judgment. And the weights on the scale are equal. It has been an inclination in me as one who persists in looking at the bright side, to throughout find the greater weight on the side of progress and hope, but that inclination really runs counter to what I am saying about these plays. Along with all he does for Andrei and (at times) the sisters, Chekhov's Chebutykin is an irresponsible lout, and Jamie Tyrone's *dead* part will always be a force equal to his live part. If we ignore the permanence of the split, we verge toward the sentimentality the critics deplore.

Whether the emphasis be on the major characters or on the plays' underlying ideas, vital contradictions have been my theme—vital because they enhance our sense of the humanity of the characters, vital because contradictions about existence are so much a part of the way we look at the world at the beginning of our new millennium. Alfred E. Kahn, the prominent economist, once jokingly said that people who do not see things in schizophrenic terms are just are not thinking very clearly. Such an assessment, however humorously intended, is what makes the plays I have been looking at so particularly immediate.

---

[2]   The one in which Jim was inadequate was performed by a road company of the Dublin Abbey Theatre, which I saw at Dartmouth College in the early 1990s; while in the 1999 New York production of the play starring Gabriel Byrne and Cherry Jones, Byrne was a highly contradictory Jim (though still no match for Jason Robards in the 1970s), but Jones did not sufficiently emphasize Josie's contradictions.

Works Cited

Bagchee, Shyamal (ed.). *Perspectives on O'Neill: New Essays.* U of Victoria, B.C., 1988.

Bentley, Eric. *The Dramatic Event.* N.Y. Horizon,1954

Berlin, Normand. "The Beckettian O'Neill." *Modern Drama* 31 (March 1988): 28–34.

Black, Stephen. *Eugene O'Neill: Beyond Mourning and Tragedy.* Yale UP, 1999.

————— "Tragic Anagnorisis in *The Iceman Cometh.*" In *Perspectives on O'Neill.* Edited by Shyamal Bagchee. U of Victoria, B.C.,1988, 17–32.

Bloom, Harold. *Shakespeare: The Invention of the Human.* N.Y.: Riverhead Books, 1998.

Brantley, Ben. Review of original production of Edward Albee's *Play about the Baby. New York Times,* 2 February, 2001.

————— Review of 1999 New York revival of *The Iceman Cometh. New York Times,* 9 April 1999.

Brietzke, Zander. *The Aesthetics of Failure: Dynamic Structure in the Plays of Eugene O'Neill.* Jefferson, N.C.: McFarland, 2001.

Brooks, Peter. *The Melodramatic Imagination.* New Haven: Yale UP, 1976.

Brustein, Robert. *The Theatre of Revolt.* Boston: Little, Brown, 1964.

Canby, Vincent. Review of 1999 New York revival of *The Iceman Cometh. New York Times,* 18 April 1999.

Cargill, Oscar et al. (eds.). *O'Neill and his Plays.* New York UP, 1961.

Carlson, Harry G. *Strindberg and the Poetry of Myth.* U California P, 1982.

Chekhov, Anton. *Chekhov: The Major Plays.* Translated by Ann Dunnigan. N.Y.: Signet, 1964.

————— *Letters.* Selected, translated, and edited by Avrahm Yarmolinsky. N.Y.: Viking, 1973.

Chothia, Jean. *Forging a Language: A Study of the Plays of Eugene O'Neill.* Cambridge UP, 1979.

————— "Trying to Write the Family Play." In *The Cambridge Companion to Eugene O'Neill.* Edited by Michael Manheim. Cambridge UP, 1998.

Clurman, Harold. *Ibsen.* N.Y.: Macmillan, 1977

Eisen, Kurt, *The Inner Strength of Opposites: O'Neill's Novelistic Drama and the Melodramatic Imagination.* U of Georgia Press, 1994.

Fergusson, Francis. *The Idea of a Theatre.* Princeton UP, 1949.

Fjelde, Rolf. "*Peer Gynt,* Naturalism, and the Dissolving Self." *The Drama Review* 13 (Winter, 1968): 28–43.

Floyd, Virginia. *Eugene O'Neill at Work.* N.Y.: Frederick Ungar, 1981.

Fuchs, Elinor. *The Death of Character.* Indiana UP, 1996.

Gassner, John. "The Duality of Chekhov." In *Chekhov: A Collection of Critical Essays.* Edited by R.L. Jackson. N.Y.: Prentice-Hall, 1967.

Gelb, Arthur and Barbara. *O'Neill.* NY: Harper and Row, 1962; second edition, 1987.

Gerhardie, William. *Anton Chekhov: A Critical Study.* N.Y.: St. Martin's Press, 1974.

Gilman, Richard. *Chekhov's Plays: An Opening into Eternity.* Yale UP, 1995.

Golden, Joseph. *The Death of Tinker Bell.* Syracuse UP, 1967.

Hays, Michael and Anastasia Nikopoulou (Eds.). *Melodrama: The Cultural Emergence of a Genre.* N.Y.: St. Martin's Press, 1996.

Haugen, Einar. *Ibsen's Drama: Author to Audience.* U of Minnesota Press, 1979.

Heilman, R. B. *Tragedy and Melodrama: Versions of Experience.* Seattle: U of Washington Press, 1968.

Ibsen, Henrik. *Four Major Plays.* Translated by Rolf Fjelde. N.Y.: Signet, 1965.

––––– *Peer Gynt.* Translated by Rolf Fjelde. Minneapolis: U of Minnesota Press, 1980.

Jackson, Robert Louis. "Chekhov's *Seagull.*" In *Chekhov: A Collection of Critical Essays.* Edited by Jackson. N.Y.: Prentice-Hall, 1967.

Johnston, Brian. *Toward the Third Empire: Ibsen's Early Drama.* U of Minnesota Press, 1980.

Kierkegaard, Soren. *The Sickness unto Death.* In *Fear and Trembling.* Translated by Walter Lowrie. Garden City, N.Y.: Doubleday Anchor, 1954.

Koht, Halvdan. *Life of Ibsen.* N.Y.: Blom, 1971.

Lamm, Martin. *August Strindberg.* Translated by Harry Carlson. N.Y.: Ayer Company Publishers, 1971.

Lyons, Charles R. *Henrik Ibsen: The Divided Consciousness.* Carbondale: Southern Illinois UP, 1972.

Manheim, Michael. "At Home with the Harfords." *Eugene O'Neill Review* 20 (Spring and Fall, 1996): 102–109.

----- *Eugene O'Neill's New Language of Kinship.* Syracuse UP, 1982.

----- "Mother-Son Dialogue in Chekhov's *The Sea Gull* and O'Neill's *Long Day's Journey into Night. Eugene O'Neill Newsletter* 6 (Spring, 1982): 24–29.

----- "The Stature of *Long Day's Journey into Night.*" *Cambridge Companion to Eugene O'Neill.* Edited by Manheim. Cambridge UP. 1998, 206–216.

Martine, James (ed.). *Critical Approaches to Eugene O'Neill.* Boston: G.K. Hall, 1984.

Maufort, Marc (ed.). *Eugene O'Neill and the Emergence of American Drama.* Amsterdam: Rodopi, 1989.

McCarthy, Mary. "Dry Ice" [review of the original production of *The Iceman Cometh*]. *Partisan Review* 13 (1946): 577–579.

Meyer, Michael. *Ibsen: A Biography.* Garden City, N.Y.: Doubleday, 1971.

----- *Strindberg.* N.Y.: Random House, 1985.

Mitchell, Stephen A. "The Path from Inferno to the Chamber Plays: *Easter* and Strindberg." *Modern Drama* 24 (1986): 157–168.

Murry, J. M. "Thoughts on Tchekhov." In *Aspects of Literature.* London, 1920.

O'Neill, Eugene. *Complete Plays.* 3 volumes. N.Y.: The Library of America, 1988.

Pfister, Joel. *Staging Depth: Eugene O'Neill and the Politics of Psychological Discourse.* U of North Carolina Press, 1995.

Pitcher, Harvey. *The Chekhov Play.* N.Y.: Harper and Row, 1973.

Redmond, James (ed.). *Melodrama.* Cambridge UP, 1992.

Scheibler, Rolf. *The Late Plays of Eugene O'Neill.* Berne: Francke Verlag, 1970.

Shapiro, Bruce G. *Divine Madness: Ibsen's 'Peer Gynt' and the Philosophy of Kierkegaard.* N.Y.: Greenwood,1990.

Shaughnessy, Edward L. *Down the Nights and Down the Days.* U of Notre Dame Press, 1996.

----- *Eugene O'Neill in Ireland.* Westport, CN: Greenwood, 1988.

Sheaffer, Louis. *O'Neill: Son and Artist.* Boston: Little, Brown, 1968.

----- *O'Neill: Son and Playwright.* Boston: Little, Brown, 1962.

Sheldon, Richard. "Cathartic Disillusionment in *The Three Sisters.*" In *Russian Literature and American Critics.* Edited by Kenneth N. Bostrom. Ann Arbor: *Papers in Slavic Literature* 4 (1984).

Sprinchorn, Evert. "The Logic of *A Dream Play.*" *Modern Drama* 5 (1962): 352–365.

----- *Strindberg as Dramatist.* Yale UP, 1982.

----- "The Unspoken Text of *Hedda Gabler.*" *Modern Drama* 36 (1993): 353–367.

Strindberg, August. *'Miss Julie' and Other Plays.* Translated by Michael Robinson. Oxford UP, 1998.

----- *Selected Plays II.* Translated by Evert Sprinchorn. U of Minnesota Press, 1986.

----- *Six Plays.* Translated by Elizabeth Sprigge. Garden City, N.Y.: Doubleday, 1955.

Stroupe, John H. (ed.). *Critical Approaches to O'Neill.* N.Y.: AMS Press, 1988.

Styan, John L. *Chekhov in Performance.* Cambridge UP, 1971.

Tiusanen, Timo. *O'Neill's Scenic Images.* Princeton UP, 1968.

Valency, Maurice. *The Breaking String: The Plays of Anton Chekhov.* Oxford UP, 1966.

----- *Flower and the Castle: An Introduction to Modern Drama* [primarily on Ibsen and Strindberg]. N.Y.: Macmillan, 1963.

Vitins, Ieva. "Uncle Vanya's Predicament." *Slavic and East European Review* 22 (1978): 454–463.

Wikander, Matthew. "Eugene O'Neill and the Cult of Sincerity." *Cambridge Companion to Eugene O'Neill.* Edited by Michael Manheim. Cambridge UP, 1998, 217–235.

Dramaturgies

Texts, Cultures and Performances

This series series presents innovative research work in the field of twentieth-century dramaturgy, primarily in the anglophone and francophone worlds. Its main purpose is to re-assess the complex relationship between textual studies, cultural and/or performance aspects at the dawn of this new multicultural millennium. The series offers discussions of the link between drama and multiculturalism (studies of minority playwrights—ethnic, aboriginal, gay and lesbian), reconsiderations of established playwrights in the light of contemporary critical theories, studies of the interface between theatre practice and textual analysis, studies of marginalized theatrical practices (circus, vaudeville etc.), explorations of the emerging postcolonial drama, research into new modes of dramatic expressions and comparative or theoretical drama studies.

The Series Editor, **Marc MAUFORT**, is Professor of English literature and drama at the *Université Libre de Bruxelles*.

Series Titles

No.6– Michael MANHEIM, *Vital Contradictions. Characterization in the Plays of Ibsen, Strindberg, Chekhov and O'Neill*, Brussels, P.I.E.-Peter Lang, 2002, ISBN 90-5201-991-6.

No.5– Bruce BARTON, *Changing Frames. Medium Matters in Selected Plays and Films of David Mamet* (provisional title), Brussels, P.I.E.-Peter Lang (forthcoming 2002), ISBN 90-5201-988-6.

No.4– Marc MAUFORT & Franca BELLARSI (eds.), *Crucible of Cultures. Anglophone Drama at the Dawn of a New Millennium*, Brussels, P.I.E.-Peter Lang, 2002, ISBN 90-5201-982-7.

No.3– Rupendra MAJUMDAR, *Central Man. The Significance of Heroism in Modern American Drama* (provisional title), Brussels, P.I.E.-Peter Lang (forthcoming 2002) ISBN 90-5201-978-9.

No.2– Helena GREHAN, *Mapping Cultural Identity in Contemporary Australian Performance*, Brussels, P.I.E.-Peter Lang, 2001, ISBN 90-5201-947-9.

No.1– Marc MAUFORT & Franca BELLARSI (eds.), *Siting the Other. Revisions of Marginality in Australian and English-Canadian Drama*, Brussels, P.I.E.-Peter Lang, 2001, ISBN 90-5201-934-7.